I0817376

SPECTRALITY IN THE NOVELS OF TONI MORRISON

Spectrality in the Novels of Toni Morrison

MELANIE R. ANDERSON

The University of Tennessee Press / Knoxville

First Edition.

An earlier version of the section on *Paradise* in chapter three appeared as "'What would be on the other side?' Spectrality and Spirit Work in Toni Morrison's *Paradise*" in *African American Review* 42.2 (Summer 2008).

The paper in this book meets the requirements of American National Standards Institute / National Information Standards Organization specification Z39.48–1992 (Permanence of Paper). It contains 30 percent post-consumer waste and is certified by the Forest Stewardship Council.

LIBRARY OF CONGRESS CATALOGING-IN-PUBLICATION DATA

Anderson, Melanie.
Spectrality in the novels of Toni Morrison / Melanie Anderson. — 1st ed.
p. cm.
Includes bibliographical references and index.
ISBN-13: 978-1-57233-858-6 (hardcover)
ISBN-10: 1-57233-858-X (hardcover)
1. Morrison, Toni—Criticism and interpretation.
2. Ghosts in literature.
3. Future life in literature.
I. Title.

PS3563.O8749Z537 2013
813'.54—dc23
2012026773

For my parents—Paul and Deborah Anderson

I think of ghosts and haunting as just being alert. If you are really alert, then you see the life that exists beyond the life that is on top. It's not spooky, necessarily—might be, but it doesn't have to be. It's something I relish, rather than run from.

Toni Morrison
Interview on NPR, September 20, 2004

The latter [scholar] would finally be capable, beyond the opposition between presence and non-presence, actuality and inactuality, life and non-life, of thinking the possibility of the specter, the specter as possibility.

Jacques Derrida
Specters of Marx

CONTENTS

Acknowledgments ix

INTRODUCTION

"What Does it Mean to Follow a Ghost" in Toni Morrison's Fiction? 1

CHAPTER 1

Spectral Beginnings in *The Bluest Eye* and *Sula* 19

CHAPTER 2

"Why Not Ghosts As Well?" The Presence of the Spectral in *Song of Solomon* and *Tar Baby* 37

CHAPTER 3

"What Would Be on the Other Side?" History as a Spectral Bridge in *Beloved* and *Paradise* 65

CHAPTER 4

"The Specter as Possibility": Ghostly Narrators in *Jazz* and *Love* 101

CHAPTER 5

"Slave. Free. I Last": Spectral Returns in *A Mercy* 131

Conclusion 145

Notes 149

Works Cited 159

Index 171

ACKNOWLEDGMENTS

I have many people to thank, even beyond those mentioned here. This project began as my dissertation at the University of Mississippi, and during those early stages, the J. L. and Diane Holloway Dissertation Fellowship provided a respite from teaching and greatly expedited the writing process. For reading drafts of this work, I first need to thank my former committee members at the University of Mississippi: Annette Trefzer, Ethel Young-Minor, Benjamin F. Fisher, and Kirsten Dellinger. In particular, I am grateful to Professors Fisher, Trefzer, and Young-Minor for their encouragement from my original seeds of thought about spectrality and hauntings to this project. In northern Kentucky and in Oxford, Mississippi, I have been blessed with excellent groups of friends who have been supportive and inspirational. Among those, individuals who have provided feedback on drafts of this manuscript include Jeff Stayton, Gray Kane, Lisa Kröger, Lorraine Dubuisson, Travis Montgomery, Matt Saye, Pip Gordon, Michaela St. John, and Bethany Miller. I also wish to thank the readers engaged by the University of Tennessee Press for their incisive comments on the manuscript.

I have presented this material in various stages at several academic conferences, and the feedback from those gatherings has been valuable. These conferences include meetings of the Toni Morrison Society, the American Literature Association, the South Central Modern Language Association, the Society for the Study of Southern Literature, and the Mississippi Philological Association. My students have helped to sharpen my thinking on Morrison's work when I have had the opportunity to teach it, and I have especially valued the discussions of *Beloved* in my haunted literature classes.

This list would not be complete if I did not acknowledge the people who influenced the course of my life toward academe. When I was an undergraduate at Thomas More College, James Schuttemeyer introduced me to the work of Toni Morrison through *Song of Solomon;* Sherry Cook Stanforth assigned *Beloved* in a memorable "American Novels" class; and Sister Colleen Dillon served spectacularly in her roles as teacher and advisor.

Even though I met them well before even the possibility of this project existed, their influence is apparent.

Most important, I am deeply grateful to my family: Paul, Deborah, Stephanie, and Justin Anderson; my grandparents Earl and Aline Beil; and finally, my grandmother Helen Anderson, who unfortunately passed away during the writing of this book. They offered unconditional love and support throughout this process, and they put up with much rambling speculation about spectrality. Their patience and enthusiasm have kept me moving forward even when I began to question where I was going and then, if I figured that out, whether I would ever get there. Without them, I could not have ventured forth upon this journey and completed it.

INTRODUCTION

"What Does it Mean to Follow a Ghost" in Toni Morrison's Fiction?

Among Toni Morrison's nine novels, *Beloved* (1987) is the obvious ghost story since one of the integral characters of the novel is a revenant, but supernatural events and ghosts are present throughout her canon. Labeling Morrison's other works "ghost stories" may initially seem to be an exaggeration, but in reading the trilogy (1987–97), *Song of Solomon* (1977), *Tar Baby* (1981), *Love* (2003), and *A Mercy* (2008) as "ghost stories," I do not mean to suggest that they are preoccupied with conventional fireside stories of haunted houses or apparitions. Once Morrison's novels are read as haunted texts, peopled by ghosts and "ghostly" characters, connections within her work as a whole become clearer. What if the specter of Beloved is a "type" of character that readers should notice throughout the novels, not just as "the beloved" but as a figure of spectrality mediating personal and cultural history?[1] I posit that Morrison connects her novels not only through cultural history but also through a preoccupation with spectrality and the haunting, disjointed natures of both personal and cultural history. As Kathleen Brogan notes, "In contemporary haunted literature, ghost stories are offered as an alternative—or challenge—to 'official,' dominant history" (17). In her work, Morrison plays with the boundaries of American culture and life, showing where the past is still present, even if certain groups' histories seem separate or invisible to the "mainstream's" eye. "The ghost is that which interrupts the presentness of the present," writes Jeffrey Andrew Weinstock, "and its haunting indicates that, beneath the surface of received history, there lurks another narrative, an untold story that calls into question the veracity of the authorized version of events" (*Spectral America* 5).

To understand why Morrison would write spectral literature to subvert the master narrative, one can turn to Carlos Fuentes: "The role of the marginal cultures is that of the guardians of memory. A memory of what the West sacrificed in other cultures through imperialist expansion and what it sacrificed within its own culture" (qtd. in Zamora, *The Usable Past* 123). But how can a writer engage this silenced history through the use of spectrality? Specifically she can do the subversive cultural work of imagining a communal past and origin. In spectral literature, even if the original ancestors are no longer alive, they are present. Therefore, in books like Morrison's *Beloved,* the work of the specter is cultural and generational, helping the second generation understand specific cultural moments of dispossession and slavery, important events that are often elided in the greater American historical purview. The specter provides connection and identity to confused and, subsequently, "ghosted" characters. Ghosts create spaces that indicate issues of dispossession and trauma, and they can create places for memorializing and healing.

Shining a light on this very issue of the ghostly relationships between cultures, Morrison's study *Playing in the Dark* (1992) traces the African American presence as a shadow that refused to be ignored in the works of canonical, predominantly white American writers. She posits that "[t]he contemplation of this black presence is central to any understanding of our national literature and should not be permitted to hover at the margins of the literary imagination" (5). Critic Tammy Clewell identifies this underlying motivation in Morrison's fiction as well: "While Morrison uses her fiction to recover black histories ignored by dominant Western traditions, she also manages to emphasize what has been irretrievably lost—those personal memories, communal traditions, and unrealized possibilities that have disappeared without benefit of permanent documentation" (130). Through the metaphoric power and the poststructural binary-busting possibilities of the specter, Morrison does her cultural work of emphasizing African American history in America and of reestablishing the connections among past and present, life and death, and generations. Her spectral figures elicit an awareness of the actual lived experience of the African American past situated within historical events, and by writing about these memories and personal experiences, she calls attention to the unique position of this past as a haunting presence in relation to mainstream American history. As a Pulitzer and Nobel Prize–winning author, she certainly is one of the most important presences in twentieth- and twenty-first-century American critical and creative thought, and she uses her position to call attention to the cultural amnesia surrounding past events such as slavery and physical and cultural dispossession. Morrison accomplishes this work against the background of Latin American magical realism and within the African American literary context of the supernatural. This latter context includes the interaction between individuals and their haunted pasts *and* the silence that often accompanies the black experience in America.

The Magically Real Presence of the Supernatural

The appearance of fictional specters that exhibit temporal and border-crossing capabilities is often found under the larger literary rubric of magical realism, and any study exploring ghosts must acknowledge and develop out of this background. As Lois Parkinson Zamora notes, "Magical realist texts ask us to look beyond the limits of the knowable, and ghosts are often our guides" ("Magical Romance/Magical Realism" 498). While magical realism may be identified primarily with Latin American fiction, particularly that of the "Boom" period of the mid-twentieth century, Zamora and Wendy B. Faris consider the mode to be "an international commodity" (2).[2] Faris makes a connection between magical realism and postcolonial writing: "Magical realism has become so important as a mode of expression worldwide, especially in postcolonial cultures, because it has provided the literary ground for significant cultural work; within its texts, marginal voices, submerged traditions, and emergent literatures have developed and created masterpieces" (*Ordinary Enchantments* 1). Stephen Slemon agrees that magical realist texts "recuperate the lost voices and discarded fragments that imperial cognitive structures push to the margins of critical consciousness" (415). For these critics, during the last half of the twentieth century magical realism became the literary mode of choice for writers who wished to "unghost" elided history and write from the spaces between their native cultures and that of the West. These texts "can be read as reflecting in [their] language of narration real conditions of speech and cognition within the social relations of a postcolonial culture" (Slemon 411).

Spinning this thread of minority writers working within the cultural interstices, Zamora asserts that the seamless and nonchalant use of the supernatural is a primary characteristic of U.S. magical realist texts.

"Ghosts are liminal, metamorphic, intermediary," Zamora writes; "they exist in/between/on modernity's boundaries of physical and spiritual, magical and real, and challenge the lines of demarcation" ("Magical Romance/ Magical Realism" 498). Supernatural figures have an uncanny ability to violate the limitations of physical and temporal spaces and to dissolve traditionally Western binaries. Elizabeth T. Hayes writes, "U.S. magic realist narratives are postmodernist texts that destabilize, that question, that challenge ideological assumptions, that refuse closure, unity, totality; and they do so through their juxtaposition of seeming contraries" (169).

For Amaryll B. Chanady, this interplay of contraries, or of contrasting codes, defines magical realism: "What the magical realist does . . . is to present a world view that is radically different from ours as equally valid. He neither censures nor shows surprise" (29–30). In her *Magical Realism and the Fantastic: Resolved Versus Unresolved Antinomy,* Chanady sets forth criteria for judging the difference between magical realism and the fantastic in literature. She views magical realism as "a mode, or particular quality of a fictitious world that can characterize works belonging to several genres, periods or national literatures" (2). She argues that magical realism occurs in texts primarily when "the supernatural does not disconcert the reader" (Schroeder 13). According to Chanady, the difference between fantastic literature and magical realist texts lies in the manner in which the two modes handle antinomy, or "the simultaneous presence of two conflicting [textual] codes" (12). In fantastic literature, the reader never stops hesitating between a rational explanation and the paranormal. The fantastic "cannot be explained by any coherent code" (12). Within the plot of the fantastic work, there are supernatural elements imposed upon the real world, or at least upon the characters who are denizens of the mimetic world similar to that of the reader. For instance, in C. S. Lewis's *Narnia* series, the children begin in the real world of England with the war in the background, but their adventures take place in a magical world that cannot be explained through any but its own logic—the codes of realism and magic are separated within the works. Chanady's definition of fantastic literature finds its origins in Tzvetan Todorov's analysis of the literary mode in his study *The Fantastic: A Structural Approach to a Literary Genre.* He posits that "uncanny" literature is a type of the "supernatural explained" where the paranormal has rational causes that can be discovered, the "fantastic" involves the perpetual hesitation of the reader between the rational and supernatural poles, and "marvelous" fiction accepts the paranormal as a part of rational experience (41–42).

Chanady posits that magical realism resolves the antinomy that can arise from the presence of two conflicting codes within the text—mimetic realism *and* the magical, or the marvelous (12). This resolution results in the reader's inability to question "the fictitious world view" that is presented (123). "The supernatural, which is the product of an alien imagination," she writes, "is juxtaposed with everyday reality in order to create a more complete picture of the world" (27).[3] Indeed, when asked about magical realism, Isabel Allende responded: "Magic realism is a literary device or a way of seeing in which there is space for the invisible forces that move the world: dreams, legends, myths, emotion, passion, history. All these forces find a place in the absurd, unexplainable aspects of magic realism. . . . Magic realism is all over the world. It is the capacity to see and to write about all the dimensions of reality" (Snell 238–39). According to Chanady and Allende, magical realism allows for a more truthful and complete picture of the world beyond the privileging of stark, mimetic realism. It opens texts (and readers) to other worldviews and experiences outside the Western literary orientation. Creating a link between her work and the postcolonial uses of magical realism, Chanady notes, "If this mode of literary expression is characterized by the presentation of two different world views, why could it not be found in any country that has more than one ethnic or racial group?" (20). This awareness of liminality and multiplicity "works to establish indigenous and other marginalized histories as a site of 'truth' in literature" (Schroeder 126).

To be sure, critics who analyze magical realist works emphasize its "goals of displacing Eurocentric notions of reality" (Schroeder 23), and the natural place for this work to occur is the New World, but there are problems with this categorization. In his *Posts and Pasts: A Theory of Postcolonialism,* Alfred J. López identifies the problems inherent in using "magical realism" as a label for certain literatures that are written predominantly by marginalized individuals. For him, use of the term can result in a neocolonial exoticizing of an "alien" literature (39). He describes magical realism as a "process of naming—which is already itself an act of appropriation, a bid to harness the wild, 'exotic' text within a reasonable European critical framework" (143). I tend to lean toward Zamora's and Hayes's emphasis on the poststructuralist tendencies of magical realism to explode confining Western binaries, as the mode "exceed[s] and escape[s] the impositions of a Western desire or will-to-mastery" (López 172), but I agree that there are problematic aspects of the term, particularly if it is used as a name for literature that seems "other." Rather than simply labeling novels that contain the supernatural as "magical realist," I agree with López that critics should employ an intersubjective reading that works to understand the multiplicitous worldviews being presented (40, 209). This practice allows for an analysis that is culturally sensitive.

These issues surrounding the labeling of works as "magical realist" have affected Morrison's own understanding of the term. Because her characters and readers accept magical happenings, such as the presence of ghosts or the ability to fly, as part of her narrative worlds, she would seem to fit into this convenient category, but her acceptance of the label "magical realist" has fluctuated over the course of her career. Though she initially embraced magical realism, she later distanced herself from the movement (Bowers 85). In an interview with Mel Watkins in 1977, she cited Gabriel García Márquez and Miguel Asturias as "among those authors that she envies," but she did not "feel that their work consciously influenced her" (47). Ten years later, she told Gail Caldwell, "I felt the preachers, the storytelling, the folklore, the music was very accessible to me. . . . I didn't have any precedent for what I was trying to do with the magic" (243). In a more forthright repudiation to Paul Gilroy, Morrison asserted that "[*Beloved*] is outside most of the formal constricts of the novel but you've got to call it something. Just as long as they [critics] don't call me a magical realist, as though I don't have a culture to write out of. As though that culture has no intellect" (Gilroy 181). For Morrison, dismissing the supernatural in her fiction as out of the ordinary or superfluous to reality ignores the cultural traditions that inform her writing.

Regardless of Morrison's protests against magical realism, critics have placed her within this international group of writers, particularly in criticism of her novels *Beloved, Song of Solomon,* and *Tar Baby.*[4] By contrast, Morrison's rejection of the term "magical realism" for her own work highlights how her fiction oversteps and exceeds the label's bounds, calling for an "intersubjective" and culturally prescient reading. I see her making creative use of African spirituality and the openness in African American literature to other realms and possibilities of existence as methods of countering Western binaries and creating "a more complete picture of the world" (Chanady 27), and these beliefs are central to the worldviews of her characters. According to Morrison, "Ghosts are not difficult [to write] because everybody believes in them, even those of us who don't believe in them, because we don't put our hands outside the bed when we sleep. We're convinced that there's something underneath. . . . You can use that remembrance that's in me, in you, in everybody" (*The World* 46). She is describing her creation of a culturally realistic world that cannot be illustrated without recourse to the supernatural. Ultimately, she uses the spectral to deconstruct constraining and opposing ways of seeing the world, stressing the interconnectedness of memory, history, and lived experience for individuals often caught in the cracks between cultures.

"Learning to Live" in the Interstices: Poststructural Specters and Social Ghosts

Morrison's spectral work continues the emphasis that is present in twentieth-century African American writing on tracing the relations between past and present, often allowing for spectral eruptions of the traumatic past that accompany the return of an ancestor-figure. These concerns with the fluidity of past and present and with remembering those who have come before are integral parts of the bridge between African American culture and what Therese E. Higgins terms "the African American's Africa." For Higgins, "much of the material in Morrison's fiction closely parallels African culture and cosmology," and these aspects "resonate . . . by implication, connotation, and nuance" (ix). In other words, this cultural legacy haunts Morrison's books, and an important part of this legacy is the belief in the transitory nature of death from one state of being to another, rather than as a passage to oblivion or to an ephemeral paradise.

In his general study of the religious beliefs of African peoples, Joseph S. Mbiti describes the acceptance of death as another stage of an individual's life that does not necessarily end communal connections with the living. He writes, "We have repeatedly emphasized that the spiritual universe is a unit with the physical, and that these two intermingle and dovetail into each other so much that it is not easy, or even necessary, at times to draw the distinction or separate them" (74). He later adds, "For the majority of African peoples, the hereafter is only a continuation more or less as it is in its human form" (157). In anticipation of Morrison's liminal spectral figures who, I will argue, have one foot in the world of the living and the other in the beyond, Mbiti describes what he terms the "living-dead." The "living-dead" is a departed individual who has not fully transitioned into the world of the spirits and can still communicate with the living, either for good or, in some cases, if angered, for ill. Memory is closely tied to this process, because "when the last person who knew a particular living-dead also dies, then in effect the process of death is now complete as far as that particular living-dead is concerned" (83). These "living-dead" beings are inherently liminal: "But the living-dead are bilingual: they speak the language of men, with whom they lived until 'recently'; and they speak the language of the spirits and of God, to Whom they are drawing nearer ontologically. These are the 'spirits' with which African peoples are most concerned: it is through the living-dead that the spirit world becomes personal to men" (82). This play between accepted oppositions, such as life and death, is transformative and disruptive. The communication between the living and the dead that occurs in Morrison's work, with its African cultural antecedents, begins the crucial work of breaking down exclusionary binary barriers and essentialisms.

A list of Morrison's predecessors and contemporaries in African American literature who allow for the presence of the supernatural in their work would include, but not be limited to, Toni Cade Bambara, Octavia Butler, Gloria Naylor, Paule Marshall, Lucille Clifton, August Wilson, Randall Kenan, and Tina McElroy Ansa. The presence of the supernatural often indicates the deconstructive cracks that this literature creates in the binaries of the larger Western worldview of American literature. Morrison continues this work, in particular that of her female creative counterparts, in her novels. While writers such as Wilson and Kenan may foreground ghosts and hauntings in their plays and fiction, Morrison develops the often-ignored black female experience in America as it has been lived during the historical periods that she re-creates, including slavery and the turbulent movements of the 1960s and 1970s.

Morrison's comments on her fiction show that she eschews "either/or" dichotomies and is attracted to the slippery spaces on the boundaries.

She often belabors the importance of open endings: "In order to be as free as I possibly can, in my own imagination, I can't take positions that are closed. Everything I've ever done, in the writing world, has been to expand articulation, rather than to close it, to open doors, sometimes, not even closing the book—leaving the endings open for reinterpretation" (Jaffrey 140). Therefore Morrison can frustrate readers with her common "both/and" answers to queries: Beloved can be both an escaped slave and the ghost of Sethe's daughter (Darling 247); the racial makeup of the Convent women can remain ambiguous; the Convent women might have escaped the shooting and they might be ghosts; and *Song of Solomon* can remain open-ended. Morrison's fiction is replete with scenes of uncertainty that are not explained where previously defined areas of meaning bleed back and forth among each other. For my study of the specter in Morrison's work, Jacques Derrida's definitions of the spectral and the "Spectrality Effect" and Avery F. Gordon's theory of the ghost as a "social figure" together form a viable frame for analyzing those moments in Morrison's work where there is communication between the living and the dead and those characters who appear to be alive but may have more in common with the spirits of the story as largely silent presences.

Of the poststructural possibilities of the specter, Derrida notes, "If it—learning to live—remains to be done, it can happen only between life and death. Neither in life nor in death alone. What happens between the two, and between all the 'two's' one likes, such as between life and death, can only maintain itself with some ghost, can only talk with or about some ghost" (xviii). In this passage, he questions what happens in the spaces "betwixt and between," and his answer shows that it is not so much the permanent ideas of life or death facing one another across a gulf. It involves, rather, the bleeding of the meaning of one into the meaning of the other through a medium, the medium of a ghost. Moreover, mixed into this medium of communication is "a politics of memory, of inheritance, and of generations" (xix). The transition from the living to the dead is one of gradation and not of complete disconnect, and the dead still effect a powerful sway upon the living. In this light, individuals who may seem to be biologically alive may very well be spectral, depending upon where they may lie in the transition. Furthermore, the idea of a haunting (an obsession, a constant fear, a fixed idea, a nagging memory) becomes a method whereby a space for self may be opened between generations and communication may flow freely from one generation to another (4).

Not only does the ghost work as a mediating presence within and throughout a liminal space between binaries; the ghost itself is a liminal entity. According to Derrida, a "spectral moment" is a "moment that no longer belongs to time" (xx). The ideas of present and past merge into timelessness: "[H]aunting, by its very structure, implies a deformation of linear temporality" (Buse 1). With ghosts, the past is never over, the present is never secure, and the future is certain only of the spectral return. Specters "serve to destabilize any neat compartmentalization of the past as a secure and fixed entity, or the future as uncharted territory" (Buse 14). Ghostly entities and moments play with and deconstruct the very concepts of time that Western thought has identified as chronological. These ghostly encounters account for the actual malleability of lived time and memory.

This concept of "spectrality" is expanded beyond the moment and conditions of appearance when Derrida further develops the "specter" as a "paradoxical incorporation, the becoming-body, a certain phenomenal and carnal form of the spirit. It becomes, rather, some 'thing' that remains difficult to name: neither soul nor body, and both one and the other" (6). The specter is an ultimate paradox, both there and not there at the same time, and "still nothing that can be seen when one speaks of it" (6). The powerlessness of reason to completely grasp the specter for analysis is posited as well: "One does not know: not out of ignorance, but because this non-object, the non-present present, this being-there of an absent or departed one no longer belongs to knowledge" (6). Buse and Stott describe this aspect of the ghost as an "absence-presence" (17). A ghost, or a ghostly presence, has the "power to see without being seen" (Derrida 8) and to appear at will. When discussing "spectrality" itself, Derrida reiterates the lack of definition and the inability of reason to pin down exactly what, when, or where a specter is: "If there is something like spectrality, there are reasons to doubt this reassuring order of presents and, especially, the border between the present, the actual or present reality of the present, and everything that can be opposed to it: absence, non-presence, non-effectivity, inactuality, virtuality" (39). For Derrida, the "Spectrality Effect" can undo the opposition "between actual effective presence and its other" (40).

Since ghosts are liminal "beings" who disjoint and interrupt temporal existence, how can one react to their presence in literature? Buse and Stott note the incredulity of some when taking the presence of ghosts literally and not searching for their metaphorical meaning: "[G]hosts, of course, fall very firmly in the camp of unreason and therefore become fair game for empiricists eager to demonstrate that ghosts are in fact the product of illusion or hoax, or mere hallucination" (3). Acceptance of this aspect of unreason inherent in the ghostly presence is, however, necessary when analyzing it. As Derrida notes, "The latter [scholar] would finally be capable, beyond the opposition between presence and non-presence, actuality and inactuality, life and non-life, of thinking the possibility of the specter, the specter as possibility" (12). Ghosts do not inhabit one state of being or another, life or death; rather, they inhabit the space between and serve as a conduit of knowledge from one to the other. Specters are the perfect vehicles for emphasizing the multiplicitous experiences that lie beneath master narratives.

Derrida posits that "being-with specters would also be . . . a politics of memory, of inheritance, and of generations" (xix). This concern with the spectral and the flexibility of time and reality recurs in Morrison's fiction, where it often connects with "memory," "inheritance," and "generations." Spectral figures, or characters who are open to spiritual realms, include Pilate, Thérèse, Beloved, Consolata, the Convent women, Wild and Dorcas, and even the narrators of *Jazz* and *Love*. Each of these figures can cross borders and serve as a guide for other characters: Pilate guides Milkman; Thérèse returns Son to the supernatural, liminal side of the island; Beloved interacts with Sethe, Denver, and Paul D; Consolata leads the Convent women; and Wild and Dorcas both affect Joe, Violet, and Felice. In *Love,* Morrison introduces a spectral narrator reminiscent of the disembodied narrator of *Jazz,* so that the two novels can be read as spectral spaces. Without the intervention of these liminal characters who disregard physical and temporal limits, these novels would lack the individual and communal healing that takes place.

Standing in contrast to the power of the spectral figures in Morrison's novels are the characters who are biologically alive, but who are ghostly because they are marginalized, silenced outcasts. I call these characters social ghosts. Kathleen Brogan describes the ghost as not only a transitional figure that is a "go-between, an enigmatic transitional figure moving between past and present, death and life, one culture and another" (6), but also as a metaphor for silenced characters, particularly women. For Brogan, "ghosted" individuals signal an "absence made present," or a kind of living ghost (25), recalling both Derrida's and Buse's descriptions of the specter. She writes, "As an absence made present, the ghost can give expression to the ways in which women are rendered invisible in the public sphere. . . . [Women] are ghostly both because they are socially unrecognized and because they have acquired an illegitimate strength" (25). Abused and outcast women are silent, social ghosts haunting the margins of society.

Nevertheless, the relation of the female to the ghostly is not always that of invisibility and loss; within their marginality these female characters can discover a power that is healing but not socially accepted. Power is evinced through the connection of the female and the "other world," or, in my reading of Morrison, through the spectral guides who are often female: Pilate, Thérèse, Beloved, Consolata, Wild and Dorcas, and L. As Barbara Hill Rigney notes, women have different "ways of knowing" and "are the primary tale-tellers and the transmitters of history as well as the singing teachers; only they know the language of the occult and the occult of language and thus comprise what Morrison has called a 'feminine subtext'" (*The Voices* 15, 10–11). Morrison claims for women a "special knowledge" (qtd. in Rigney): these guides offer an alternative knowledge grounded in the spiritual and the communal. Women with a close connection to spirits and ghosts, and women with the power to control spirits and ghosts, are fearsome and strong characters.[5]

In this vein, according to Patricia Hill Collins, African American women must come to terms with "intersecting oppressions of race, class, gender, sexuality, ethnicity, nation, and religion" (9). These intersecting oppressions form the nexus that silences and, for my purposes, turns women attempting to achieve social justice into ghosts. For Collins, "on the individual level, [there are] connections among lived experiences with oppression, developing one's own point of view concerning those experiences, and the acts of resistance that can follow" (30). In a move that is reminiscent of the tendency of spectrality to cross boundaries of even the most rigid binaries,

Collins calls for a "dialogical relationship" with oppressive structures that "characterizes Black women's collective experiences and group knowledge" (30). Some of the experiences that Collins believes that African American women can bring to this social work come from roles in the labor force, urbanization, the family, and community institutions. For Collins's work, as for Morrison's fiction, actual lived experience is as important as intellectual pursuits in attempts to achieve social justice and historical awareness.

This issue of social ghosting does not, however, apply only to women. In her critical work, Morrison has commented on the ghostly position of the black presence in the fiction of the "mainstream" American literary canon. Collins notes: "Suppressing the knowledge produced by any oppressed group makes it easier for dominant groups to rule because the seeming absence of dissent suggests that subordinate groups willingly collaborate in their own victimization" (3). "Maintaining the invisibility of Black women and our ideas," she writes, ". . . has been critical in maintaining social inequalities" (3).[6] It is this problem of social ghosting that Ralph Ellison describes in *Invisible Man* (1952): "I am an invisible man. No, I am not a spook like those who haunted Edgar Allan Poe; nor am I one of your Hollywood-movie ectoplasms. I am a man of substance, of flesh and bone, fiber and liquids—and I might even be said to possess a mind. I am invisible, understand, simply because people refuse to see me" (3). The narrator of *Invisible Man* is not a supernatural ghost in a Gothic horror story or film. He is a human being who is ignored by others because of his social position. Later in the novel, the "Invisible Man" identifies this perceptual problem of African American personhood when he finally notices the people on the street, the people he was supposed to be helping through his work in the Communist Party, but of whom he was completely unaware: "They'd been there all along, but somehow I'd missed them. I'd missed them even when my work had been most successful. They were outside the groove of history" (443). This concern with people "outside the groove of history" plays directly into Morrison's literary concern with "unghosting" African American history, and it is precisely these socially ghosted people whom Morrison's spectral guides are sent to aid.

In an important passage from her *Ghostly Matters,* Avery F. Gordon describes the concept of a "haunting" as a social moment:

> If haunting describes how that which appears to be not there is often a seething presence, acting on and often meddling with taken-for-granted realities, the ghost is just the sign, or the empirical evidence if you like, that tells you a haunting is taking place. The ghost is not simply a dead or a missing person, but a social figure, and investigating it can lead to that dense site where history and subjectivity make social life. The ghost or the apparition is one form by which something lost, or barely visible, or seemingly not there to our supposedly well-trained eyes, makes itself known or apparent to us, in its own way, of course. The way of the ghost is haunting, and haunting is a very particular way of knowing what has happened or is happening. Being haunted draws us affectively, sometimes against our will and always a bit magically, into the structure of feeling of a reality we come to experience, not as cold knowledge, but as a transformative recognition. (8)

Similar to Derrida's emphasis on spirit work always involving transformation, Gordon's primary emphasis is on the transformative power of the haunting experience. She also defines a ghost as not necessarily a returning deceased individual, but rather, as a "social figure" and a sign of the haunting that is taking place. When this definition is wedded to Derrida's work on spectrality, the "spectral figure" becomes not a returned lost one but a liminal figure enmeshed in a specific social situation, catalyzing change in the lives of the surrounding characters.

Gordon asks, "What kind of a case is a case of a ghost?" For her, "It is a case of the difference it makes to start with the marginal, with what we normally exclude and banish, or, more commonly, with what we never even notice" (24–25). This formulation of ghostliness, or of what it means to be haunted, when slotted with Gordon's insistence that "to write stories concerning exclusions and invisibilities is to write ghost stories" (17), helps illuminate the many manifestations and permutations of haunting and spectrality within Morrison's writing. Ghosts as presence and metaphor shape and connect her novels and play an important role in her project to represent African American history creatively. In her fiction, the bind of being socially powerless because of gender, race, class, or all three, and yet having access to a liminal position of power to play with signifiers and to mediate between cultures, past and present, and living and dead occurs repeatedly. Throughout her creative work, there is a preponderance of socially ghosted characters who find power and/or peace through a spectral guide. These characters include, among others, Milkman, Son and Jadine, Sethe, Denver, the Convent women, and Violet and Joe. These characters are abused, silenced, and practically invisible. They haunt the margins of their communities, even if they are the main characters in the novel. Although they seem powerless, once they have come into contact with the spectral guide(s), there is a renegotiation of position, and the spaces between cultures, classes, life and death, past and present, begin to become permeable and useful. Historical and cultural wounds are healed, and contact with the spectral guides reconnects these living apparitions to their communities, their families, and their personal, cultural, and national history. These reconnections that are so vital for the social ghost would be impossible without the catalyst of interaction with the spectral figure and its acceptance of liminality.

The Trajectory of Morrison's Canon

Single-author studies of Morrison's fiction have explored various aspects of her work including trauma, double-consciousness, class concerns, motherhood, the fragmentation of identity, folklore, bicultural readings by white and African American critics, feminist theories, revisionist postcolonial historiography, masculinity, and the development of the artist's identity.[7] While Morrison stresses the presence of "ancestors" in her novels, and in various articles critics have dealt with the presence of ghosts in her work as emblems of the ever-present past, there is no other comprehensive critical work that traces this spectral Beloved presence and Morrison's concern with social ghosts throughout her canon. There is no analysis of how she may be using her deconstructive ghosts and their accompanying liminality to signal issues of historical and sociopolitical conflict and trauma.[8]

By looking at the revisionary and complementary nature of Morrison's canon, I tease out the implications of the spectral in her novels from *Song of Solomon* through *A Mercy*. The primary thread that links all of the novels in Morrison's canon is the presence of the ghost. In each of her books, Morrison comments upon the ghosted experiences of African Americans, and she increasingly meditates upon the positive possibilities of liminality and the options that exist in the spaces between false oppositions like past and present. In this study, I focus on the seven novels published from 1977 to 2008 because I believe they illustrate the importance of the transformative interaction between the spectral figure and its ghosted charges most explicitly. The seeds of the ghosted characters and the spectral figure are present, however, in her first two books, *The Bluest Eye* (1970) and *Sula* (1973). These two novels serve as precursors to the powerful spectral work to come in that Morrison's first novel can be read as a primer on social ghosting and the second as a gesture toward creating her first spectral figure. I begin in chapter one with a brief look into their gestures toward spectrality before delving into the other books.

For the following six novels, I structure my analysis dialectically and discuss two novels in each chapter. In the second chapter, I explore the seeds of the relationship between the spectral figure and the ghosted characters as presented in *Song of Solomon* and *Tar Baby.* Here, Morrison begins her cultural work with young characters who are unaware of a larger family past that has slipped away over generations. Milkman, Jadine, and Son are all disconnected from their personal and cultural histories, and class divisions fragment their relationships. Milkman is unaware of his family's origins and its history during slavery and Reconstruction. Because she is an orphan, Jadine, like Milkman, is oblivious to her heritage as an African American woman, and for her, a reconnection to a maternal lineage is most important. These characters are in need of connection. In each novel, the protagonists are placed in the middle of seemingly insurmountable extremes. For example, in *Song of Solomon,* Milkman is trapped between the materialism of his father and the revolutionary tendencies of his friend Guitar. In *Tar Baby,* Son and Jadine's conflict encapsulates the binaries in the text based on class, race, and culture. In each case, tenuous links are formed through interactions with mysterious and powerful female mentors, who privilege liminality and experiential knowledge.

From 1987 to 1997, Morrison published her trilogy, *Beloved, Jazz,* and *Paradise.* My third chapter is focused on the bookends of this trilogy—*Beloved* and *Paradise.* I see these two novels forming the apogee of Morrison's endeavor to highlight African American history through spectral means. Beloved is the ultimate Derridean "becoming-body." Because she defies compartmentalization and comprehension—her identity is impossible to pin down—she is a manifestation of the "Spectrality Effect." She helps transmit knowledge of the past from Sethe to her daughter Denver, unghosting both women in the process. In *Paradise,* Consolata picks up where Beloved left off and helps the Convent women deal with their traumas resulting from physical and political violence. As spectral guides, Beloved and Consolata help the other characters relive and work through African American history from the Civil War to the civil rights movement. *Paradise* also is the culmination of Beloved's work in that the reader sees at the end of the novel the actual space of spirits where the specters' haunting work continues after physical death. I posit that the presence of this spectral paradise at the end of the trilogy is the key to understanding the importance of the power of liminality in Morrison's canon.

The fourth chapter is centered on *Jazz* and *Love,* novels in which Morrison is primarily interested in the haunting, layering effects of history and in creating "historiographic metafictions," to use Linda Hutcheon's term. While the overarching historical narratives of the Jazz Age and the civil rights movement form the backgrounds of these books, Morrison focuses on the individual's experience of and reaction to these moments. Moreover, her use of spectrality evolves to incorporate the narrators and the text itself. In *Jazz,* the narrator is so impossible to pin down that its gender, age, and corporality are all questioned. In *Love,* the reader discovers that the occasional first-person narrator of the novel is dead in the fictional present but still aids the reader in sifting through the various interpretations of reality offered in response to the changing political environment of the 1960s and 1970s. The very spectrality of narration in these two texts points to the fluid, shifting, and multivalent aspects of an inclusive American history that recognizes and values multiple perspectives.

In the fifth chapter, I discuss the implications of the spectral for Morrison's latest novel, *A Mercy* (2008). In this novel, Morrison revisits themes of her earlier work: the destruction of the family unit by slavery; mother and daughter relationships; obsessive love; degrees of freedom; the importance of community; class, gender, and race conflicts; and patriarchal dominance. *A Mercy* can be read as a companion piece to *Beloved,* and the two novels haunt each other in conversation about the effects of slavery. By creating Jacob Vaark's homestead, Morrison reveals valences of slavery that connect the New World to its European antecedents, America to the Caribbean, settlers to Native Americans, and women to the patriarchy. All of these relationships are present even if they appear to be visually absent or ignored. Finally, this novel continues the spectral narration of *Jazz* and *Love* through Florens's narration of her story by writing it on the walls of her deceased master's home and the appearance of Florens's mother, who has been a haunting presence in her daughter's life, at the end of the book. Even though Florens never learns why her mother abandoned her, the ghostly presence of this woman explains her choice to the reader.

In her essay "Rootedness: The Ancestor as Foundation," Morrison defines ancestors as "not just parents, they are sort of timeless people whose relationships to the characters are benevolent, instructive, and protective, and they provide a certain kind of wisdom" (343). She asserts that the absence of an ancestor is "frightening" and that "when you kill the ancestor you kill yourself" (343–44). She writes, "I want to point out the dangers, to show that nice things don't always happen to the totally self-reliant if there is no historical connection" (344). Building on this description of ancestors, I read the guides of her novels not just as shamans or as members of an older generation, but rather as spectral "entities" actively haunting characters and repairing mental damage and separation. Each specter serves as a bridge for the people she haunts, connecting individuals to cultural and personal history and generations to one another.

CHAPTER ONE

Spectral Beginnings in *The Bluest Eye* and *Sula*

As a figure of transition, mediation, and connection, the specter enters into a relationship with the social ghosts of the text, and this relationship catalyzes a transformative healing and seals the ruptures that have resulted from oppression and silence. If Morrison's canon is connected through this thread of haunting history uncovered, emphasized, and re-created by the interaction between social ghosts and spectral figures, then this process must start at the beginning. While the two types of ghostly figures that I have identified are manifested most powerfully from *Song of Solomon* onward, it is possible to discern the seeds of these concepts in Morrison's first two novels, *The Bluest Eye* and *Sula.* These two books can be read as primers that prepare the reader for the appearance of later characters such as Beloved and Consolata.

When looking at Morrison's first novel, *The Bluest Eye,* through this ghostly framework, pointing out haunting aspects is not necessarily a new thing when we take into consideration explorations of influence such as John N. Duvall's suggestion that Ellison's *Invisible Man* "haunts" Morrison's first narrative and Michael Awkward's contention that Morrison uses this novel as a "self-conscious rejection of the models of . . . James Baldwin and Ralph Ellison" in favor of a celebration of the influence of Zora Neale Hurston as a literary predecessor (58). Moreover, many critics have looked at her use of the school primer that heads each of the sections and how these snippets show the difference between the reality of Pecola's family and the too-perfect-to-be-true, supposedly "typical" American family represented in the "Dick and Jane" reader. As the snippets repeat and deteriorate structurally, thus Pecola's mental life also spins out of control. For me, however, the haunting moments in the work focus around Pecola and her family. Using the metaphor of the ghost for female and ethnic invisibility from the critical work of Kathleen Brogan and Avery F. Gordon, I read the Breedloves, and in particular Pecola, as social ghosts who haunt the periphery of their community as they struggle with poverty and racism. While Pecola may experience tragedy and may not find a spectral figure in her text to help her negotiate her painful path, I see *The Bluest Eye* as an important anticipation of the social conditions that will silence characters in Morrison's later fiction. This text is an important precursor to the powerful haunting work that appears in later books such as *Beloved* and *Paradise,* therefore creating intertextual and dialogic relationships in her work. Pecola is the initial haunting signal in her canon that cries for the presence of a Beloved.

According to Philip Page, "Underlying Morrison's fiction is the paradox of dangerous freedom." For him, characters that I have termed social ghosts, such as Cholly Breedlove, Sethe, Denver, and Joe and Violet Trace exhibit this paradox in that they "are in varying degrees unconventional, wild. They are relatively free from social norms, free to create themselves, to experiment with identity formation and with relationships with others. . . . Yet simultaneously and necessarily, this wildness is also dangerous, for it forces the characters to rely on themselves for their continuing spiritual growth and their precarious stability, and it throws them into uncharted territories of experimental identities" (*Dangerous Freedom* 27). While Page sees these characters as "dangerously free," I read them through the framework of Brogan's use of the ghost as a metaphor for ethnic female experience and Gordon's work on the sociological implications of ghosts, for they share more than an opportunity to shape their identities. Several of the characters that he identifies begin their stories isolated and disconnected from their communities and their pasts. Their freedom is indeed "dangerous," as it requires a deconstructive force to counteract their marginalized and compartmentalized existence. For Brogan, "ghosted" individuals signal an "absence made present," or a kind of living ghost (25). As being ghostly implies a lack of substance or visibility even when present, it is the perfect metaphor for the manner in which many women and minorities find themselves unrepresented in the life of society. Gordon, a sociologist, came to the conclusion in her work that "[t]o study social life one must confront the ghostly aspects of it" (7). She notes, "The available critical vocabularies were failing (me) to communicate the depth, density, and intricacies of the dialectic of subjection and subjectivity . . . of domination and freedom, of critique and utopian longing" (8). According to Gordon, "[t]o write stories concerning exclusions and invisibilities is to write ghost stories" (17). The social ghost is a natural by-product of the national power structure of domination and freedom. In a binary relationship, the social ghost is the haunting signifier of the broad and generative space between. Without some sort of deconstructive ability to break down these impermeable borders, however, the marginalized figure becomes an apparition—one of the invisibilities that Gordon seeks to illuminate.

In *The Bluest Eye,* Morrison precisely limns the condition of social ghosting in the tragedy of the Breedlove family, in particular Pecola, and many of the struggles that slowly chip away at this family resurface in Morrison's later work. For example, Pecola's parents, Cholly and Pauline, are marginalized because of their race and their poverty, issues that will reappear in *Song of Solomon, Tar Baby,* and *Love,* and they are progenitors of Joe and Violet Trace in *Jazz* in that they are haunted by horrible incidents they experienced in the South before migrating to Ohio. When the narrator introduces the reader to the Breedloves' storefront home, the family's location on the periphery of the community is emphasized:

> So fluid has the population in that area been, that probably no one remembers . . . when the Breedloves lived there, nestled together in the storefront. Festering together in the debris of a realtor's whim. They slipped in and out of the box of peeling gray, making no stir in the neighborhood, no sound in the labor force, and no wave in the mayor's office. Each member of the family in his own cell of consciousness, each making his own patchwork quilt of reality. (34)

Like Sethe, Baby Suggs, and Denver in 124 after it is haunted, the Breedloves are marginalized from the larger community. They are part of a long line of tenants in the abandoned storefront, from shopkeepers to gypsies, and no one pays attention to their existence except to collect a rent check. Even the furniture is impersonal and damaged during delivery, with the family having no recourse to complain or get a replacement. Besides a lack of contact with the outside world, the family members do not have relationships with each other as each lives in a separate world of pain and fear. The reasons for the pain and the violence in the family are apparent in the "patchwork quilt" of the parents' pasts.

Part of the reason for Cholly's abuse of his wife and his rape of Pecola can be found in his traumatic memories of his first sexual experience and his parents' rejections of him. When he is a young man in Georgia, after his aunt's funeral, he leaves the gathering with his friend Darlene and the two begin to make love. Suddenly, white hunters who have been following their dogs interrupt the pair and then force them to continue intercourse while being watched in the glare of flashlights and under the aim of guns. Cholly becomes angry with Darlene for causing him to be there in the first place. He knows that he cannot hate the white men or defend himself or Darlene because they have guns and all the power in this situation. Thus begins Cholly's coping mechanism of misdirected rage. After this traumatic experience, he makes the decision to run away and try to find his father. When he does find him, he cannot talk to him, and his father threatens him. The effect of the abuse and rejection is that Cholly gives up on relationships and becomes entirely self-reliant. As Morrison writes, "Abandoned in a junk heap by his mother, rejected for a crap game by his father, there was nothing more to lose" (160). He wanders rudderless and only cares for his own "perceptions and appetites" (160). Family life bores him with its "sameness," and he has no clue about how to interact with his children. He is rendered "totally dysfunctional" by them and has no stable connection; he can only react to them rather than provide emotional support (160–61). Before he rapes his daughter, he realizes that he is haunted by her very presence, as it is an accusation of his responsibility for her misery. He cannot fathom what he could possibly give her or how he could comfort her. His abuse of his family can be read as an attempt to reclaim agency and presence in a situation in which he has had no viable models of behavior, but his violence only serves to silence and destabilize these intimate relationships, in particular with his daughter.

Cholly's wife, Pauline, feels isolated throughout her life. As a child, she suffered an injury to her foot that left her with an acute limp, and it is in this self-perceived "deformity" that she identifies the root of her "separateness" within her own family, a condition that was more likely the result of the economic strain of a thirteen-person family in the rural South. She lacks nurturance: she never receives a nickname, never has any stories told about her, never gets special food cooked or saved for her, "never felt at home anywhere, or that she belonged anyplace" (111). Once she and Cholly move to Ohio, this marginal feeling intensifies: "*Everything changed. It was hard to get to know folks up here, and I missed my people. I weren't used to so much white folks. The ones I seed before was something hateful, but they didn't come around too much. . . . That was the lonesomest time of my life*" (117). Even though Cholly and Pauline migrate northward for a safer life and more opportunities, this move also means a loss of those southern relationships of family and friends. The couple has no support group in Ohio.

The final straw that breaks the Breedloves' relationship surfaces when Pauline becomes increasingly concerned with money and her appearance, unconsciously downloading the dominant culture's "ideals" of beauty during her trips to the movie theater. She feels that her perceived ugliness and her deformity are disconnecting her from her community: "Money became the focus of all their discussions, hers for clothes, his for drink. The sad thing was that Pauline did not really care for clothes and makeup. She merely wanted other women to cast favorable glances her way" (118). These money disputes lead to the family being "put outdoors" for some time. The simple difference between eviction and being *outdoors* encapsulates the Breedloves' ghostly position on the periphery without hope: "If you are put out, you go somewhere else; if you are outdoors, there is no place to go. . . . But the concreteness of being outdoors was another matter—like the difference between the concept of death and being, in fact, dead. Dead doesn't change, and outdoors is here to stay" (17–18). Unlike later Morrison characters, the Breedloves do not have hope for transformation—they are condemned to being socially dead without recourse to digesting the past and re-creating a future.

This violence and displeasure trickle down to the children, Pecola and Sammy. Sammy, on the one hand, deals with the family situation by participating in the fights between his parents and constantly running away from home. Pecola, on the other hand, is forever thinking about invisibility. She either notices that others ignore her, or she desires to be invisible until she can acquire blue eyes, which she thinks are the epitome of beauty. She prays "to disappear" (45), and she protects herself from the violence of her family and the scorn of the community by hiding behind a mask: "She hid behind hers. Concealed, veiled, eclipsed—peeping out from behind the shroud very seldom, and then only to yearn for the return of her mask" (39). Her fellow students at school torment her for being too black, and the whites and middle-class African Americans of her town ignore her presence. As Madonne M. Miner notes, "[*The Bluest Eye*] contains repeated instances of Pecola's negation as other characters refuse to see her" (187). In a telling scene in a candy store, Pecola finds in the clerk's eyes "a total absence of human recognition—the glazed separateness" (*The Bluest Eye* 48). The narrator tells us, "He does not see her, because for him there is nothing to see" (48). There is an uncrossable chasm between Pecola and this white immigrant. He does not even want to touch her hand to take her money.

When Pecola's despair over her loneliness and perceived ugliness intensifies after her father has impregnated her, she reaches out to Soaphead Church, who is a "Reader, Adviser, and Interpreter of Dreams" (165). This moment would seem to presage the later appearance of Pilate, Baby Suggs, or Consolata in Morrison's canon. In this vein, we learn that because he "palm[ed] himself off as a minister" upon his arrival in Lorain, Ohio, and because of his unusual celibacy, the women of the town, "not being able to comprehend his rejection of them, decided that he was supernatural rather than unnatural" (171). This belief in his supernatural aura feeds directly into his success as a kind of conjure person who helps the townspeople fix problems with "love, health, and money" (172). Unfortunately, Soaphead Church is exactly what Pecola does not need: he is a con man. Unlike Morrison's future spiritual guides, who are grounded in both bodily and spiritual experience and accepting of life as it is lived, Church is a sterile misanthrope who "disdain[s] human contact" (165). He also is affected deeply by the very class and racial politics that have destroyed Pecola's self-perception. We know that "he had been reared in a [West Indian] family proud of its academic accomplishments and its mixed blood" (167), and he shares Pecola's anguish that she cannot, as he puts it: "rise up out of the pit of her blackness and see the world with blue eyes" (174). Instead of aiding her by transforming her reaction to her circumstances, he exacerbates her disconnect and self-hatred and uses her for his own ends in the process. He gives her poisoned meat to give to a dog that he hates and tells her that if the "animal behaves strangely, your wish will be granted on the day following this one" (175). Once Pecola has left, convinced that she will have blue eyes, Church writes an accusatory letter to God, blaming the deity for the lack of love in his life and announcing that he will do God's job for him, and in Church's *mercy* help girls like Pecola. Instead of explaining Pecola's beauty to her and helping her to reconnect to a larger community, Church's lack of true care for others and his belief in the prevailing values that created Pecola's problem result in her complete disconnect from the world and a spiral into madness. This behavior stands in stark contrast to a guide like Consolata, who will help others face and digest painful memories and create relational support networks in the present.

In the final section of the novel, Claudia describes the madness that Pecola experiences after her baby dies. According to Claudia, "The damage done was total. She spent her days, her tendril, sap-green days, walking up and down, up and down, her head jerking to the beat of a drummer so distant only she could hear. Elbows bent, hands on shoulders, she flailed her arms like a bird in an eternal, grotesquely futile effort to fly" (204). In an effort to "fly" away from her dire situation, Pecola has a final break with reality and creates an imaginary friend, or a ghostly alter ego, so to speak, that only she can see. Pecola wonders why this friend she never saw until she believed she had blue eyes has just appeared, and the ghost of her subconscious answers, "*You didn't need me before*" (196). Pecola is so lonely that she has created a companion, and this friend is the only person who can see her new blue eyes. Even her mother has rejected her: Pauline beat Pecola for being raped and ignores her daughter when they are at home together. Pecola has finally buckled under the pressures of isolation, poverty, and racism. She believes that she has blue eyes, and she lives in her mind, haunted by conversations that she has with her ghosted split self. Since her mother and the community simply ignore her predicament, this is the only place where she can speak of the horrors she has experienced and tried to repress. Several times during their conversation, this ghost of herself questions whether Pecola tried hard enough to stop the rape and reminds her that she was assaulted twice, something Pecola violently denies. The fear and shame that she buries deep inside refuse to lie quietly; these emotions erupt into her everyday reality through an alternate personality. This alternate self is a space for all her self-hatred and shame. It brings up things that Pecola violently represses. This figure is not spectral because it supports her belief that she has blue eyes, and it cannot help her deal with her painful past, since she refuses to engage it on any subject other than her blue eyes. Instead of helping her reach out to others, it allows her to retreat further into herself. Her desire for beauty and the abuse from her father haunt her and lead to her painful marginalization from her family, the community, and her own sanity.

Pecola and her family haunt the narrative, and they haunt their community, with no access to connection with the surrounding townspeople. There is no rejoining the community at the end of *The Bluest Eye,* as in *Song of Solomon* and *Beloved.* Rather, the community scapegoats the family and allows it to fall apart. In a shining example of why Pauline could not feel welcome when she and Cholly moved north, Claudia and Frieda overhear the adults discussing Pecola's situation. Rather than offering help or at least sympathy, the grown-ups partially blame Pecola for her rape and hope that the resulting baby dies. This hostility shocks Claudia and Frieda, who want the baby to live for precisely the reason that if it does not survive, then the prevailing social values that have destroyed Pecola will win. Claudia thinks, "I felt a need for someone to want the black baby to live—just to counteract the universal love of white baby dolls, Shirley Temples, and Maureen Peals" (190). Claudia does not want the damaging reification of whiteness to continue into the next generation. Moreover, there is the implication in Claudia and Frieda's concern that they know that without their tight sisterly bond and their close family relationships, they might have succumbed as Pecola has. The Breedloves, in contrast to the MacTeers, are barely surviving economically and allow these concerns to disrupt the family relationships. On top of that, the larger community ignores them until there is a scandal. There is no safety net for Pecola once she leaves the MacTeer home to return to her family. Except for Claudia and Frieda, no one takes an interest. Indeed, the gossips regard the entire family with suspicion: "Don't nobody know nothing about them anyway. Where they come from or nothing. Don't seem to have no people" (189). Because they are migrants, the Breedloves are seen as outsiders and no one comes to their defense or even seems to try to understand their situation. Their personal histories and origins are publicly erased and privately tear them apart.

Pecola's madness makes her the town's eccentric, not an object of pity or a call to guilt. Similar to Sula's position in Medallion, but without that character's self-confidence, she becomes the space where the community places its "waste," as the members view her problems and are relieved that they do not have them. She is shunned as people "tr[y] to see her without looking at her" (204). The only people who feel some responsibility are Pecola's girlfriends Claudia and Frieda, who try to help her but are powerless to address her entrenched inferiority complex. Pecola's presence on the outskirts of the town, "searching the garbage," talking to her split self, and believing that she has magical blue eyes (206), is a haunting presence. As Morrison posits in the "Afterword," Pecola is the sign of unspeakable things unspoken—the danger to anyone in the community of the "damaging internalization of assumptions of immutable inferiority originating in an outside gaze" (210). Claudia points to this overarching social problem in her final words: "I talk about how I did *not* plant the seeds too deeply, how it was the fault of the earth, the land, of our town. I even think now that the land of the entire country was hostile to marigolds that year. This soil is bad for certain kinds of flowers" (206). Claudia correctly places a share of the blame on the larger communities that fail Pecola and perpetuate this terrible definition of idealized beauty, including the town and the nation. As Gordon posits, "It is essential to see the things and the people who are primarily unseen and banished to the periphery of our social graciousness" (196). Instead of acting as if the problems that hurt Pecola do not exist, actually *seeing* Pecola and the damage done to her psyche is the first step toward exorcising the social forces that gave rise to this broken girl, and Morrison continues to direct her penetrating and recovering gaze into silent lives throughout her later novels. Still to come in her work are characters like Milkman, Sethe, Denver, and Joe and Violet, to name a few, who will begin their journeys isolated and in thrall to loss, but end in a space of connection to the past, loved ones, and the larger community.

Whereas *The Bluest Eye* is a primer on later issues of social ghosting in the Morrison canon, her next novel, *Sula,* continues this concern with social apparitions and edges toward the creation of the spectral figure that is so important to her later works. The titular main character is a precursor to figures such as Pilate and Beloved, but she does not share their spectral predilection for crossing boundaries and for exploding expectations within her community. Sula alienates others rather than healing them. In anticipation of Pilate, Sula is ambiguous. She escapes definition as evinced by a birthmark over her eye, which is variously interpreted as a flower, a tadpole, or a snake, depending upon who is observing it. She defies the traditional roles for women of wife and mother; instead, she leaves her home to attend college and travel the country. Like Pilate's wandering through her geography book, Sula searches across the country for something new: "Nel was one of the reasons she had drifted back to Medallion, that and the boredom she found in Nashville, Detroit, New Orleans, New York, Philadelphia, Macon and San Diego" (*Sula* 120). A bizarre "plague of robins" signals her return to the Bottom (89), where she becomes a marginalized figure because of her wanton sexuality and her disregard for her grandmother, whom she commits to a charity rest home. As Duvall observes, both Sula and Pilate are on the margins of society, but whereas Pilate focuses outward on nurturing others, Sula turns inward and is rejected by the larger community (56). On her deathbed, she tells Nel, "Girl, I got my mind. And what goes on in it. Which is to say, I got me" (*Sula* 143). She, like Cholly before her, has decided to forego personal relationships and instead pursue only her own appetites.

Morrison signals Sula's initial openness to liminality by creating in her childhood home a house that anticipates Pilate's home, 124, and the Convent—a borderless, spectral zone of connection and possibility. Sula lives with her grandmother Eva Peace and her mother, Hannah, in a rambling carnivalesque home of excess:

> Sula Peace lived in a house of many rooms that had been built over a period of five years to the specifications of its owner, who kept on adding things: more stairways—there were three sets to the second floor—more rooms, doors and stoops. There were rooms that had three doors, others that opened out on the porch only and were inaccessible from any other part of the house; others that you could get to only by going through somebody's bedroom. The creator and sovereign of this enormous house . . . was Eva Peace, who sat in a wagon on the third floor directing the lives of her children, friends, strays, and a constant stream of boarders. (30)

This Gothic maze of confusing rooms and stairways is a female space, as Eva rules the ever-changing group of people who live there and visit. Hannah handles all the housekeeping, and she cultivates a reputation for sleeping with most of the men from town wherever she and a potential paramour happen to be in the house together. Sula's best friend, Nel, who comes from the highly ordered world of her mother, where everything is in its place and where Nel must regulate even her appearance by wearing a clothespin on her nose to thin it, loves this disordered space of life and experience. For a young child with a rigid mother, Eva's house is one of endless possibilities: "[S]he preferred Sula's wooly house, where a pot of something was always cooking on the stove; where the mother, Hannah, never scolded or gave directions; where all sorts of people dropped in; where newspapers were stacked in the hallway, and dirty dishes left for hours at a time in the sink, and where a one-legged grandmother named Eva handed you goobers from deep inside her pockets or read you a dream" (29). This passage could be describing Pilate's house, or the Convent of *Paradise,* or even 124 before the death of the "crawling-already" infant. Eva's home has the potential to be a spectral zone of transformation and possibility, but as the family disintegrates and Sula inherits the family home, the flux and development begin to dissipate.

When Sula returns home from her rambling around the country, she and Eva argue over the deaths of Plum and Hannah. Sula resents Eva's belief in her power of life and death over her children, and Eva resents Sula's apparent disinterest in the burning of her mother: she made no move to help Hannah and simply watched the woman burn to death. In addition to a deep misunderstanding between two strong-willed women, there is a generational disconnection. Even though Tar Baby and the Deweys still live in (haunt) the home, it is darkened from its earlier days of company and conversation. Eva is alone in her room with her porch window boarded over so that she cannot watch the proceedings of the town below and participate as she did before the trauma of Hannah's death. She is isolated, and once Sula returns, instead of a happy reunion, both women lock their doors against each other in an eerie anticipation of the separate living quarters in one house that Heed and Christine will later share in *Love.* Instead of developing the home into its former glory as a communal meeting place, Sula makes herself Eva's guardian and power of attorney and banishes her grandmother to a nursing home. She then proceeds to live in the house alone.

According to Deborah Guth, the real center of the novel is Eva, not the selfish Sula. She writes, "through the narrative of Sula's failed journey to selfhood, it is in fact Eva's inner potency, her black ancestral knowledge and their loss that is being explored" (319). She reads Nel's conversation with Eva at the end of the novel as "Eva's uncanny return," which "reinstates the full authority of the past" (319). While Eva does exhibit some tendencies toward spectrality—for example, she haunts Nel by implicating her in Chicken Little's death, and she is the ancestral figure of the novel—I read her as more evidence of Sula's failed spectral possibilities in her attempts to limit the powers of her grandmother. She isolates her grandmother. Eva does not connect with anyone at the end but Nel. Unlike later spectral characters, Eva's effects are limited by Sula's rejection of valuing others. Sula could continue her grandmother's work in the community, but she gradually closes rooms in the house and withdraws from a community that is already pulling away from her because it blames her for any negative or harmful occurrence. She does not pay much attention to the Deweys or Tar Baby, and her ultimate sin in the eyes of the community—putting Eva in a home—violates one of the tenets of Morrison's essay "Rootedness." Sula mistreats her ancestor, and as Morrison asserts, "when you kill the ancestor you kill yourself" ("Rootedness" 343–44). With this warning in mind, it is not surprising that Sula contracts a mysterious illness and dies before the end of the novel. Sula rejects the communal carnivalesque nature of her grandmother and her home; she focuses on the excesses of her own pleasures.

Unlike Pilate and Beloved, who create connection, Sula denigrates most relationships, except for her friendship with Nel. According to Laurie Vickroy, she "sacrifice[s] connection for freedom" (306). Her positive effects come from her identity as a community scapegoat, and they dissipate after she dies. The townsfolk do improve because of her, but this is because she forms the baseline for evil that everyone wishes to rise above: "Their conviction of Sula's evil changed them in accountable yet mysterious ways. Once the source of their personal misfortune was identified, they had leave to protect and love one another" (*Sula* 117). This effect on the community only lasts as long as she is physically present, however. After her death, the townspeople forget their insistence on being better than she: "The tension was gone and so was the reason for the effort they had made. Without her mockery, affection for others sank into flaccid disrepair" (153). The only person who experiences lasting effects from Sula's life and death is Nel, who finally understands that her despair over the disintegration of her marriage was actually her anguish over losing Sula, not her husband. This epiphany is poignant, but it changes nothing between Sula and Nel, or even the Bottom. It is Nel's personal tragedy, and it is a moment of devastating loss, rather than uplift or redemption.

Sula's ability to affect Nel after she has died and her reaction at the moment of death point to her liminal possibilities, which she has hitherto ignored. Even at the end, Sula is pleased by her isolation and the finality of death. Instead of accepting Shadrack's promise of life in spite of death, "always," she glories in a room that is closed off from the world. She is in Eva's room, and the window from which Eva leaped in an attempt to save her daughter is sealed, illustrating Sula's broken relationships and self-centeredness. She finds comfort in this womb-like space: "And looking at those four wooden planks with the steel rod slanting across them was the only peace she had. The sealed window soothed her with its sturdy termination, its unassailable finality. It was as though for the first time she was completely alone—where she had always wanted to be—free of the possibility of distraction" (148). This is a remarkable reversal of the openness to possibility in later works, in particular *Paradise.* In *Paradise,* the townspeople see an open window or door that piques their curiosity about what happened to the Convent women and what is to come, whether helpful or harmful. Sula so relishes death as the end of her life journey of exploration that she is astonished when she learns the power of the open door or window between life and death. Her death is a painless passage. She realizes that she has died after the anticlimactic fact, and she evidently still can speak: "Well, I'll be damned . . . it didn't even hurt. Wait'll I tell Nel" (149).

Remarkably, she does tell Nel, in a way, during Nel's epiphany, which ends the novel. When Nel is walking home from Sula's funeral, thinking about how Sula must have caused the rain to fall on the singing women as a kind of vengeance, she passes the other town outcast, Shadrack, and has a painful realization. As if she has heard Sula's voice call out to her through her musings on the past, Nel responds, "Sula?" and "gaze[s] at the tops of trees" (174). At this moment, Nel's ball of grief and anger bursts, and she realizes that her grief has been for the loss of her friend Sula, not for her husband, Jude. Morrison writes, "And the loss pressed down on her chest and came up into her throat," and Nel cries out to her lost friend, "We was girls together. . . . girl, girl, girlgirlgirl" (174). Nel does have an epiphany, but it only deepens her loss. Even though there is the possibility that Sula is influencing and directing Nel's grief from beyond the grave, there is no conversation, no connection for the friends after death as there will be between Heed and Christine in *Love.* Nel calls to Sula, but Sula does not seem to be able to answer, and Nel's call is composed of "circles and circles of sorrow" (174). She understands her pain and can verbalize it, but she cannot fix her relationship with her friend because Sula is dead and gone.

Tellingly, Nel feels Sula's presence after she passes Shadrack, who is connected to Sula in the community's mind. Because of this and the trauma of his past, Shadrack becomes another complex character in this novel. He is a social ghost who exhibits spectral tendencies at the end, tendencies that, like Sula's, are not fully realized. He is linked to Sula through the community's decision to lump them together as outcasts. Town gossips note that Sula is the only person whom Shadrack does not "cuss," and he tips his hat to her. The verdict is that they are "two devils" (117). While Shadrack finds comfort in remembering when he found Sula in his cabin, "his visitor, his company, his guest, his social life, his woman, his daughter, his friend" (157), the two only meet in that one moment when he tells her the cryptic one-word message "Always." There is no continuing connection between the two except that they are both labeled outcasts by the larger community.

In an interview with Morrison in 1976, Robert B. Stepto equates Soaphead Church and Shadrack as "two crazies," but Morrison marks an important contrast between the two men, in that while they are both "eccentrics" and "outside the law," "Shadrack's madness is very organized" (388). Unlike Church's claim to be able to manipulate dreams and conjure, when he actually is a false spectral guide who only reinforces the self-hatreds of his clients, Shadrack attempts to deal with his painful past alone. Instead of creating connections and being open to possibility, Shadrack exercises extreme control over himself and his surroundings. Moreover, whereas Church is the opposite of a spectral figure because of his hatred of his community, Shadrack, like Pecola before him, is the consummate social ghost who makes tenuous grasps toward an oblivious community. He is so traumatized by his World War I experience of seeing a fellow soldier's face blown away that he awakes in a hospital completely unnerved. He believes that "anything could be anywhere," and he is horrified by his inability to control his hands. Every time that he tries to eat his food, his hands appear to grow and expand so quickly that he must hide them immediately (*Sula*

8–9). Either because of the hospital's need for more space, or because of Shadrack's panicked violence at the growth of his hands, he is discharged and given no personal information to help him find his home. He simply is given his release papers, a suit of clothes, and some money and then set adrift in a world that seems unpredictable and dangerous. His memory is chaotic and full of holes, and he admits to himself that he does not "even know who or what" he is (12). In a passage that anticipates Morrison's description of Consolata's ghosted state in *Paradise,* the narrator explains Shadrack's predicament in a list of what he lacks: "no past, no language, no tribe, no source, no address book, no comb, no pencil, no clock, no pocket handkerchief, no rug, no bed, no can opener, no faded postcard, no soap, no key, no tobacco pouch, no soiled underwear and nothing nothing nothing to do" (12). Since his hands seem unchecked and monstrous, his own body is alien to him, and, from this litany, it is clear that he has neither family nor means to take care of whoever he is. Shadrack's identity is a gaping absence. He was used in war, damaged, and set completely free with no assistance. Part of his terror is his "skittish apprehension that he was not real—that he didn't exist at all" (13). He only accepts his bodily existence when he sees his reflection staring back at him in a toilet in a jail cell. He needs to find his place and purpose.

Rather than allowing for life's possibilities, no matter how dangerous they may be, and facing his war past, Shadrack returns from the trauma of war to his grandfather's cabin in Medallion with a desire to order life as strictly as he can. He wants to repress the terrifying memories through routine and ceremony, like Violet's obsessive chores in *Jazz* and Sethe's beating back of memories while she beats dough in *Beloved.* He creates an even stronger binary between life and chaos and life and death by attempting to corral all life's dangers into one day of the year. He calls this day "National Suicide Day": "It was not death or dying that frightened him, but the unexpectedness of both. In sorting it all out, he hit on the notion that if one day a year were devoted to it, everybody could get it out of the way and the rest of the year would be safe and free" (14). The town is not affected much by Shadrack's mission. Life continues without much disturbance, since "once the people understood the boundaries and nature of his madness, they could fit him, so to speak, into the scheme of things" (15). "National Suicide Day" becomes a byword in the town as people note its passing and refuse to marry on that day, among other things, but the community is not transformed by the day at all. As with Sula's defiance of social boundaries for her own selfish interests, Shadrack works out his own demons on his holiday; it does not have outward reach until after the hard winter following Sula's death. Because of their eccentric behavior, Shadrack and Sula are pushed to the fringes of society. They affect the community only in that the community creates boundaries against the madness and perceived deviance that each represents.

After Sula's death and the subsequent hard winter, the community is struggling and Shadrack's call has a new power for them, but not for Shadrack. Sula's death has affected him deeply. In his mind, her death, despite his admonition of "always," is the proof that he cannot control life and death. He is a lonely man, aware of his lost connections with the local community, and he no longer orders his surroundings with "precision" (156). When Sula came to him as a child, Shadrack told her "'always' to convince her, assure her, of permanency" (157). He believes that her death is evidence that he is "wrong," and he "suspect[s] that all those years of rope hauling and bell ringing were never going to do any good" (157–58). Unlike Sula's realization that death is not the end of life, only a transition, Shadrack views her death as the end, as loss. He cannot move beyond the line between life and death; he cannot see the value of transcending opposition. When he goes out on his final "National Suicide Day," he is despondent, and "he no longer cared whether he helped them or not" (158). Unfortunately, it is at this time that the community follows him.

Even though Shadrack does not believe in his mission, the members of the town leave their homes and gather in a release of tension and fear. They parade behind Shadrack all the way to the unfinished tunnel they were not allowed to build. This display is described as a "curious disorder," and the people dance as "though the sunshine would last, as though there really was hope" (160). This effusion of connection is short-lived, like the sunshine, which cannot last. The sight of the tunnel is a concrete representation of dead promises: "Their hooded eyes swept over the place where their hope had lain since 1927. There was the promise: leaf-dead. The teeth unrepaired, the coal credit cut off, the chest pains unattended, the school shoes unbought, the rush-stuffed mattresses, the broken toilets, the leaning porches, the slurred remarks and the staggering childish malevolence of their employers" (161). The people fall upon this symbol of the economic hardship and oppression they are barely surviving, and they try to "kill . . . the tunnel they were forbidden to build" (161). Rather than a moment of triumph over these struggles, this is a moment of death, as the tunnel and its associations swallow many of the townspeople. Their actions are ineffectual because the tunnel collapses and drowns the attackers while Shadrack rings his bell. In a way, the community has committed suicide on "National Suicide Day," but Shadrack has not transformed anything. People only have died on a specific day. The survivors are still where they were before, still struggling against the forces that so damaged the Breedloves before them.

In these two novels, we see the beginnings of the issues of oppressive binary ways of viewing the world and the liberating fluidity of liminality that will interact in every following book in Morrison's canon. Isolated and marginalized characters like Pecola and Shadrack have been damaged and cast away by the larger American society as a result of poverty, violence, and racism, and they need some way to negotiate from these positions of loss toward connection with the larger community and a stronger sense of self-confidence. Acceptance of liminality and the "other side" is problematic and tenuous in these early texts. Unlike in novels to come, such as *Song of Solomon, Beloved,* or *Paradise,* characters who die, such as Plum and Hannah, do not exercise the possibility of return. Sula may offer a tenuous movement toward some form of acceptance of the fluid boundaries between past and present and life and death, but she does not realize this until after she dies; and she does not use this knowledge to help any marginalized characters deal with pain or create relationships. In life, she denigrates connection. She cuts off her grandmother from the community, and she helps isolate Nel. In a sea change from Sula and her belief that her freedom is in developing herself at the expense of interaction with others, Morrison's next novel, *Song of Solomon,* will show Milkman's leap, which as Guth notes, gives us a character who "embraces the present as well as the legendary past and defines freedom as complex connectedness" (324). These issues of marginalization, spectrality, and the search for origins and relational networks begin in flux, but they will develop throughout Morrison's writings, both in her fiction and nonfiction.

CHAPTER TWO

"Why Not Ghosts As Well?" The Presence of the Spectral in *Song of Solomon* and *Tar Baby*

Before we see Beloved in her ultimate and fully developed spectrality bridging life and death and confusing the area betwixt and between, we are introduced to the spectral in *Song of Solomon* (1977) through the character of Pilate and her interactions with her nephew, Milkman, and in *Tar Baby* (1981), where the spectral interrupts the lives of the characters, hinting at the loss of heritage and disavowal of the past that cause them to be marginalized. Many critics have noted the similarities between these two novels, even suggesting that *Tar Baby* might be a sequel to or revision of the previous book.[1] There are indeed many likenesses between the two works, even though one takes place as a journey that moves south from Michigan and then returns home, and the other one is set on a fictional Caribbean vacation island. Each novel problematizes class and race and the characters' relationships to issues of generational awareness and connection. The protagonists, Milkman and Jadine, are both rising stars in the real estate and fashion worlds, respectively. They have money and the opportunities it affords, but they are figuratively "dead" in that they are disconnected from their family heritage and cultural past: Milkman's father is consumed by his work and greed, and Jadine is an orphan who gets ahead on the dime of her aunt and uncle and their employers, her white patrons. While Milkman finds a bridge to his past in Pilate, a woman who lives in the space between the extreme positions that surround him, Jadine and her fellow characters find no connection despite the many supernatural places and presences that erupt at certain points in the text. These surges of the supernatural illustrate something more that the characters, particularly Jadine, cannot grasp. At the end of *Song of Solomon,* Milkman makes the leap into the mythic world of his family past and accepts his place in that lineage, but in *Tar Baby,* Jadine, while affected by her spectral encounters, returns to the safety of self-exile in Europe, refusing to face her past—at least not yet.

In 1977, *Song of Solomon* was chosen as a Book-of-the-Month-Club selection, the first by an African American since Richard Wright's *Native Son,* and the next year Morrison received the National Book Critics' Circle Award. The novel has since generated a large body of accompanying critical work that approaches it from various angles, most often addressing Morrison's use of folklore and the magical elements interpolated into Milkman's quest.[2] The book is also filled, however, with many supernatural details—from spectral figures to ghosted characters to actual ghosts that haunt various individuals. As Morrison told Salman Rushdie, "[L]ife is not as small as many people think it is, it's not completely repressed, it's not wholly scientific. . . . That's what makes life original. That part of it seemed to me absolutely part of the warp and woof of African-American life" (60). Crossings between life and death, certainty and speculation, and past and present are not clear-cut; and it is figures such as Morrison's later ghost, Beloved, that prod characters toward these liminal realizations.

Morrison's first incarnation of the Beloved-type spectral figure can be witnessed in the person of Pilate. According to many critics, she is the *griot* of *Song of Solomon*—the receptacle for both familial and cultural stories that she shares with the protagonist, Macon Dead III, or Milkman, as he is nicknamed by the Southside community.[3] In addition to being the young man's paternal aunt, she is clearly a guardian and mentor for Milkman in that she guarantees his birth and protects his life. Her brother, Macon Dead II, "remembered when his son was born, how she seemed to be more interested in this first nephew of hers than she was in her own daughter, and even that daughter's daughter" (*Song of Solomon* 19). Because of the barrenness of Milkman's parents' relationship, Pilate creates a powder that, when ingested, makes the elder Macon Dead visit his wife, Ruth, until she conceives a son. Then, in the face of Macon's attempts to abort Milkman, Pilate comes to Ruth's aid once more by using her conjure powers to scare

Macon. Pilate ensures Milkman's existence, and she sings during the initial scene of the novel as Robert Smith commits his suicidal leap from the top of the hospital and Ruth goes into labor with Milkman. Later, she even beats her granddaughter, Hagar, to try to keep her from killing Milkman after he has callously jilted her, his cousin and longtime lover. Finally, it is Pilate's journey north that Milkman must travel in reverse by going southward to Virginia so as to recover and digest his tangled family origins in slavery and Reconstruction. His journey begins as a part of his father's tortured search for the gold that caused the rift between him and his sister, Pilate, but it ends with Milkman's realization that the gold is gone and never really mattered in comparison to understanding the story of his ancestors—Solomon and Jake.

Pilate's home has many of the qualities of a borderless, spectral zone of connection and possibility, clearly anticipating later incarnations of this space in the island in *Tar Baby,* 124 in *Beloved,* and the Convent in *Paradise.* Her home is a communal place where she, her daughter Reba, and her granddaughter Hagar share responsibilities and avoid the normal indicators of society's progress. The home is on the edge of both the black and white neighborhoods and on the edge of the surrounding urban area too: "Her house sat eighty feet from the sidewalk and was backed by four huge pine trees, from which she got the needles she stuck into her mattress" (27). Macon notes that she and her house smell like "a forest." She has no electricity, no gas, and no city water, and lives "pretty much as though progress was a word that meant walking a little farther on down the road" (27). Like the Convent in Morrison's *Paradise,* Pilate's house is a female crossroads of production, trade, and consumption. She, Reba, and Hagar create wine to sell to the community mostly through trade of goods rather than for money. They do not hoard the profits or live by a set schedule: "They ate what they had or came across or had a craving for. Profits from their wine-selling evaporated like sea water in a hot wind—going for junk jewelry for Hagar, Reba's gifts to men, and [Macon] didn't know what all" (29). Macon, a harsh landlord who lives for the acquisition of things and people, views Pilate's home as a place where he can find in secret "just a bit of music" (28). While listening, he "thinks of fields and wild turkey, and calico" (29), and he feels himself "softening under the weight of memory and music" (30). His wife, Ruth, seeks Pilate whenever she needs help, first for the conception of

Milkman and then for his protection, and she also feels that the home is a "haven . . . an inn, a safe harbor" (135). Pilate's home is a safe zone of female community, and it is a space of memory, family heritage, and responsibility. Perhaps part of what triggers Macon's memory is the irony that his own father's bones are in Pilate's home. She firmly believes in her father's injunction that "[y]ou just can't fly on off and leave a body" (208), though she is not quite sure of the meaning of the phrase until she and Milkman finish the story of the Deads and bury Jake's bones in Virginia.

Indeed, Milkman's father tells him, "Pilate can't teach you a thing you can use in this world. Maybe the next, but not this one" (55). Macon means that this lesson should teach Milkman the importance of "own[ing] things" (55), but he is unconsciously telling Milkman exactly what he needs from Pilate. As his guide, she is a supernatural nexus of important family history that Milkman needs, and her belief in communal and extraordinary ways of knowing and being, rather than his father's love of wealth and status, transforms Milkman in the end. He cannot understand what truly happened to his great-grandfather Solomon and his grandfather Jake until he opens up to the possibility of spectral figures and events. He needs the dry facts and the well-worn oral stories of the past. Morrison indicates the tension between what is known and unknown, and she illuminates the presence of many layers of information underneath the surface of accepted knowledge through a conversation between Milkman and Freddie, his father's handyman and the man who gave Milkman his nickname. Milkman's eventual acceptance of ghosts and the supernatural is foreshadowed early in his life when community women speculate that his "deepness" as a child is a result of being born in a caul and caution Ruth that he may "see ghosts" (10).[4] As an adult, however, Milkman admits to Freddie that he is not sure about the existence of ghosts, but he offers, with a smile, that he is "willing to" believe. This mocking apathy shocks Freddie, whose worldview encompasses the supernatural as an everyday occurrence. He tells Milkman, "You better believe [in ghosts], boy. They're here. . . . I mean they in the world" (109). In an intriguing turn, after this conversation about spectral matters, Freddie cryptically reveals some information about Empire State and Milkman's radically political friend Guitar. Freddie describes the very real, but secretive, activities of the Seven Days revenge group as "strange things" of which Milkman is unaware in addition to his lack of knowledge about the supernatural.

Morrison emphasizes the necessity of this openness to ghosts in a discussion of *Song of Solomon* in her essay "Rootedness." In this novel, she wanted to "blend the acceptance of the supernatural and a profound rootedness in the real world at the same time with neither taking precedence over the other. . . . That kind of knowledge has a very strong place in my work" (342). Ghosts are often harbingers of strange and previously unknown information, and only after Milkman believes in ghostly happenings can he fit together his family's past. After his first meeting in Virginia with Susan Byrd about his grandmother Sing, Milkman discovers three important facts. First, Pilate's father's command for her to sing was really a call for his wife, a Native American woman named Sing. Second, he realizes that his "interest in his own people, not just the ones he had met, had been growing" since his initial foray into Danville, Pennsylvania (293). Third, he knows that his growing acceptance of the supernatural is vital to successfully deciphering the evidence left of his family: "Here he was walking around in the middle of the twentieth century trying to explain what a ghost had done. But why not? he thought. One fact was certain: Pilate did not have a navel. Since that was true, anything could be, and why not ghosts as well?" (294).

By contrast, Pilate's belief in ghosts diverges sharply from Milkman's inability to accept the supernatural *until* he has traveled to Shalimar, Virginia, and decoded his family's history; but his softening toward this magical side of experience comes partially from her and her strangeness—her lack of a navel and her conversations with her dead father. As Milkman asserts, "Pilate did not have a navel. Since that was true, anything could be" (294). Macon remembers her miraculous birth:

> After their mother died, she had come struggling out of the womb without help from throbbing muscles or the pressure of swift womb water. As a result, for all the years he knew her, her stomach was as smooth and sturdy as her back, at no place interrupted by a navel. It was the absence of a navel that convinced people that she had not come into the world through normal channels; had never lain, floated, or grown in some warm and liquid place connected by a tissue-thin tube to a reliable source of human nourishment. (27–28)

For all the bizarreness that other people attach to this aspect of Pilate, the young Macon "thought [it] no more strange than a bald head" (28). This lack of a navel, though, is the chief reason for Pilate's power and her unease in the community. Her oddity separates her at the same time as it affords her special powers: Pilate "never bothered anybody, was helpful to everybody, but . . . also was believed to have the power to step out of her skin, set a bush afire from fifty yards, and turn a man into a ripe rutabaga—all on account of the fact that she had no navel" (94). Remarkably, Pilate's stomach is not the only place that is preternaturally smooth. Part of what scares Ruth when she sees Pilate is something that is quite Beloved-like: "Ruth was still frightened of her a little. Not just her short hair cut regularly like a man's, or her large sleepy eyes and busy lips, or the smooth smooth skin, hairless, scarless, and wrinkleless" (138). Pilate seems to be a timeless woman. Life and age do not show on her skin.

In addition to Pilate's eerie lack of a navel and the typical marks of aging, she can change her physical appearance when necessary.[5] After Milkman and Guitar steal Pilate's bag of bones because they think it contains the gold that divided her and Macon, the police stop the two young men for no apparent reason other than that they are African American. The police find the bag of human remains and arrest them. While Macon tries to appease the police officers by offering money, Pilate appears and creates an elaborate persona of a weakened old woman from the South who kept her husband's bones after he was lynched in Mississippi because she could not afford the price of a proper burial (206–7). Milkman is amazed at Pilate's shape-shifting abilities, noting to his father that she changed her voice and her physical height, appearing shorter than her true stature, which equals that of Macon and Milkman. Macon believes that Pilate's ability to change her appearance and demeanor points to her evil "snake"-like powers (205), but Milkman has a different interpretation. He is ashamed of his behavior toward Pilate and that she, the victim of his crime, came to the station to help him: "But nothing was like the shame he felt as he watched and listened to Pilate. Not just her Aunt Jemima act, but the fact that she was both adept at it and willing to do it—for him. For the one who had just left her house carrying what he believed was her inheritance" (209). Far from being a show of weakness, Pilate's caricature of an older African American woman plays to all of the stereotypes that the police expect and allows her to manipulate them and recover her "inheritance." As Brenda Marshall writes, "She was someone else. Not Pilate, but someone who fit the cop's expectations. Pilate slips into the shapes and forms that society recognizes when it suits her purpose, as an actress slips into a role" (487).

While signaling a type of female conjuring power, these physical peculiarities concurrently push Pilate to "the boundaries of the elaborately socialized world of black people" (*Song of Solomon* 149). Because her body is marked by the lack of a navel, "every other resource was denied her: partnership in marriage, confessional friendship, and communal religion" (148). This isolation results in her becoming a migrant, a placeless person, and she uses her geography book as a guide, "planting her feet in each pink, yellow, blue or green state" (148). This borderless wandering continues until she pauses to "decide how she wanted to live and what was valuable to her" (149). Once she tracks down Macon and establishes her winemaking business near Southside, she spurns normal manners of behavior in order to focus on "a deep concern for and about human relationships" (149). For Susan L. Blake, "Pilate represents the spirit of community inherent in the folk consciousness" (78). The surrounding community may shun her, but it respects her powers, tacitly accepting her business, her healing talents, and her openness to the spiritual side of existence. According to Joseph T. Skerrett Jr., "Pilate functions as a priestess or *shaman;* she is a figure of power and mystery. . . . Pilate is the frightening source of uncomfortable questions and liberating truths" (198–99). This woman crosses every boundary through her fluid existence and agelessness. She is a free radical, concurrently outside and inside of the community, and she can even change her physical appearance to suit her purposes.

This acceptance of non-material and spiritual matters is illustrated in her close communication with her father after his death. He first appears when Pilate and Macon are children lost in the woods. Although they saw their father's dead body after he was killed, they now see him as if he is alive, and this specter leads the scared children to a cave for shelter overnight. Unbeknownst to them, this cave is the place where their father's body will be ditched by his murderers. After her daughter is born, Pilate's father begins visiting her regularly. Pilate informs Ruth that her father tells her what she needs to know: "All kinds of things. It's a good feelin to know he's around. I tell you he's a person I can always rely on. I tell you somthin else. He's the *only* one. I was cut off from people early" (*Song of Solomon* 141). Evidently, posthumous communication is not startling for Pilate. As with most other spectral manifestations, the meaning of Jake's appearance is not fixable or stable. He appears first to Pilate and her brother, and after that, only to Pilate, until Milkman sees him in Pennsylvania. He could be a manifestation of her memory of her father, or, more likely, he is her spectral guide, since he attempts to give her a message about her mother when he visits. Pilate believes that when he says, "Sing. Sing," and "You just can't fly on off and leave a body" that he wants her to sing for him and to find the body of the white man whom Macon murdered in the cave (147). Milkman discovers instead that Jake's wife was named "Sing" and that Pilate has Jake's bones, not the white man's, in her sack. Rather than asking Pilate to sing, Jake is calling his wife's name, and he is telling Pilate to bury him, so that he finally can rest. Even though she misinterprets her father's requests, Pilate still is a proponent of the interrelationship between the past and present; she thinks that "[l]ife is life. Precious. And the dead you kill is yours. They stay with you anyway, in your mind" (208). She transmits this care for family to Milkman, and his tentative steps toward this mindset are evident when he sees his grandfather's ghost upon his arrival in Danville, Pennsylvania. When Jake appears to Pilate, he wears a "white shirt, a blue collar, and a brown peaked cap" (150), and when Milkman looks for someone to ask for directions on the first leg of his journey retracing his family's migration, he meets a helpful "elderly" man wearing "a brown peaked cap and an old-fashioned collar" (227). This man points Milkman in the direction of people who know his family. If Pilate's spectral guide and a helpful ancestor is haunting Milkman, then he must be on the right track.

In direct opposition to Pilate's communal and nurturing existence, which is firmly rooted in her past and the "other side," stands the Dead household.[6] Wilfred D. Samuels notes that the family's "very name signifies forfeited beings, empty lives: inauthentic existence" (6). Unlike Pilate's home, which serves her surrounding community, the Dead house is Macon's monument to his wealth. When Macon thinks of his home, he sees "his wife's narrow, unyielding back; his daughters, boiled dry from years of yearning; his son, to whom he could speak only if his words held some command or criticism. . . . There was no music there" (*Song of Solomon* 28). He may be upwardly mobile, but he is not content. He evicts tenants, like Guitar's grandmother, with alacrity, even when there is good reason for a missed payment; he beats his wife into a kind of twisted submission; and he parades his daughters, Lena and Corinthians, for show, thereby effectively cutting them off from others and preventing them from creating independent lives outside of the family. By taking Milkman into the family business, he is attempting to inculcate his son with his materialistic and patriarchal values. Aware of her shadowy life under their father's thumb, Milkman's sister Lena accuses her brother of urinating on all the women in the family just as he did to her during a Sunday drive when they were children. She believes that Milkman is simply filling his father's shoes as the family oppressor through his control of Corinthians's first romantic relationship and his protection of their mother from abuse. Lena thinks that Milkman is not helping but continuing Macon's stranglehold on the family members' lives. At one point, Milkman realizes that he had never "thought of his mother as a person, a separate individual, with a life apart from allowing or interfering with his own" (75).

Growing up against this background of oppression and turmoil, Milkman is in dire need of some sort of connection before he sets off on his journey southward. Doreatha Drummond Mbalia calls Milkman "the living dead who sucks the life force from his people" (127). Unlike Pilate with her deep concern for others, Milkman could not care less about his family, and when he tries to show some sort of protective instinct, he replaces his father's violence: he hits his father to save his mother, and he denies Corinthians a relationship outside the home, even though she is a woman in her forties, because her partner, Porter, is a member of the Seven Days secret revenge society. His ultimate rejection of his cousin Hagar destroys her. After a lengthy romantic relationship that, for Milkman, is not monogamous, he drops Hagar by sending her a business-like thank you letter with a final Christmas gift. He thinks that this decision to break up with her is influenced by his middle-class sensibility and because she has become too easy. Besides his callousness toward his family and his lover, he has even less of a connection to his community. People whom his father has dispossessed refuse him service and avoid him, and he has no political awareness of the larger black community. This political ignorance drives a wedge between him and his friend Guitar, who joins the Seven Days. In an alarming display of selfishness, after being completely disconnected from the rage in the barbershop over the murder of Emmett Till, Milkman tells Guitar, "Yeah, well, fuck Till. I'm the one in trouble" (*Song of Solomon* 88). According to Mbalia, Milkman needs to develop "people consciousness" (126).

Morrison signals Milkman's lack of agency and his ghostly, ungrounded existence throughout the first part of the text before he leaves on his journey. When Hagar comes to kill him in Guitar's apartment, Milkman hopes for a moment that she will succeed: "Above all he wanted to escape what he knew, escape the implications of what he had been told. And all he knew in the world about the world was what other people had told him. He felt like a garbage pail for the actions and hatreds of other people. He himself did nothing" (*Song of Solomon* 120). Milkman is surrounded by extreme oppositions that he cannot reconcile. His father believes in the power of property and money, but he is stifling his family's development. His mother is obsessed with class and being known as Dr. Foster's daughter. Guitar believes strongly in the protection of the black community as a whole, but he joins a group that produces random violence to answer random violence.[7] All the people in Milkman's life tell him their stories to justify their actions, but they all compete for his loyalty. Instead of constructing his own viewpoint, he feels pressured to choose a side. He is incomplete, his very face "lacked coherence, a coming together of the features into a total self. It was all very tentative, the way he looked, like a man peeping around a corner of someplace he is not supposed to be, trying to make up his mind whether to go forward or to turn back" (69–70). The point of Milkman's journey becomes one of reconciliation with and the development of empathy for others. He does not have to choose his father's interpretation of his mother's love for her father over his mother's story, and he does not have to either ignore the African American community or join Guitar. He simply must listen and let the two perspectives stand by each other. Morrison symbolizes his immature inaction when he looks out of the back window of his father's car: "It was becoming a habit—this concentration on things behind him. Almost as though there were no future to be had" (35). Milkman feels that he does not have a future because he is not grounded in his past. He needs to look back into his family's past in order to heal his present and move into the future. He does this by journeying south, initially to find his father's gold, but he ends up discovering the origins of his family.

Once Milkman begins his search for the gold Macon and Pilate left behind, he encounters a black community in Danville, Pennsylvania, that is deeply connected to and still affected by the Dead family:

> They talked on and on, using Milkman as the ignition that gunned their memories. The good times, the hard times, things that changed, things that stayed the same—and head and shoulders above all of it was the tall, magnificent Macon Dead, whose death, it seemed to him, was the beginning of their own dying even though they were young boys at the time. Macon Dead was the farmer they wanted to be. (235)

Milkman's grandfather is the symbol of everything that they could achieve if they would work hard, and his death at the hands of the Butler family kills something inside of them. It is in this place, surrounded by his father's contemporaries, that Milkman, for the first time, "glittered in the light of their adoration and grew fierce with pride" (236). He tells the men stories of his father's triumphs, which they interpret as a continuation of the first Macon's successes, but while Jake nurtured the land and the surrounding community, Milkman's father is isolated and miserly with his wealth.

Besides the community of men who admired his grandfather, Milkman also meets the woman—Circe—who hid Pilate and Macon in the very home of their father's murderers. Circe becomes Milkman's spectral guide while he is en route, following Pilate's path without her.[8] According to A. Leslie Harris, every questing hero must seek answers in the Underworld, and for Harris, this is Circe's function in the text: "He could not reach the dream-like core of his quest, his journey into Virginia, without direct contact with the world of the past and the dead" (74). Indeed, Circe is a liminal figure, connected to the past and to the dead. She is an ancient woman who interacts with Milkman in the ruins of the Butler estate, but she is dead in the novel's present time frame. In a conversation with Reverend Cooper, Milkman notes that Circe "must have been a hundred years old when she died," but the clergyman tells him that she had to have been older than that because she was "a hundred when I was a boy" (*Song of Solomon* 233). Her abode, the Butler mansion, is a typical haunted house that looks "dark, ruined, evil," has what seems to be a ghostly child's eyes peeping from the second-story window not yet covered by ivy, and exudes a sharp smell of decay that mysteriously turns into a "sweet spicy perfume" when Circe appears (238–39). Milkman cannot rationalize what he is seeing. Circe is not dead because she is physically talking to him, but she cannot be alive because she died a long time ago. She is between Milkman's binary concepts of a separation between life and death and past and present. Her unfixable position is clear in that she welcomes Milkman because she thinks that he is Macon returning to visit her, and she cannot seem to understand the generation gap. She is a physical incarnation of the Dead family's past come to guide Milkman, and she tells him of his grandmother Sing, the family's origins in Virginia, and the location of the cave that he believes still holds the abandoned gold.

Circe even claims a kind of vengeful triumph in that she has supernaturally outlasted her mistress. At first during her story, it seems as if Circe was alive when the last Butler died—"there was nobody here but us" (243)—but later, it becomes clear that the reason the woman killed herself was that Circe was gone. Milkman accuses Circe of staying in the house because she loved the family, and this enrages the specter who knows that she is staying in the house *in spite of* the family. She explains:

> Do you know why she killed herself? She couldn't stand to see the place go to ruin. She couldn't live without servants and money and what it could buy. . . . She saw the work I did all her days and *died,* you hear me, *died* rather than live like me. Now what do you suppose she thought I was! If the way I lived and the work I did was so hateful to her she killed herself to keep from having to do it, and you think I stay here because I loved her, then you have about as much sense as a fart! (246–47)

The last Butler had no servants left at the end of her life, and she killed herself to keep from having to do Circe's work. If the woman "*died* rather than live like" Circe, then Circe, most likely, was already dead. This bearer of Milkman's family's past is deeply intertwined with class and racial conflict, but she is triumphant through her power to endure where her mistress could not. Circe has outlasted the conniving Butler family through her eternal return, and she oversees the mansion as it "crumbles and rot[s]" (247). She will not take care of the Butlers' property in any way, and it seems as if her presence will not be needed much longer as she tells Milkman that "the dead don't like it if they're not buried." She hopes, too, that someone will "find me soon enough and somebody'll take pity on me" (245). While she is congratulating Milkman here for his (pretended) concern over burying his grandfather, it also seems as if she is yearning for a proper burial for her own remains.

After speaking with Circe, Milkman is still obsessed with finding the gold in order to prove himself to his father and the men of Danville, but when he finds the cave after tramping through the forest, there is no gold. At this point, tired and tattered from the woods, he decides to keep following his family's original path and find Shalimar, Virginia, which is not easy since it does not appear on any maps that he can procure from AAA. For Denise Heinze, Shalimar is "an atypicality—no commerce, no transportation, no government. It even defies the myopic eye of the map. For all intents and purposes, Shalimar does not exist in civilization" (140). Shalimar is a spectral and indeterminate space, and it is where Milkman has his final epiphany about his ancestors. His family history haunts this place. The locals pronounce the town name "Shalimar" in a manner very similar to his great-grandfather's name, "Solomon"; every family in town claims a lineage to that patriarch; and the children even play a chanting game that tells the story of how Solomon flew back to Africa and left behind his wife and twenty-one children, including Milkman's grandfather Jake.

While in this small, southern town, Milkman develops the knowledge apparatus required to crack this familial and historical code. He goes on a hunt with the older men of the town. This is a communal ritual that ultimately allows him entrance into their group and furnishes another clue to his mystery, for the older men tell him how to find his cousin Susan Byrd, who knows about his grandmother Sing. During the nighttime bobcat hunt, however, Milkman begins, on his own, the painful process of self-reflection that has been absent from his thinking up until this point. He realizes that he has never thought of others and only complained about whether or not he "deserved" anything—from hearing about politics from Guitar, to listening to his parents' quarrels, to putting up with Hagar's murder attempts. He thinks, "But why shouldn't his parents tell him their personal problems? If not him, then who? And if a stranger could try to kill him, surely Hagar, who knew him and whom he'd thrown away like a wad of chewing gum after the flavor was gone—she had a right to try to kill him too" (*Song of Solomon* 276–77). At this moment, Milkman is learning lessons about "people consciousness," and he will soon emulate Pilate's careful concern for others. At the very moment when he is listening to the children's chanting song about Solomon and Jake, Milkman is thinking of home and Pilate: "Milkman smiled, remembering Pilate. Hundreds of miles away, he was homesick for her, for her house, for the very people he had been hell-bent to leave" (300). While he does think also of his parents and sisters and now understands their motivations in a way he never had before, he first thinks of his spectral guide and her home. As he contemplates this newfound empathy for others, he is struck by certain phrases in the children's song. He translates this game, incorporating it directly into his memory and consciousness, using all the bits and pieces he has learned during his travels from the men in Danville, from Circe, from his cousin Susan Byrd, and, of course, from Pilate's blues song, which she sings at important moments in the text, in particular on the day his mother went into labor with him.

An important aspect of Milkman's heritage that he must discover is one that haunts American history itself: a Native American presence. He finds out that his grandfather married the daughter of his Native American foster mother, and early in the novel Guitar foreshadows the Native American presence in Milkman's past by alluding to the violent history of America: "The earth is soggy with black people's blood. And before us Indian blood" (159). After Milkman learns about his ancestors and leaves the South to return to Pilate, he takes the time to think about the land as a palimpsest of historical presences that were real and must be remembered: "He read the road signs with interest now, wondering what lay beneath the names. The Algonquins had named the territory he lived in Great Water, *michi gami.* How many dead lives and fading memories were buried in and beneath the names of the places in this country. Under the recorded names were other names. . . . Names that had meaning" (329). Milkman has learned another lesson from Pilate, his spectral guide: real names are important. Why else would she wear her name in a box hanging from her ear? His quest must deconstruct the layers of names, memory, and history in his family's past, a search that is redolent of the nation's contested history as well.

Once Milkman has proven himself to the men of Shalimar in the hunting ritual, experienced a healthy reciprocal relationship with Sweet, and puzzled out his family history, he has forgotten the gold and is excited about returning home to tell Pilate about his discoveries. He goes to see her before even setting foot in his own home and learns one more lesson about responsibility to others. While he has been on his self-actualizing quest, Hagar has passed away after completely losing any conception of self along with her loss of Milkman's love. Michael Awkward describes this deflation of Milkman's triumphant return as Morrison's "liter[ally] breaking Milkman's male heroic quest with the specifically antithetical story of Hagar's demise"

("Unruly and Let Loose" 107). Milkman's quest is not simply for his own benefit; it also helps make him more aware of his interactions with others, and he accepts his part in Hagar's demise: "He had hurt her, left her, and now she was dead—he was certain of it. He had left her. While he dreamt of flying, Hagar was dying" (*Song of Solomon* 332). He now fully understands the command of Pilate's father—"You just can't fly on off and leave a body" (332)—and he understands the pain of Solomon's wife Ryna and the children he left behind who kept the story of his flight aloft. With his newfound knowledge, he can tell Pilate that the bones she has been carrying are actually her father's and require burial, and he takes Hagar's hair with him to signify his responsibility for her. When he returns home, he has none of the things with which he left, but "he return[s] with a box of Hagar's hair" (334).

As another step forward in Milkman's development of compassion, responsibility, and awareness of his family's origins, Milkman returns to Shalimar to bury Jake's remains, this time accompanied by his spectral guide, Pilate. Unfortunately, Guitar is still chasing the nonexistent gold for very materialistic reasons reminiscent of Milkman's old worldview. Guitar wants the gold so that he can, in his mind, prove his love for the African American community by seeking revenge for the church bombing. Just as Milkman predicted earlier, Guitar's single-minded pursuit of revenge has resulted in his ability to kill anyone, marring his altruistic intentions. In anger, he shoots Pilate after she and Milkman have buried the bones. In a move typical of Morrison's novels, the book ends with uncertainty as Milkman leaps toward Guitar from Solomon's Leap, where his great-grandfather flew: "As fleet and bright as a lodestar he wheeled toward Guitar and it did not matter which one of them would give up his ghost in the killing arms of his brother. For now, he knew what Shalimar knew: If you surrendered to the air, you could ride it" (337). According to Marianne Hirsch, "The novel does not determine this end for us but remains inconclusive, undecidable, unreadable. Yet it ends in several moments of nurturing and connection" (157). These moments of "nurturing and connection" indicate Milkman's full understanding of his past and of Pilate's importance to that journey of discovery. As Pilate dies, she passes her spectral mantle to him. She asks him to watch over her daughter Reba, and she asks him to sing to her. Tellingly, he decides to sing her own song to her, only substituting "Sugargirl" for "Sugarman." In singing this changed song, he inserts

Pilate as a healing ancestor into the family tradition; as he notes, "Without ever leaving the ground, she could fly" (*Song of Solomon* 336). He also takes upon himself the role of griot and the keeper of the family past.

Most critics offer a positive reading of the end of the novel, but James Coleman has a more muted response to Milkman's leap, seeing it as a transcendent moment of knowledge for him, but not in any way related outward to the community: "[A]t the end there is no way to transfer the significance of Milkman's journey from the level of the mythical and symbolic to the practical level of the majority" (160). While I agree that this moment is more centered on the individual than in later Morrison works such as her trilogy, it is unclear whether Milkman is truly jumping to his death like Robert Smith at the beginning of the novel. He may be repeating Smith's action, but there is a difference this time. Because there is a possibility of his survival in the open ending, I do not believe the communal implications of his new awareness can be ignored. When he leaps, he understands his great-grandfather's escape, but, unlike the abandonment of the earlier flight, his is one of connection and mediation. He has learned and accepted his family's history, and he is leaping *toward* Guitar, who has been trying to kill him but whom he still calls "brother man" (*Song of Solomon* 337).

Pepsi Charles asked Morrison in an interview if *Song of Solomon* has what she would consider to be a "happy ending." Morrison responded: "Happy ending? I thought it was a book of absolute triumph! . . . Because a man learns the only important lesson there is to learn. And he wins himself, he wins himself. And the quality of his life improves immeasurably. Whether its length improves or lengthens is irrelevant. And his friend knows he has improved" (22). For Milkman, life and death are irrelevant binaries that are part of all the extremes that have stifled him his whole life and that he must transcend. Charles Scruggs posits that "Milkman's triumph is that for one brief second he sees man's potentiality for transcendence" (333), but this awareness does not last only for one second, regardless of whether his life ends or not. In a later interview on *Paradise,* Morrison emphasizes how an end to a character's life is not the point: "To say that the women lost is to forget all that they learned. . . . And at the end of the book their lives take on other dimensions. . . . The person who has the vision, converses with it, becomes larger than themselves" (Hostetler 197). In an anticipation of the women of *Paradise,* Milkman has learned of his own individual, family, and cultural pasts; he has experienced the vision; and he is now ready to accept new spectral and communal dimensions to his life regardless of what they may mean for his physical body. In her next novel, *Tar Baby,* Morrison shows the inherent danger to individuals who inhabit binaries without negotiation and may not experience the vision or Milkman's spectral development.

The follow-up to *Song of Solomon, Tar Baby,* published four years later in 1981, initially seems to be a departure for Morrison with its Caribbean island setting and a fully developed set of white characters joining the cast. The plot shares, however, some affinities with its predecessor. Once again, readers face a socially mobile African American individual who is cut off from the cultural past. Instead of a middle-class Milkman, in *Tar Baby* there is the orphan-turned-world-famous fashion model, Jadine Childs, who is more comfortable in the wealthy upper-crust world of her patron, Valerian Street, than around her working-class aunt and uncle or among Son's rural southern roots. In a manner similar to that of *The Bluest Eye,* all the characters in *Tar Baby* are socially marginalized in some way and they all, Valerian and Margaret, Sydney and Ondine, and Jadine and Son, haunt the Street household on Isle des Chevaliers. Unlike in *The Bluest Eye,* a few of these ghostly characters do have economic power, but as in *Song of Solomon* this fails as a substitute for personal development, compassion, and communal connection. Even the seemingly most privileged character is damaged in some way, and status does not heal wounds: it merely covers the pain. While there is not in this novel a complete transformation through spectral mediation such as Milkman's decision to fly like his ancestor or the Convent women's survival in another realm, there are still eruptions of the spectral that affect Jadine and pull her toward an encounter with her heritage. These moments of spectrality include her meeting with the African woman in canary yellow at the Paris supermarket, her vision of the night women in Eloe, Isle des Chevaliers itself, and the old conjurer Thérèse. Unlike Milkman, none of the characters in this novel make significant changes, but Son does show openness to spectral space at the end when he immerses himself in the mythos of the island at the urging of Thérèse. In *Tar Baby,* as in *The Bluest Eye,* Morrison shows the danger of binary thinking without the mediation of a liminal spectral figure; only this time, elements of spectrality surround the protagonist, Jadine, and she does not engage them. She remains locked in her self-reliant perceptions.

Among the "ghosts" of the Street mansion, Margaret is a victim of childhood neglect and the pitfalls of being a young trophy wife for the wealthy candy baron Valerian Street. While arguing with her husband over the length of their stay on the island, which lengthens from a six-month retirement vacation to a three-year self-imposed exile, she describes the limbo of her life: "*This* is crazy. I live in airplanes now. Nowhere. Not in Philadelphia where I at least have friends. Not here boiling under a palm tree with nobody to talk to" (*Tar Baby* 28). She feels homeless as she is forever jetting between the island and the mainland with no permanent address. Margaret and Valerian are not only separated by age, but they are also from different classes. Valerian grew up knowing that he would take over his family's candy company, but Margaret was the child of working-class Italians in Maine. Her parents ignored her because of her beauty, thinking that it would take her far: "They gave her care, but they withdrew attention" (57). Once she marries Valerian, she loses herself in the lifestyle of vacuous leisure; but she is unable to participate in the dinner party conversation, and she is shunned by the Street family, who believes that she is "from a family of nobodies" (54). When Margaret thinks she has found a friend in Ondine, the household's black cook, Valerian puts a stop to the relationship. The two women bond while talking about their roots in South Suzanne, Maine, and Baltimore. Fittingly, Valerian is offended by the class implications: "[S]he should guide the servants, not consort with them," and "the point was her ignorance and her origins" (59). Margaret is forever sublimating herself to the whims of another: "back down beneath it [her beauty] where her Margaret-hood lay in the same cup it had always lain in—faceless, silent and trying like hell to please" (83). She spends most of the novel waiting and desperately hoping for her son, Michael, to come for Christmas dinner, and much is made of her suffocating love for him. Michael will not come, though, because of the abuse he was subjected to as a child at her hands. The son is a pawn between her and Valerian and neither parent takes the time to create a true relationship with him that is defined outside of their desires.

While Valerian as the wealthy head of the household would appear to be in charge, he is in self-exile from the States, living in the limbo of a semi-vacation on the island. His wealth is a result of the Caribbean labor that produced sugar and chocolate for his candy factory, and he returned the favor by destroying the natural world of Isle des Chevaliers to build his vacation home and sell parcels of land to the wealthy for other pleasure palaces. He is ignorant of these sources of his power, viewing himself as kind to his servants, laborers, and Jadine. Son describes this total non-comprehension of brutality when he hears that Valerian has dismissed Gideon and Thérèse: "[T]hey [whites] could defecate over a whole people and come there to live and defecate some more by tearing up the land" (203). Valerian's power over his "family" is shown to be a sham after the Christmas dinner when he learns that he was ignorant of, and thus complicit in, Margaret's abuse of their son, Michael, by burning him with cigarettes and sticking him with pins. Valerian never troubled himself to find out why Michael was upset, and he is tormented by his false "innocence" and his impotence to fix the problem or comfort Michael. At the end of the novel, he is aged and becoming senile under the care of his wife and servants, who tell him what to do as his greenhouse and home slowly fade back into the natural world. Sydney tells Valerian that he and Ondine do not want to return to Philadelphia, and he helps himself to some of the wine. Valerian can tell that he is losing something, demanding, "What's happening here. Something's happening here" (287). Sydney calms him as if his employer were a child, assuring him that he and Ondine will "give you the best of care. Just like we always done. That's something you ain't never got to worry about" (287). Valerian may have financial security, but it comes at the expense of others and has alienated him from his home, his environment, and his loved ones. He is unmoored.

Sydney and Ondine Childs, the Streets' butler and cook and Jadine's uncle and aunt, are tied to Valerian and Margaret, dependent upon them for their very livelihood, as indicated by their last name. They are in a precarious position in the Street household, forever defining themselves against others by class and rank. They are the servants, but they have been with Valerian so long that they can exercise some freedom. Margaret complains to Valerian at one breakfast, "They tell *us* what to eat. Who's working for who?" (23). Moreover, the Streets and the Childses are a mingled family in that Valerian provides for the older couple financially with gifts of stock, and he and Margaret are Jadine's patrons, having paid for her education and travel. This identification causes Sydney and Ondine to separate themselves from the islanders who come to do odd jobs and from Son once he appears on the scene. The house servants never take the time to learn the names of the islanders. They call Gideon "Yardman" and every female is called "Mary." Sydney follows Son with a gun when he is discovered in the house and demands proper deference because he is a butler. He tells Son, "I know you but you don't know me. I am a Phil-a-delphia Negro mentioned in the book of the very same name. My people owned drugstores and taught school while yours were still cutting their faces open so as to be able to tell one of you from the other" (163). Obviously, Sydney is choosing to forget his Baltimore roots, even though that city is the setting of the refreshing dream he has each night, and he is lumping Son into a subgroup, which for him includes "Yardman" and the "Marys." Ondine and Sydney only have limited agency in the behind-the-scenes work that keeps the Street house functioning. Their feeling of superiority over the island workers is a sense of false bravado, and they are placeless and isolated like their employers.

While many critics see Son as the possible savior figure for Jadine and the voice of reason in the text, he is just as placeless and lost as everyone else, and his relationship with Jadine makes it clear that dangerous binary thinking is his downfall, as it is for all the other characters.[9] While he accuses Jadine toward the end of their relationship of not being "*from* anywhere" (266), he is just as rootless and not in a positive way. He may be from Eloe, Florida, but he has been traveling for years, hiding his true identity and trying to avoid prison for killing his wife in a fit of passion. Jadine may only hope that her aunt and uncle can take care of themselves and never offer them help, but Son has not worked very hard to stay connected to his father either. He did send money orders as regularly as he could, but he never wrote a note to let his father know how he was. When he tells his father that he did not write so as to keep others ignorant of his whereabouts, "it was too lame an excuse to carry on with" (250). The first time he appears in the novel, he is jumping ship and drifting at sea with no apparent origins or direction. When he gains land, he haunts the Street household, slipping through the rooms, watching Jadine as she sleeps, and slipping out "just before dawn when the kitchen came alive" (138). Son accuses Jadine of lacking true connection to anything and of being a puppet for Valerian and Margaret, but he "had been alone so long, hiding and running so long. In eight years he'd had seven documented identities and before that a few undocumented ones, so he barely remembered his real original name himself" (139).

Besides Son's marginalization and disconnection from his family and past, it is hard to imagine that he could be a successful guide for Jadine when he knows that his weakness is violence. One of his most vivid memories is of losing his temper and bashing in a snapper's head while working on a fishing boat. His Mexican crewmate then identifies him as a true American and gives him a picture of a bloody "Uncle Sam" devouring land and children (167). He basks in Jadine's fear of him when he admits to killing his wife (177); he punches Jadine (264); he dangles her out of a window (265); and he forces a sexual encounter while calling her a "tar baby" created by Valerian to trap him (270–71). After this last violent sexual incident, Jadine leaves him without a backward glance. He never attempts to meet her halfway, always asking, "Why do you want to *change* me?" (266). Even when she leaves him, he simply decides to do whatever she wants just so he can be with her again. There is no possibility of negotiation.

Numerous critics see Jadine as an assimilationist and a "cultural orphan" (Mobley 765), mainly citing her white patrons, her European education, and her modeling career.[10] She is dramatically disconnected from her family and her cultural roots, but it would be unwise to see her as completely wrong just because she is the opposite of what Son wants her to be. Like Milkman before her, she must discover her past and her lineage, this time a maternal heritage, to be a complete individual. The most damning evidence of her disconnection is her refusal to take care of her uncle and aunt, who have sacrificed for her. Instead of feeling empathy for them and wishing to do her part in their care, she feels put-upon. Ondine says to her, "A daughter is a woman that cares about where she come from and takes care of them that took care of her," and Jadine's response is telling: "You want me to pay you back. You worked for me and put up with me. Now it's my turn to do it for you, that's all you're saying" (281). Jadine, like Milkman, is caught up in who owes whom, instead of feeling any empathy for the only family members who cared for her. She has no altruistic motivations. She only thinks of the future and how to succeed. She needs to see the future in relation to where she has come from.

It is also interesting that Jadine sees herself as trying to *correct* and *avoid* simplistic binaries, yet she creates them in all her relationships. While she constantly thinks that she wants to be an individual and avoid the ways in which Margaret "stirred her into blackening up or universaling out" (64) and she accuses Son of pulling "black-woman-white-woman shit on me" (121), she completely writes off Son's hometown of Eloe as unsophisticated and marshals all her power to change him to her ways. She and Son as a couple represent the strongest opposition in the book, and neither will back down. As the narrator describes their conflict: "Each knew the world as it was meant or ought to be. One had a past, the other a future and each one bore the culture to save the race in his hands" (269). They cannot have a present because each is wrapped up in what he or she thinks is important: ties to a romanticized past in the rural South versus extreme urban and material progress. She insists on conditions that he does not want, and then, instead of seeking the support of her family after the relationship fails, she makes Sydney and Ondine a simple pit stop on her way back to the French fashion scene.

The Street household is quite dysfunctional, as Denise Heinze notes (66), and the mansion is filled with conflicting views and oppositions that will not be negotiated, not even after the ill-fated Christmas dinner at which everyone discloses secrets that throw the group into tumultuous violence, sending Son and Jadine back to the States. Although the dinner conflict has brought into view long-held and disturbing secrets about the true feelings of Sydney and Ondine for their employers, Margaret's child abuse, and Valerian's ignorance of the abuse, "the family remains the same, locked together in a lifeless, static existence. What had kept them together before—fear of losing their jobs, of losing a husband, of losing access to the world of fashion—keeps them together now" (Heinze 90). Sydney and Ondine remain because they have nowhere else to go; Margaret and Valerian keep up their charade of a marriage; and Son and Jadine flee the scene—Son because he catalyzed the explosion and Jadine because she does not want to be bound to her uncle and aunt.

While Son may be the physical catalyst for the fight because he dares to question why Valerian would fire Gideon and Thérèse, there is another absent presence who fuels this disagreement: Michael. Maria DiBattista calls Michael a "ghost" (103); he is the dinner guest who never appears but is still the subject of conversation. Son reminds Valerian of his son, and this is why the candy mogul lets the intruder stay. Margaret is obsessed with mothering Michael properly now that he is an adult, and Ondine felt it was her duty to try to protect him when he was a child. He even makes Jadine uncomfortably aware of her disconnection from her culture when she remembers his pressing upon her the need for political action, not a European education: "He said I was abandoning my history. My people" (*Tar Baby* 72). Michael's absence is filled by whatever emotion or quality that each family member feels that he or she lacks.[11] He is also the harbinger of ghostly reminders of Jadine's disconnection that are still to come—reminders that she will not heed.

Through this conflict in the Street household, Morrison establishes these binary relationships that play white employers against black housekeepers, the wealthy and liberated supermodel against the southern and patriarchal male, the Western-educated female sophisticate against the male steeped in African American community, and the barons of capitalism against their labor force. She does not, however, simply let these dichotomies stand. She allows for eruptions of spectrality that begin to mediate these rigid oppositions. The first spectral moment of the text occurs in a Paris supermarket when Jadine is shopping for a celebratory dinner: she has three men in her life, has been chosen for the cover of *Elle,* and has been informed that she passed her orals for her art history degree. As she is shopping and enjoying her good fortune, an African woman in a canary yellow dress enters the store. Susan Willis includes this scene in her discussion of "eruptions of funk." For her, "funk" is woman's "spontaneity and sensuality" (87), and these eruptions are (in a very spectral manner in this instance) the "intrusion of the past into the present" (108). At first, Jadine is so struck by the woman that she tellingly ponders whether the "vision" of the woman "is not all part of the list" and "another piece of her luck" (*Tar Baby* 45). It is as if Jadine is meant to see this woman, who is so striking that everyone in the store openly gawks at her. The woman is larger than life and timeless; she is the epitome of the feminine: she buys only three eggs, which symbolize fertility; and she is supremely confident in that she buys them in spite of the cashier's protests. This woman is not the type of beauty that Jadine would typically value. She is excessive and escapes all Western definitions of beauty, being "much too tall" with "too much hip" and "too much bust" (45). She seems so unearthly and ghostly that the shoppers believe she will "float through the glass the way a vision should" (46). This African woman, a symbol of Jadine's ignored heritage, transcendent of all meaning and definition, is described as a "woman's woman—that mother/ sister/ she; that unphotographable beauty" (46). Her very gaze is "so powerful it had burnt away the eyelashes" (45). Jadine's vision ends with the woman spitting at her, breaking the spell and showing precisely how much space there is between this woman's perceptions and Jadine's fashion-world conceptions of beauty, success, and life. Even more important, Jadine feels that she must leave Paris and return to her aunt and uncle after seeing this vision, though she does not know why she feels that imperative: "[W]hy leave the show? . . . She couldn't figure out why the woman's insulting gesture had derailed her" (47). The vision dislodges Jadine's self-confidence and pricks at her lack of self-awareness: "The woman had made her feel lonely in a way. Lonely and inauthentic" (48). Regardless of the direction in which Jadine's life takes her, the woman in yellow reminds her that she should know from where she comes. The woman is the initial reminder that Jadine needs what Milkman finds. She is a spectral catalyst because she sparks Jadine's desire to go back to Isle des Chevaliers, the place where her adoptive parents are and where nature achieves mythic and supernatural proportions.

Heinze notes the liminal character of the island: "The reality that Morrison attempts to fend off [by creating a supernatural island] is one in which whites are set against blacks, women against men, culture against primitivism, and civilization against nature" (168). The island is a space of mediation, which holds all of the characters and their extreme positions in an uneasy mixture.[12] It is a location that seems out of phase with time, space, and the reality of the outside world that its inhabitants are avoiding, and it is where Son eventually finds a space that transcends the conflicts that separate him and Jadine. It is, appropriately, where Jadine and Son begin their ill-fated relationship. When the two leave Isle des Chevaliers, they are torn apart by their oppositions. From the very beginning, the island is a place of mysteries where different myths exist side by side. Valerian believes that there are one hundred French horsemen riding across the island, while Thérèse thinks that a group of blind horsemen rides across the island, composed of Africans who were brought there as slaves and struck blind by the prospect of abject slavery in the New World. In addition to the myths, one of colonial origin and the other a link back to Africa, Morrison heightens the island's supernatural awareness of the people living on it by personifying nature: "When laborers imported from Haiti came to clear the land, clouds and fish were convinced that the world was over, that the sea-green green of the sea and the sky-blue sky of the sky were no longer permanent. . . . Only the champion daisy trees were serene" (*Tar Baby* 9). According to Karla Holloway, this representation of nature "develops a thematic interpenetration of natural elements—an explicit thematic interplay basic to an African view of the universe" (117), and she identifies the island as "a place suspended in time" (127). The timeless properties of the island are clear in that nature is not fully eradicated and is always attempting to grow back over the buildings. Pointing to the island's transformative possibilities, Sydney thinks, "This place dislocates everything" (*Tar Baby* 284), as the ants invade the greenhouse and the bricks pop out of the earth.

Significantly, Jadine experiences her second encounter with the spectral once she has returned to her home on this island. After her lunch picnic with Son, when she begins fantasizing about what it would be like to be with him, she finds herself in a dangerously close encounter with the swamp. At first, the lighting and the "lawn" charm her; she wants to sketch this beauty, capture this quality, and make it artificial. Not understanding nature, she steps into a swampy "slime" that begins to suck her into it and scare her. She realizes that "every Girl Scout" knows what to do in this situation; but she does not, and she fears "worms or snakes or crocodiles" (182). According to Marilyn E. Mobley, "[T]he central reasons for Jadine's divided consciousness have to do with her rejection of the cultural constructions of race and mothering that are part of her Afro-American heritage" (763). The ancient "tree women" who watch Jadine struggle recognize this situation: "[The women] were delighted when first they saw her, thinking a runaway child had been restored to them. But upon looking closer they saw differently. This girl was fighting to get away from them. The women hanging from the trees were quiet now, but arrogant—mindful as they were of their value, their exceptional femaleness" (*Tar Baby* 183). Their "sacred properties" defy time, building the world itself and Moses's crib with the "pace of glaciers" (183). Jadine does not learn anything from these women because she is not even open to their presence as she attempts to escape. She does not see the stretch of time and the sacredness behind the island's natural setting. For her, this is a life and death struggle to escape the muck, but even though she does get away, she is marked with the swampy blackness in which she was submerged as a reminder of this encounter and of her incomprehension of her cultural and maternal lineage, as symbolized by the women in the trees. Jadine needs to see beyond the surface level of the people and the world that surround her.

Jadine's final spectral experience occurs in Eloe and hurries the end of her relationship to Son. During her second night in Son's hometown, a group of ghostly women crowd her room, showing their breasts to her, and the woman in yellow brings forth her eggs. This group includes women from her past, her present, her family, Son's friends and family, and even Thérèse. It is an amalgamation of all the female presences in Jadine's life, known and unknown. The women seem to be insisting on the generational and nurturing aspects of womanhood—what Jadine refuses to do. This is not necessarily a call for childbearing, but rather for connections between generations. Jadine wishes to move forward in her own life, and it is clear that she feels no family ties to Sydney and Ondine, even though they gave her everything they had for her education. These spectral women are offering her a maternal link that she lost when her mother died and that she ignores in her negligence of her adoptive parents. She even thinks, "Nanadine and Sydney mattered a lot to her but what they thought did not" (49). She has no respect for or connections to the "sacred properties" of the previous generations. Like Milkman, she is being called to create connections to her familial and cultural heritage—her lineage. She refuses this call, however, and the next morning she makes her final judgment on Eloe: "There was no life there. Maybe a past but definitely no future and finally there was no interest" (259). While Son romanticizes this past to the point that he cannot function in the present or future, Jadine rejects it outright for her independence and her future. She is completely ungrounded, and she flees from Eloe just as she ran away from her responsibilities to her aunt and uncle on the island.

She may run, but the night women's lessons are not completely lost. She is still contemplating their message at the airport before she leaves for France. While she angrily believes that the woman in yellow "could discredit your elements," on the plane she does concede that she must deal with the women and her past: "She would go back to Paris and begin at Go. Let loose the dogs, tangle with the woman in yellow—with her and with all the night women who had *looked* at her" (290). Morrison told Charles Ruas of this moment of possible growth: "She has a glimmering on the plane she thinks that *she* is the safety she has longed for, that there is no haven, and being the safety you have longed for is not only taking care of yourself; you are the safety of other people. . . . She now knows enough—she hasn't opened the door, but she knows where the door is" (108). Like the door or window at the end of *Paradise,* there is a glimpse here of possibility. This tiny opening for contemplation and possible future transformation is echoed in Son's journey back to Isle des Chevaliers.

Son returns to the island in search of Jadine, but he learns that she left the Streets' mansion for Europe a week before his arrival. He goes to the home of Gideon and Thérèse, the workers Valerian fired, and asks them to take him to Isle des Chevaliers as soon as possible. He is so deeply in love with Jadine that his view of his hometown has been skewed, and he has decided to do whatever is necessary to get her back, even if it means completely changing himself. Thérèse correctly identifies his problem as a lack of choices but offers to take him to the island that night. Gideon is afraid that they will not reach the island because Thérèse is blind. She is an ancient wise woman, a conjurer with magical breasts that still give milk in her old age, and a descendant of the blinded slaves who hid on the island and still ride through the rain forest: "What they saw, they saw with the eye of the mind, and that, of course, was not to be trusted" (*Tar Baby* 152). Thérèse evidently has the power of "insight," and as a character she anticipates Connie in *Paradise.* She can see beyond the physical into the spiritual realms, and she identified Son as an island rider and kindred spirit when she first became aware of his presence on the island. For Judylyn S. Ryan, this blindness is a form of protest: "The fact that these Africans 'went blind' must be seen as a willed and self-conscious act of survival" (69). It would appear that from Thérèse's perspective, Son has this spirit of survival and opposition; he has what it takes to transcend the hold of the present and to merge into the timeless space of the island.[13] Thérèse straddles past and present, life and death, and she can see into the beyond. She is the Pilate figure in this novel, and she is the connector for Son into his mythic past and into the future. After dropping Son off on the opposite side of the island from the Streets' mansion, she tells him that the island is "the place. Where you can take a choice" (*Tar Baby* 305), and that he cannot see, but rather must "feel" where he is going (304). She believes that Jadine has "forgotten her ancient properties" but that Son can find his if he joins the riders and the nature spirits of the island (305). Earlier, Valerian and Jadine asked Son if he believed in the swamp ghosts, and he indicated his openness to "the far side" (304): "Sometimes. . . . In a swamp, I believe" (93). Like Milkman's mythic leap into the air, Son runs "looking neither to the left nor to the right," into the mythic, timeless, spectral side of the island (306). Even though we do not see the transformation of a Milkman, Son is taking steps toward that overarching connective view among people and generations.

"Toni Morrison's fiction," writes Lauren Lepow, "embodies a powerful critique of dualistic thinking. Dualism—any system of thought that polarizes what we perceive—is a narrowing world view" (165). In *Song of Solomon* and *Tar Baby,* Morrison creates individuals who are caught in the extremes of dualistic, binary thinking about race, class, and the place of the past and culture in the lives of individuals. Milkman is trapped between the competing views of his capitalist father and his revolutionary friend Guitar. Issues of class, race, and the question of how to move forward in a world controlled by men like Valerian Street polarize Jadine and all her fellow characters. While Milkman, through his relationship with his spectral guide, Pilate, finds the middle ground that is communal and empathetic and becomes aware of the past and of his family heritage, Jadine and Son get lost in the abyss between their opposing ways of being in the world. In both novels, Morrison uses figures, places, and moments of spectrality to "disjoint" time and jog the characters out of their oppositions into more fully aware relationships with each other and with their cultural history. Milkman jumps into the space between with full knowledge and confidence; Son runs at full speed into the wild, timeless space of Isle des Chevaliers; and Jadine boards a plane to cross the Atlantic now pondering her place in a maternal lineage and, hopefully, truly willing to "tangle" with and learn from the night women. I do not see Son or Jadine as failures in their quests simply because they do not have the epiphany that Milkman has. Moving beyond the faint traces of spectrality in *Sula* that were discussed in the first chapter, *Tar Baby* shows, rather, the individual in process, interacting with the supernatural and moving toward understanding. Morrison deals with the complexity of real journeys in a polarized America that leaves both Son and Jadine feeling fragmented and cut-off.

CHAPTER THREE

"What Would Be on the Other Side?" History as a Spectral Bridge in *Beloved* and *Paradise*

In a 1983 interview, Toni Morrison told Nellie McKay: "I am very happy to hear that my books haunt. That is what I work very hard for, and for me it is an achievement when they haunt readers" (146). Like her previous novels *Song of Solomon* and *Tar Baby,* Morrison's fifth and seventh books, *Beloved* (1987) and *Paradise* (1997), are set in the area between "all the 'two's' one likes" (Derrida xviii). Unlike her previous works, these bookends to her trilogy together form the apogee of her project to conjure African American history through a spectral guide.

According to Marsha Darling, for the characters in the environment that Morrison creates, "Ghosts or spirits are real. . . . And the purpose of making [them] real is making history possible, making memory real" (249). In *Beloved,* the presence of a ghost makes real the personal and cultural history of Sethe, a runaway slave who attempts to kill her children rather than see them enslaved. This choice results in isolation from her community and a tainted relationship with her remaining children. Ultimately, for Sethe and her daughter Denver to repair their broken bonds and become healthy individuals, a bridge must be constructed to connect them. Sethe must find a conduit through which she can communicate all the horrors of her past to her daughter so that Denver can understand her mother and then begin to forge a place for herself in the world. This bridge of personal and historical memory is the ghost: Beloved.

In her seventh novel, *Paradise,* published ten years later, Morrison continues this thematic thread of haunting as she depicts supernatural events occurring in and around an all-black town in Oklahoma and a neighboring former convent school for Native American girls. The rigid town of Ruby and the unconventional Convent are in conflict until a group of men decides to empty the Convent of its five female inhabitants. After the massacre of the five women, their bodies disappear, and the town must make sense of the attack and the subsequent strange disappearances. All the characters in the novel are haunted by past events, from the "Disallowings" that result in Ruby's stagnant existence to the violent episodes that each Convent woman endures before her arrival. For the characters of Morrison's novel to "learn to live," they must negotiate borders not only between life and death and past and present, but between all binaries. Throughout *Paradise,* Morrison privileges liminality, as the Convent women, erased and negatively "ghosted" by the larger society like their predecessors Sethe and Denver, find empowerment through their communal spiritual experiences in the Convent with their own spectral guide, Consolata. She helps the women carve out spaces of negotiation that ultimately begin to heal not only them but also many citizens of Ruby.

As a frame for analyzing the spectrality in these two novels, I read Beloved as a time-shifting, border-crossing character who embodies Derrida's "Spectrality Effect," or the "undoing [of] this opposition, or even this dialectic, between actual, effective presence and its other" (Derrida 40). She is an intense spectral appearance of traumatic history in a physical form, a "becoming-body" (6), and through her very "spectrality," she merges and undoes rigid barriers between life and death and past and present. Through her use of 124 as a spot for apparition, Beloved creates a spectral moment, which is "a moment that no longer belongs to time, if one understands by this word the linking of modalized presents (past present, actual present: 'now,' future present)" (xx). In this sense, Beloved is a timeless and subversive figure, who can cross and recross borders between binaries and defy compartmentalization. As a specter, she serves as a translation point, a medium, between Sethe and Denver, processing the traumatic memories of slavery and Sethe's personal response to it. If Beloved is interpreted as a child spirit attempting to deal with the trauma of slavery, then Consolata,[1] a character in *Paradise,* becomes a more mature spirit guide with one foot in the real and another in the beyond, memorializing and healing the scars of slavery, Reconstruction, and the civil rights movement through her interaction with the four women in the Convent and the townspeople of Ruby. In both *Beloved* and *Paradise,* Morrison privileges the liminal power of spectrality that illuminates personal memory and cultural history while concurrently "unghosting" silenced individuals who are disconnected from that transformative space where personal experience, memory, and history merge.

In *Beloved,* history is very dangerous and very real in the present, and this reality and concomitant danger go beyond the actual specter and exist within the fabric of the characters themselves. For Sethe, moments of graphic terror from her past continue in a time that is not temporal but repetitive and otherworldly. She tells Denver, "What I remember is a picture floating around out there outside my head. I mean, even if I don't think it, even if I die, the picture of what I did, or knew, or saw is still out there. Right in the place where it happened" (*Beloved* 36). This is a remarkable description of the spectral as a moment that is in the mind, yet physically outside of the individual, and in the past but still forever recurring in the present. It is an obsessively repetitive trauma that can be experienced by people other than the original participants, which is why Sethe warns her daughter against visiting these haunted locations either imaginatively or physically.[2] For Sethe the past haunts and hurts, and death is no certain release from the haunting, since she is already caught in a traumatic, temporal limbo. Furthermore, she unwittingly cuts herself off from Denver by giving incomplete explanations of the danger of experiencing past horrors. At first she tells her, "You won't understand" (35). But for Denver to fully understand Sethe's warnings not to "go there" with respect to the past (36), she must actually "go there," experience her mother's past, and see for herself Sethe's reasons for her actions. Even with a limited amount of information available, Denver seems to pick up on the importance of Sethe's warning when she notes, "If it's still there, waiting, that must mean that nothing ever dies" (36).

With this observation, Denver correctly diagnoses the problem for the characters in *Beloved* as the line between the living and the dead is blurred, and nothing ever dies. In this worldview, pain continues, and a ghost is just another obstacle to peace. Sethe and the baby ghost are tied together through her past actions; and in the process, "[t]he invisible becomes visible, the unsaid, said. Sethe carries with her the dead incarnate" (Rand 29). This incarnate dead connected to Sethe is the thought-picture, which will soon return in the flesh through the specter of Beloved.[3] It is not surprising that Morrison would build a ghost story around this trauma. According to Lynette Carpenter and Wendy K. Kolmar, women's ghost stories traditionally include the ascent of the supernatural over reason and the natural; the bleeding back and forth between the living and the dead and the respective concerns of each; the parallel relationship between the concerns of women's experiences and the concerns of their ghost stories; and the empowerment afforded to the powerless by life after death. In *Beloved,* the supernatural events result from a family's experience of infanticide and affect Sethe and her children, particularly her daughters, Denver and the ghost-child. The violence, which causes Beloved's haunting, comes from a problematic place of maternal love and opens a permeable space between the living and the dead. Unfortunately, Denver cannot possibly understand Sethe's past, her actions resulting from that past, or her love, since Denver was an infant when the incident took place and she does not remember slavery. I believe that Beloved functions in the text as a spectral bridge that conveys historical and cultural information from Sethe to her remaining daughter, Denver: she is a vital connection between generations. Beloved's presence in the text as "spectral history" and her resulting "Spectrality Effect" help Denver "learn to live" and to respect her mother as well.

The importance of spectrality is clear in that Morrison immediately immerses the reader in the spirit world. A haunted house is introduced on the first page, and 124 is occupied by "three phantoms (after Sethe's sons run away) and a ghost" (Lawrence 50).[4] Once again, there are two kinds of "ghosts" operating here. Because of Sethe's actions and her pride, her family is cut off from the surrounding community and each woman is trapped in memories of the past that can take over the present moment without warning. The three isolated and ghost-like women of 124 haunt the building just as much as the baby's spirit does. The "real" ghost—the baby—is the typical ghost of a haunted house, and it changes its manifestations as the book progresses. The contact that the ghost desires is at first satisfied through childlike crawling on the main stair, shattering mirrors, and placing handprints in desserts. These paranormal manifestations make 124 a link in the long chain of haunted houses and their representations of generational haunting in American literature, including the work of writers such as, to name a few, Nathaniel Hawthorne, Edgar Allan Poe, Henry James, Edith Wharton, Shirley Jackson, Richard Matheson, and even William Faulkner. Indeed, the house itself is described as an instrument of a child's revenge on a parent: "124 was spiteful. Full of a baby's venom" (*Beloved* 3).

This otherworldly atmosphere of 124 Bluestone Road is described by Carol Schmudde as a type of crossroads: "124 is a point of intersection for powerful antithetical forces: North and South, black and white, past and present, this world and the other" (410). Seen from this liminal perspective, 124 has much in common with Pilate's house, the island in *Tar Baby,* and the Convent in *Paradise.* 124 is a powerful, spectral space. Although 124 is on a rural road outside Cincinnati, before the haunting it is not separate from the surrounding community. Once Sethe arrives at 124, she feels not only what it is like "claiming ownership of [her] freed self," but she also experiences "days of company" (*Beloved* 95). Before Sethe's isolation, 124 is a communal place: "days of having women friends, a mother-in-law, and all her children together; of being part of a neighborhood" (173). The house is a meeting place where neighbors can freely discuss historical, political, and religious matters (173). After Sethe becomes an outcast, her house transforms into a spectral nexus between two worlds, the real and the spirit worlds, and 124 becomes the focus of Beloved's spirit work. The house is a place where physical space and time are intermixed into what Sethe terms a "no-time" space, and Stamp Paid believes that he can hear the "mumbling of the black and angry dead" putting voice to "unspeakable thoughts" from outside of the small house (191, 199).

Even though Sethe's two sons are frightened away from the house by the ghost and presumably by their fear of their mother, the characters do not seem surprised that the house can be a home to a ghost. Baby Suggs *is* surprised that her grandsons think that 124 is especially frightful: "Not a house in the country ain't packed with some dead Negro's grief" (5). At this time, Baby Suggs's thoughts center on her own ghosted existence on the cusp of death, and she ponders the interminable aspects of life even after death: "Suspended between the nastiness of life and the meanness of the dead, she [Baby Suggs] couldn't get interested in leaving life or living it," and Baby knows for certain that "death was anything but forgetfulness" (4). Both the house itself and the later appearance of Beloved illustrate the truth of Baby Suggs's thoughts on the trials of memory after death.

Of the occupants in the haunted house, the one responsible for the presence of the ghost is Sethe. She is a strong woman whose powers extend into the spirit world, and she believes that she understands the haunting powers of memory and the torment sent from occupants of the "other side." Moreover, her love for her children is so "thick," as Paul D describes it, that she commits the ultimate act of protection and possession, claiming for herself the arbitration of life and death among her children in a time of peril. When she and her children are threatened by recapture, Sethe chooses to kill them rather than to see them enslaved: "For Sethe the children are better off dead, their fantasy futures protected from the heinous reality of slavery" (Demetrakopoulos 53). She succeeds in killing the oldest daughter, the one who will become Beloved. Through this violent act, she earns the mistrust of her remaining children in addition to the ire of her murdered child. Her attempt to counteract the overpowering destruction of slavery injures her own family; as Stephanie A. Demetrakopoulos notes, "The institution of slavery, the atrocity of historical time, denies Sethe her mothering and destroys the natural cycles of maternal bonding" (52). Stamp Paid describes Sethe's protective assertion of power as love: "She was trying to outhurt the hurter" (*Beloved* 234).

Sethe is open to the supernatural world and attempts to communicate with the baby ghost long before it physically appears. Trudier Harris describes this easy acceptance of ghosts and the liminal aspect of the novel: "In a world in which several characters have experienced encounters with the world beyond, it is not farfetched that Sethe would respond to its dimensions" (*Saints* 77). Perhaps following a previous lead from Baby Suggs, Sethe and Denver conduct a séance of sorts, holding hands and calling to the ghost: "Come on. Come on. You might as well just come on" (*Beloved* 4). Sethe is sure that the ghost is her dead child, and she is insistently strong in the face of the dangerous and bizarre behavior of the spirit. She and Denver wage "a perfunctory battle against the outrageous behavior of that place; against turned-over slop jars, smacks on the behind, and gusts of sour air," and they "understood the source of the outrage as well as they knew the source of light" (4). Sethe's strength to stand up against the oppression of slavery and to survive her life of isolation is illustrated in her outburst to Paul D in defense of her daughters, both living and dead: "I got a tree on my back and a haint in my house, and nothing in between but the daughter I am holding in my arms. No more running—from nothing. I will never run from another thing on this earth. I took one journey and I paid for the ticket, but . . . it cost too much!" (15). Sethe's "tree" is a large network of horrific scars recording the terrors and abuses from her past life as a slave on Sweet Home. Not only has she paid in forced labor and demeaning abuse; she has also paid for her freedom with the destruction of her family and the haunting of her home by a horrific loss—all reminders of her painful past, a past she desperately wants to forget.

Her desire to forget the past at any cost inadvertently traps Denver in a liminal space of fear and confusion. She fears her mother's murderous maternal rage enacted in the woodshed. She fears the ultimate silencing and abandonment through death at her mother's hand. Sethe's actions against her children on that fateful day traumatize Denver, causing her not only to live in fear of her own mother's overprotectiveness but also to live in a ghosted state of isolation in a house haunted by her own dead sister. Denver must learn to "explain" herself and break her silence with the outside world to save herself and her mother from the devouring presence of an awful past in their home.

Prepared for an encounter with the spectral, Denver is born in a liminal space, the Ohio River, and she lives in seclusion in a haunted house with the mother who, she fears, could at any moment plunge her, as Sethe describes it, "[o]ver there" (163). Denver lives in a world of her own imagination between her thoughts and reality, present freedom and past enslavement, her mother's world and her sister's. She actually experiences deafness when a classmate tells her about her mother's past, and even after her hearing returns with the advent of the ghost, she lives in her own world of silence. She comes to identify with her only playmate, an otherworldly ghost-sister, to the point that she seems to understand that Beloved will take physical form. She tells Sethe, "I think the baby got plans" (37). Schmudde describes both Denver's attachment to the baby ghost and her own ghostly qualities: "The poltergeist expresses Denver's anger against her mother. Denver identifies with her dead sister; the ghost becomes her only playmate in a lonely childhood. She feels safest in the company of the ghost, both of them confined to a haunted house" (413). Denver lacks a self, either individual or communal, and after Baby Suggs dies, Denver is isolated from her cultural history, trapped in a haunted house with only her outcast mother and a ghost.

Denver's loneliness and her dependence on a ghost for company allow her to come as close as is humanly possible to the world of the dead, and her attachment to Beloved is a liability because it begs the question of what would be left of Denver if Beloved were to leave. Denver learns the horrific answer when she and Beloved go to the shed to find cider and Beloved capriciously disappears. Denver realizes that she also has disappeared; her entire identity is wrapped so tightly in Beloved's presence that she knows that "she is crying because she has no self" (*Beloved* 123). The experience continues: "Death is a skipped meal compared to this. She can feel her thickness thinning, dissolving into nothing. . . . She doesn't move to open the door because there is no world out there" (123). She feels as if the dark is "swallowing her" (123). At this point, Denver might as well be as ghostly as Beloved, since her entire being rests on Beloved's presence and the unhealthy connection she and Beloved share. Denver describes this abnormal closeness through an illustration of both life and death: "Beloved is my sister. I swallowed her blood right along with my mother's milk" (205). Denver has no identity or sense of self outside of this connection to her dead sister; it is almost as if one cannot exist fully without the other.

As a result of the stories Denver hears from her classmates before she stops attending school and of her own vague memories of her time in jail with her mother, she is aware of her mother's pathological love and her own fear of Sethe, which is tied to the horrors she hears in gossip. Instead of trusting Sethe and her strong love, she and her brothers worry that Sethe will snap and injure or kill them. The mother bond is strong but twisted. Denver tries to express her mixed feelings for her mother when she speaks during the chorus of voices in 124: "I love my mother but I know she killed one of her own daughters, and tender as she is with me, I'm scared of her because of it. She missed killing my brothers and they knew it. They told me die-witch! stories to show me the way to do it, if ever I needed to" (205). Evidently, the mother-child bond is not as nurturing as Sethe would hope, as her own children plot how to defend themselves against a maternal attack. This fear of Sethe is deeply ingrained in Denver, yet it is clear that she does not understand why Sethe committed the act. She does not seem to understand even vaguely the exact circumstances in which Sethe found herself when she made her fateful decision. Denver says:

> All the time, I'm afraid the thing that happened that made it all right for my mother to kill my sister could happen again. I don't know what it is, I don't know who it is, but maybe there is something else terrible enough to make her do it again. I need to know what that thing might be, but I don't want to. Whatever it is, it comes from outside this house, outside the yard, and it can come right on in the yard if it wants to. So I never leave this house and I watch over the yard, so it can't happen again and my mother won't have to kill me too. (205)

The only way Denver can possibly understand her mother and her actions is if she can understand the "thing that happened that made it all right for my mother to kill." In the passage, Morrison uses the word "it," an empty signifier, to leave the "thing" ambiguous for Denver and the reader. Since Denver does not know what or who caused her mother to kill, she can only wait powerlessly in the liminal zone of the haunted house, completely isolated from the surrounding community, waiting for history to repeat itself. The opportunity to understand Sethe and her strong love comes with the physical presence of what haunts Sethe's mind: the ghost. As Linda Krumholz writes, "In her lonely withdrawal from the world, due in part to Sethe's isolation, Denver is as trapped by Sethe's past and Sethe's inability to find psychological freedom as Sethe herself is" (404). For Denver, Beloved is the conduit whereby her mother's personal history and the larger cultural history of slavery and its dead can be transmitted from mother to daughter. Brogan describes a ghost as "an emblem of historical loss" and a "vehicle of historical recovery" (29), and Beloved certainly functions in both categories in the text.

The reasons for Beloved's appearance lie in the previous enslavement of Sethe and her strength and personal determination to overcome that enslavement for her children at any cost. Beloved's coming is also a kind of reckoning, a method by which the other characters in the book, including Sethe, Denver, and the surrounding community, can experience and deal with personal and cultural history. As Harris notes, "Vengeance is not the Lord's; it is Beloved's. Her very body becomes a manifestation of her desire for vengeance and of Sethe's guilt" ("Woman" 131). This avenging spirit shows many qualities that point to an otherworldly origin. A few of these qualities include that she is the age the baby Sethe killed would be; she knows things that only that child would know; she has a scar where her throat would have been slit; she appears in the text by walking directly up out of water; and, she seems able to disappear and reappear without moving from one spot. Robert L. Broad describes Beloved and her many confusing facets: "Sethe and Denver don't just get their daughter and sister back; they get a puzzled and puzzling, poly-generational, mnemonically tortured, uncertain spirit whose resurrection brings wildly unpredictable results" (192). Beloved is subversive, unpredictable, and multiplicitous: her true identity is impossible to pin down.

Beloved's primary demand is for stories. She feeds off Sethe's stories to the point that Sethe will do anything to keep Beloved satisfied and begins wasting away and becoming more ghostly herself. Deborah Horvitz writes, "As the embodiment of Sethe's memories, the ghost Beloved enabled her to remember and tell the story of her past, and in so doing shows that between women words used to make and share a story have the power to heal" (102). This storytelling in which Sethe engages for Beloved's entertainment connects Sethe and Denver in a new and vital relationship. When Denver tells Beloved the story of her own birth, she begins to feel as if she is actually experiencing the event from Sethe's perspective. As another result of Beloved's questioning, Sethe tells stories of her past that she has never shared with Denver—stories she thought she had forgotten.

One example of an important half-forgotten story involves Sethe's memories of her own mother. These remembrances haunt her and must be integrated into her consciousness no matter how dangerous they may be, which circumstance is quite similar to the impasse in communication between her and her own daughter. The only identification that Sethe knows for her unnamed mother is a brand that her mother showed her when Sethe was a young child: "Right on her rib was a circle and a cross burnt right into the skin. She said, 'This is your ma'am'" (*Beloved* 61). The loss of this family history is clear when Sethe realizes that she had forgotten this information and never shared it with her children. She is "remembering something she had forgotten she knew" (61). Denver is curious as to why Sethe's mother was hanged, since "this was the first time she had heard anything about her mother's mother" (61). Beloved's questioning initiates this connection that Sethe is forging with her long-dead African mother and also with Denver. Additionally, Sethe begins to remember bits and pieces of her mother's native language, information she had lost: "Holding the damp white sheets against her chest, she was picking meaning out of a code she no longer understood" (62). As Derrida notes, haunting is "a *politics* of memory, of inheritance, and of generations" (xix). This past must be remembered and passed on so that the generations can continue forward informed by the past, not stuck in it.

Not only does Beloved serve as the catalyst for Sethe's remembering and the subsequent empowering of Denver through family history and strength, but she also serves as a physical presence memorializing the horrors of slavery for the entire African American community. Brogan points to this aspect of the ghost: "Dedicated to the 'Sixty Million and more' Africans and African Americans killed in the slave trade, *Beloved* attempts to perform a ritual burial of the forgotten, unnamed dead" (65). Contrary to Brogan's suggestion, Morrison may not be burying the past as much as she is allowing the knowledge of it to be passed on and remembered. Beloved has *returned* from the dead with the combined knowledge of her own death and the deaths of millions during the Middle Passage. She returns in order to communicate this cultural information to both Sethe and Denver, who have become disconnected from their past and their community. Beloved knows far more than the baby ghost should know. She knows things beyond her own personal history from the realm of collective memory.[5] In her section of the trio of voices in 124, Beloved discusses what seems to be a journey on the sea surrounded by terror, violence, and death. She speaks repeatedly of "circles" around the necks of her fellow prisoners, and she says, "[T]here will never be a time when I am not crouching and watching others who are crouching too" (*Beloved* 210). Death is the only release from this forced relocation: "[W]e are all trying to leave our bodies behind" (210). According to Barbara Hill Rigney, "Beloved is a ghost, but she is also part of Sethe's lost African self and that African view of nature as imbued with spirits and life" (232). This cultural past must be remembered and "digested" (Morrison, qtd. in Darling 248) by Sethe and Denver before they can become whole and separate individuals.

Beloved's ability to remember generational information beyond what her infant self would possibly be able to remember points to her position as spectral history itself. Brogan believes that this time-shifting, which Denver and Sethe experience through Beloved's voice, is directly connected to her ghostliness: "This spatialization of memory has the effect of dissolving time; the rememberer does not mentally return in time to recall the past to the present but literally reenters the past" (74). When Beloved is present, she is not only the literal presence of an absent, murdered child, but she also has the power to twist and bend time to her own otherworldly purposes. Ellen J. Goldner describes time disjunctions and hauntings: "As hauntings preserve the dead amid the living and the past amid the present, they defy the concept of linear time, the bedrock of cause and effect that enables prediction" (62). Beloved seems to fit Derrida's descriptions of spectrality as "time out of joint." She is timeless and able to cross and recross borders between "all the 'two's' one likes" (xviii). As a specter, she is placed as a translation point, a medium, between Sethe and Denver. According to Derrida, the "Spectrality Effect" is the "undoing [of] this opposition, or even this dialectic, between actual, effective presence and its other" (40). In her very "spectrality," Beloved merges and undoes rigid barriers between life and death and past and present. This power affects every person Beloved encounters. She prods Sethe's memories of her childhood and her time at Sweet Home; she makes Denver aware of her mother's past; and she blows open Paul D's "tobacco tin" heart, so that he must face his painful past from Sweet Home and Alfred, Georgia. This mixing of time and space through Beloved also explains the whispered, jumbled "mumbling of the black and angry dead" that Stamp Paid hears when he goes to 124 during the trio of "unspeakable thoughts, unspoken" (*Beloved* 199).

This "threnody," as Morrison calls it (Darling 249), of shared thoughts, memories, accusations, and apologies begins to take its toll on the three women at 124 Bluestone Road. This ghostlike, marginal existence in a borderland of liminality is not possible in juxtaposition to the reality outside the door. Denver realizes this danger to her mother and knows that her fear of Sethe is nothing compared to Beloved's vampiric and tyrannical love. Denver must save her mother, but she cannot succeed alone. She sees that the situation is grim: "[L]ittle by little it dawned on Denver that if Sethe didn't wake up one morning and pick up a knife, Beloved might. Frightened as she was by the thing in Sethe that could come out, it shamed her to see her mother serving a girl not much older than herself" (*Beloved*

242). Denver does have the power to correct this situation since now she is empowered by knowledge of her mother's past. She can use this empowerment to reconnect with the community and ultimately to "unghost" herself, regaining agency.

Before Denver can leave the house and gather the members of the community necessary to rid 124 of Beloved, she has another, more helpful and loving supernatural experience. An ancestor appears to help her with ghostly advice.[6] Denver hears "Baby Suggs laugh, as clear as anything" (244). Denver's grandmother asks her whether she knows her family's painful past and the dangers of white people, and Denver asks in despair: what can one do when there is no defense? Baby Suggs answers with a word of assurance and endurance: "Know it, and go on out the yard. Go on" (244). Now that Denver is armed with her knowledge of her familial and cultural past, both of slavery from Beloved and Sethe and of her family and endurance from Baby Suggs, she can "know it and go on," enduring and defeating the repetitive doom of Beloved and all the guilt and despair she represents. The reader is prepared for this eventuality through Sethe's expectation that Baby Suggs can comfort her in the Clearing even though she is dead and through Denver's reminiscences of what Baby Suggs taught her. Baby Suggs made sure while she was alive that Denver knew about her father and her ghost sister. Denver knows her father's "things" (207). She knows what he liked to eat and that he bought Baby Suggs's freedom, that he believed in the power of literacy, and that he insisted, regardless of the danger, on loving people. Denver remembers:

> After the cake was ruined and the ironed clothes all messed up, and after I heard my sister crawling up the stairs to get back to her bed, she [Baby Suggs] told me my things too. That I was charmed. My birth was and I got saved all the time. And that I shouldn't be afraid of the ghost. It wouldn't harm me because I tasted its blood when Ma'am nursed me. She said the ghost was after Ma'am and her too for not doing anything to stop it. But it would never hurt me. I just had to watch out for it because it was a greedy ghost and needed a lot of love, which was only natural, considering. And I do. Love her. I do. (209)

In a way, Baby Suggs helps prepare the way for Beloved's full-body manifestation before the ghost does more than scare Howard and Buglar.

Baby Suggs's love of Denver communicated from beyond the grave is a hint of the development that is to come in the next two novels of this trilogy, *Jazz* and *Paradise.* For, rather than allowing Beloved to be the sole spectral character in the novel that bears her name, Morrison allows Baby Suggs to return from the grave and add her influence to the spectral mix. In anticipation of the spectral trio that I identify in *Jazz* (the narrator, Dorcas, and Wild) and the Convent women in *Paradise,* Morrison creates in *Beloved* two specters working in tandem to produce healing, particularly in Denver's life. Beloved is a ghost resulting from slavery: she is disconnected, angry, and, at times, violent in her demands. She opens the line of communication between Sethe and Denver, but she is so focused on Sethe and her vengeance that she cannot show Denver how to use this new knowledge. Beloved jolts Denver out of her fear and isolation by disclosing secrets of her mother's past, but Baby Suggs finishes Beloved's spirit work by comforting her granddaughter in her time of extremity and teaching her how to digest what she has learned of the past. Without Baby Suggs, Denver might have become caught up in her mother and Beloved's dance of recrimination and despair, a situation that a weakened Sethe still struggles to overcome at the end of the novel, hopefully with Paul D's help, now that he has faced his painful past and has come to terms with Sethe's as well.

Once Denver alerts the community to the situation, they come to Sethe's rescue because each member has her own demons from the past to deal with; and, as the narrator points out through Ella's thoughts, "[w]hatever Sethe had done, Ella didn't like the idea of past errors taking possession of the present" (256). The past should not control or destroy the present and the future. "Sethe's 'rememory,' in giving substance to her murdered daughter and to the painful past, casts its spell over the community," writes David Lawrence, "drawing the members of that community into one person's struggle with the torments of a history that refuses to die" (45). The tormenting history is, however, also the community's history and must be faced. The group of women that goes to 124 Bluestone Road is an amalgamation of past *and* present, Africa *and* America: "Some brought what they could and what they believed would work. Stuffed in apron pockets, strung around their necks, lying in the space between their breasts. Others brought Christian faith—as shield and sword. Most brought a little of both" (*Beloved* 257). This time the women help Sethe in her time of need.

They are there to stop her from unwittingly committing another crime. In this instance, her survival and sanity depend on the local community of African American women. In the ideal situation, her deep connection to them is a safety net.

The women use voice, pure sound, to rid 124 of the thing that symbolizes "unspeakable things unspoken." Lawrence comments, "The climactic scene shows how a culture may find it necessary in a moment of crisis to exorcise its own demons in order to reaffirm its identity" (46). Similarly, Naomi R. Rand notes that ultimately the townspeople "are not only able to relive their past, but to acknowledge Sethe as a part of it; thus it is the continuity of the African American experience, the shared suffering and finally the sense of community that banishes this ghost and resolves the conflict that generated her" (30). Denver shows her deeper understanding of what Beloved is and could be when she speaks to Paul D at the end of the novel. She has matured and is looking toward college, and when Paul D asks her whether she believes the ghost was really her sister, she replies, "At times. At times I think she was—more" (*Beloved* 267). Denver seems to be on the cusp of understanding why Beloved had to appear and that Beloved can never really be "exorcised," "banished," or "resolved," as Lawrence and Rand suggest. How can she be resolved if she was always already exceeding any meaning or label—if she was "more" than any of the identifications given to her?

The final, short section of the book deals with Beloved as if she is not permanently exorcised. Even while Morrison calls her "disremembered and unaccounted for" and insists that no one looks for her or remembers her name, she tells how she "erupts into her separate parts" and vestiges of her remain (274). In the end, Beloved's work of cultural recovery has been accomplished, but she cannot be completely laid to rest because the forgetting of generations creates her physical form: "Occasionally, however, the rustle of a skirt hushes when they wake, and the knuckles brushing a cheek in sleep seem to belong to the sleeper. Sometimes the photograph of a close friend or relative—looked at too long—shifts, and something more familiar than the dear face itself moves there" (275). Unlike Sula, Pilate, and Thérèse, who disappear by the end of their texts, Beloved seems to be absent, but traces of her presence remain on the edges of memory and perception. Moreover, the injunction to not "pass on" a cultural ghost story that has just been told hints at how Beloved's spectral presence could remain. As Karla F. C. Holloway notes, "[S]lavery itself defies traditional historiography. . . . This novel positions the consequences of black invisibility in both the records of slavery and the record-keeping as a situation of primary spiritual significance" (516–17). The spectral presence brings to the fore the experience of slavery despite holes in the master narrative's "chronicles of those events" (516). For Holloway, the repetition of the phrase "not a story to pass on" is a "consistent narrative device in black women's literature," and it emphasizes the contradictions inherent in not passing on a story that has been told. She posits that Morrison does this to "revision" the phrase, making it "mean go on through . . . continue . . . tell" (517).

The memorialization that the novel *Beloved* accomplishes is a continuation of Beloved's "spirit work," both for the future generations to whom the novel speaks and for readers. Sethe's attempts to forget result in Beloved's appearance, and Denver's attempts to learn and remember aid in her disappearance; but the cultural ghosts are necessary to future generations through memory and story. Beloved has served as a bridge from mother to daughter, and, if necessary, she will serve as a bridge again for other mothers and daughters. The reader is left with the impression that Beloved will return if ever a need for cultural "rememory" occurs again. The dynamic history that brought Beloved to life cannot be laid to rest.

Just as Beloved is the presence of an absent child, the novel represents a ghost, a presence for the absent victims of slavery and all its history. As a result of reading *Beloved,* readers can say with Denver: "At times I think she [Beloved] was—more" (*Beloved* 267). Derrida describes the actual appearance of a ghost, or haunting, as a paradox, in that it appears initially at a certain time and place to an observer, but it is also a *returning* entity in that a former living being existed before passing away and enabling the specter to reappear an infinite number of times. Derrida has named this repetitive process of being and yet not being "hauntology" (10). Viewed from this perspective, the text itself becomes the "enigmatic transitional figure moving between past and present, death and life, one culture and another" (Brogan 6), and from author to reader as well. Of the novel's ending, Goldner writes: "As Morrison's novel negotiates between the two poles of forgetting and remembering, it leaves us with ghostly traces of the haunting: the ghost of a ghost" (81). Indeed, the very definition of spectrality as a liminal zone where one must "doubt this reassuring order of presents and, especially, the border between the present, the actual or present reality of the present, and everything that can be opposed to it: absence, non-presence, non-effectivity, inactuality, virtuality" (Derrida 39), applies to *Beloved* as a novel as well as to the character. The book becomes a time-shifting, liminal space transmitting cultural information. Through a kind of *creative hauntology,* which anticipates the actual spectralization of narrative in her next novel, *Jazz,* Morrison creates a specter and a spectral novel, two Beloveds that haunt both characters and readers as a ghost-daughter and as a novel.

In an interview, Morrison said of *Beloved:* "There is a necessity for remembering the horror, but of course there's a necessity for remembering it in a manner in which it can be digested, in a manner in which the memory is not destructive. The act of writing the book, in a way, is a way of confronting it and making it possible to remember" (Darling 247–48). This credo of remembrance is intimately connected to Morrison's awareness that her "books haunt readers" (McKay 146). Just as Beloved is the presence of an absent child, the novel represents a ghost, a presence for the absent victims of slavery and all its history. Ultimately, ghosts are necessary for cultural and personal survival—"learning to live" and remembering "in a manner in which the memory is not destructive." One must be aware of the past and one's personal hauntings to survive in the present and move into the future. As Baby Suggs would say, one must "[k]now it, and go on. . . . Go on." In the culmination of her historical trilogy, *Paradise,* Morrison continues this concern with the memorialization of history, positing that cultural memory is necessary for individual and communal survival.

When *Paradise* appeared in 1997 as the final book in Morrison's trilogy alongside of *Beloved* and *Jazz* (1992), there was some critical confusion: "Although Toni Morrison herself projected her fifth, sixth and seventh novels as a trilogy, the publication of the latest work . . . left reviewers and critics in somewhat of a disarray, either ignoring its relationship with *Beloved* and *Jazz* altogether or openly acknowledging that such a relationship was not at all clear" (Tally, "Reality" 35). The connections between *Beloved* and *Jazz* seemed clear, since upon the publication of *Jazz* some critics searched for the "Beloved" character within the novel. Once *Paradise* was published, however, the desire to find "Beloved" as a character in all three novels seemed difficult and the connections became more thematic and historical. Critics focused generally on Morrison's concern with representing all of America's history (from slavery through the Civil Rights era) and in particular the transformation of the traditional Founding Fathers into the Old Fathers of Ruby expanding westward and attempting to create an ideal community.[7]

Morrison's endeavor to provide a space for the African American voice and experience within American history dovetails neatly with one of Brogan's tenets of twentieth-century ethnic women's ghost stories in that they "are offered as an alternative—or challenge—to 'official,' dominant history" (17). While Tammy Clewell does address the issue of haunting in *Paradise,* she focuses on rituals of mourning and possession in the novel's "therapeutic narration" (130). For my purposes in this chapter, there are many similarities between *Beloved* and *Paradise.* The two novels focus on specific epochs in African American history: slavery, Reconstruction, and the movement for civil rights in the 1960s and 1970s. They detail the conflicted relationship between the individual and the community, and both novels include deep concerns with the haunting aspects of personal and historical memory. Most striking is the intense and personal interaction between the spectral figures and the ghosted individuals that occurs within the spectral spaces of 124 and the Convent. In this section, my analysis of *Paradise* centers on the spectrality of Consolata and the Convent and the experiences of the "throwaway," or ghosted, women who live there (*Paradise* 4).

In her scathing 1998 review, which reduces *Paradise* to a battle between the sexes, Michiko Kakutani misses the transitional quality of Morrison's female characters, dismissing the Convent women as "two-dimensional cliché[s], thin and papery and disposable" (8). By contrast, instead of seeing these characters as clichés, I believe these women are the focus of the novel and illustrate the power of women to work through a ghosted and powerless social position into a more balanced, liminal state. Illustrating the double identity of the ghosted Convent women, the men call their targets "detritus: throwaway people that sometimes blow back into the room after being swept out the door" (*Paradise* 4); like Sethe, the women are outside the purview and acceptance of society, but they also have achieved a power that threatens the town. The rituals the women use to transcend their silenced identities appear to be witchcraft to the judgmental townspeople. The men justify the killing at first by reasoning that the women are witches, since they "don't need men and they don't need God" (276). The women are blamed for the gradual decline of the town and its people. The women achieve, however, a position of peace and integration that the rigid town of Ruby cannot understand; and it is only by working through their traumatic pasts within the confines of the spectral Convent, under the direction of Consolata, that the women can regain a sense of personal identity and transcend the boundaries between "all the 'two's' one likes" (Derrida xviii).

The building in which the five women cross and recross the boundaries between life and death and past and present is a perfect space for this process. The Convent is similar to 124 in *Beloved* in that it is a way station, a crossroads, and a meeting place. Even though it is "seventeen miles from a town which has ninety miles between it and any other," the Convent is not completely secluded (*Paradise* 3). Townspeople come and passing truck drivers stop to buy produce, peppers, rhubarb pie, and barbecue sauce (242). Connie has friendships with Lone and Soane, who live in the town of Ruby, and the Convent girls interact with other inhabitants of the town. For instance, K.D. and Gigi have an affair, and Menus arrives at the Convent drunk and recovers there under the care of the women. Arnette, worried about her pregnancy, which she has been trying to abort, makes a nocturnal visit to the Convent, and Sweetie leaves her sick children and walks to the Convent for a respite from being a caretaker. Most important, the building becomes a spiritual haven for four young women: Mavis, Gigi, Seneca, and Pallas. Each woman has been damaged and is unable to cope with life outside of the Convent. Even though they are free to leave, when they do, they eventually return to stay.

The building itself has a mottled and confused past superficially exhibited in the former nuns' attempts to demolish all traces of its racy former owner. The embezzler who built the house, then lost it when he was arrested by northern lawmen, had created a gentlemen's club complete with "female torso candleholders," "nursing cherubim," suggestive doorknobs and water spigots, and "nude statuary" (72). Gigi finds the remains of this décor, and these traces represent items that the nuns did not remove or simply coated with thick paint when they turned the building into a convent. Connie notes that her first tasks upon entering the Convent were to "smash offending marble figures and tend bonfires of books, crossing herself when naked lovers blew out of the fire and had to be chased back into the flame" (225). On top of the embezzler's remaining touches are the improvements that the nuns made to render the house habitable and functional as a convent school for native girls. Upon entering the Convent, Gigi "immediately [recognizes] the conversion of the dining room into a schoolroom; the living room into a chapel; and the game room alteration to an office" (72). The house's past and present are actually layered upon each other on its walls and in its rooms: "The Convent itself represents history as a densely layered palimpsest, a history simultaneously hidden and revealed" (Krumholz 29).

Besides its physical properties as way station, shelter, and building of vice, virtue, and education, the Convent is situated between the human and spiritual realms: a spectral place that "no longer belongs to time" (Derrida xx). When the nine men from Ruby first arrive to ambush the women, they see the Convent in the fog and "how [it] floated, dark and malevolently disconnected from God's earth" (*Paradise* 18). This image is negative and dangerous from the hunters' perspective, but it places the Convent in an otherworldly space that, at the same time, is still earthly and visible to the men.

Although the building is home to various supernatural occurrences, for the women who live there, these instances are not charged with fear or malevolency. When Mavis arrives, she can hear children's voices: "In fact she had an outer-rim sensation that the kitchen was crowded with children—laughing? singing?—two of whom were Merle and Pearl" (41). She tracks her twins' growth as the years pass, leaving "ice cream sticks" and Christmas presents out for them (258). Additionally, as she continues her life at the Convent, Mavis experiences night visits from a male figure. At first, she describes the visits as a nightmarish lion cub attacking her throat, but these feelings are not very far removed from her abusive sexual experiences with her husband and her fear of him and of her own children. As she becomes more independent, the visits change from frightening to welcome: "Perhaps she ought to admit, confess, to Connie that adding the night visits to laughing children and a 'mother' who loved her shaped up like a happy family" (171). Mavis feels comfortable in the Convent because she has found a loving family, and she does not mind that this family consists of two ghost children, a male apparition, and a spirit guide.

This spirit guide who leads the healing process of the women in the Convent is Consolata. She is the literary descendant of Beloved and the spectral figure in *Paradise.* Consolata's liminal identity becomes clear through her hybridity, her second sight and supernatural powers, and her close communication with spirits. It is appropriate that her living space, the Convent, is a spectral space where the resident women can turn their ghosted and powerless social positions into positions of healing and growth, dealing with their personal hauntings individually and as a group, and finally transitioning into a liminal space of transcendence between life and death, the real and the unreal. This transition, much like Beloved's questionable disappearance, does not end but, rather, continues in a more powerful way the "spirit work" they begin in the Convent.

Consolata's initial appearance, as she welcomes Mavis to the Convent, seems straightforward: she tells Mavis there is no telephone and offers her coffee and food (38). Soane, a visitor from Ruby, comes bearing a gift of sunglasses as a trade for the "you-know-what" mixture that Connie keeps on hand for her (44). The typical scene of a traveler receiving help ends there, however. Mavis and the reader have no idea what Soane's pouch holds or who the mysterious "Mother" is under Connie's care (42–44). Moreover, while the reason is not explained at this point, Mavis feels trepidation when she sees Connie's eyes for the first time. When Connie takes off her sunglasses in the kitchen and Mavis looks at her, she is shocked: "It was the first time she saw the woman's face without the sunglasses. Quickly she looked back at the food and poked her fork into the bowl. . . . Mavis felt, but could not face, the woman's smile. Had she washed her hands before warming up the potatoes? Her smell was walnuts not pecans" (39). The sight of Connie's eyes startles Mavis enough to become suddenly distrustful of Connie, her food, and her hospitality.

This initial meeting with Mavis opens the question of Connie's racial identity. Mavis seems unable to place her except to note that she has "[t]wo Hiawatha braids trail[ing] down her shoulders" (38). Consolata's very presence at the Convent results from a chance meeting with Mary Magna, an American nun of the "Sisters Devoted to Indian and Colored People." The location of this meeting is never specifically disclosed, although it seems to be somewhere in South America, perhaps Brazil. Sister Mary Magna cannot bear to put Connie in an orphanage because the two have formed a close connection, so Connie accompanies the Order to Oklahoma, where there is a convent school for Indian girls. Critics disagree on Connie's identity and origin, but her characteristics identify her as racially hybrid: "green eyes," "tea-colored hair," "smoky, sundown skin" (223).[8] She definitely feels a connection to the people of Ruby when she sees the horse race in town. She faintly hears a "Sha sha sha" and notes: "These men here were not dancing, however; they were laughing, running, calling to each other and to women doubled over in glee. And, although they were living here in a hamlet, not in a loud city full of glittering black people, Consolata knew she knew them" (226). This initial tenuous connection she feels as an observer becomes more concrete when she begins an affair with Deacon Morgan, Soane's husband.

In addition to her racially ambiguous identity, Connie seems otherworldly. Her movements are surreptitious to the point that neither Soane nor Mavis actually notice Connie's return to the kitchen: "Neither one of them heard the bare feet plopping, and since the swinging doors had no sound, Connie's entrance was *like an apparition*" (43, emphasis mine). Her actual physical presence at the Convent is called into question at the beginning of the novel by a slip in the thoughts of one of the invading men: "like the old Mother Superior and the servant who *used to,* still sold produce" (11, emphasis mine). Moreover, once Connie loses the Mother Superior, she feels a hopeless lack of identity: "She had no identification, no insurance, no family, no work. Facing extinction, waiting to be evicted, wary of God, she felt like a curl of paper—nothing written on it—lying in the corner of an empty closet" (247–48). At this moment, Connie resembles Brogan's metaphor of the ghost: she pictures herself as a blank piece of paper. She lacks connection to her past, and according to society, she does not exist, since she has no insurance or identification number.

Connie's eyes and her inability to bear sunlight further mark her as a ghostly character. Connie blames her age for her empty-looking eyes with just a "faint circle where the edge of the iris used to be," claiming that her eyes are "old-lady wash-out color" (70, 47). Secretly, Connie blames the loss of her vision on her indiscretion with Deek Morgan, thinking of the affliction as a punishment from God (241). Even when the town's midwife, Lone, teaches Connie how to use her power of second sight to bring back the dead, she views her "in sight" as evil and opposed to her Roman Catholic faith. Not until Connie has accepted that "in sight" is "something

God made free to anyone who wanted to develop it" can she mentor the castaway women living with her in the Convent (247). Connie's subject position becomes even more complicated when she realizes that "her colorless eyes saw nothing clearly except what took place in the minds of others" (248). Like Beloved, she can cross borders between individuals and actually know others' thoughts. Because of her mind-reading ability, Connie can identify the specific trauma of another individual, but it is hard for her to know where her mind ends and the other's begins.

Once Connie's Mother Superior has died, her lover, Deek, has left her, and she is completely blind, she becomes deeply depressed and angry. As she whiles away her time, drinking in the cellar, she enters a "void" and a period of "ghostedness" that she must pass through to constructively heal herself and the others. Paula Gunn Allen identifies this space of erasure of identity as "the void," or "the shadow" (167).[9] For Allen, the void can be a place of female renewal and power: "Women return from the spirit lands to the crossroads over and over. . . . We who are the nobody are the alive—and no one knows we're here. We are the invisible—and no one cares" (166–67). Women can find empowerment regardless of whether or not society takes notice of their presences. When Connie emerges from "the good clean darkness of the cellar," she receives a visit from a mysterious man with features similar to her own: "tea-colored hair," sunglasses, and eyes "round and green as new apples" (*Paradise* 221, 252). This figure is very similar to Connie, except that he is a male, making him her complementary other, or perhaps a contact from the other side. After this visit from a possible apparition, she changes, becoming more connected to the spirit world: "The way Connie nodded as though listening to someone near; how she said Uh huh or If you say so, answering questions no one had asked. Also she not only had stopped using sunglasses, but was dressed up, sort of, every day" (259). Connie no longer needs her sunglasses because she does not need to shade her eyes from the sun of the material world; she is fully immersed in the borderlessness of the Convent. She tells the women at dinner, "I call myself Consolata Sosa. If you want to be here you do what I say. Eat how I say. Sleep when I say. And I will teach you what you are hungry for" (262). Connie has emerged from an erasure of identity to an awareness of purpose. No longer is she that "curl of paper—nothing written on it—lying in the corner of an empty closet" (247–48). She commands that her original name, Consolata Sosa, be used rather than the shortened version, Connie. She begins instructing the women in spirit work, since she inhabits a literal "in-between" space: "a melding of opposites—that is, of young/old and male/female—into a single identity" (Bouson 209). She has passed through the void, changed her silenced and rejected identity into one of power, and reclaimed her original persona. She has transformed from a ghosted woman into a spectral guide. Consolata and the Convent are situated on the border between life and death and past and present.

While many critics discuss the Convent as a liminal location,[10] particularly in its visibly layered past, Krumholz uses the paradigm of the "nomad" to describe the Convent women "as associated with movement, multiple meanings, and shared labor and goods" (25). This fluid existence is in opposition to the more static atmosphere of Ruby, which Krumholz associates "with fixed authority, unitary meaning, and individual acquisition and control" (25). Contrasting the two locations, she points to the scene when the men discover a cross in the Convent with the figure of Christ removed: "Morrison opens up this space to reimagine ideas of sacrifice and redemption, but also to reexamine the ideas embodied by the cross itself as a symbol of doubleness, of human and divine love, of multiplicity and movement rather than purity and singularity" (26). The presence of this slightly altered cross in the Convent identifies the building as a liminal, transformative space, a space antithetical to the town.

The cross also is connected to a previous scene in Ruby. At K.D. and Arnette's wedding, a disagreement over the meaning of God's love and the cross occurs. The Reverend Pulliam tells the congregation that "[l]ove is divine only and difficult always," while Richard Misner silently holds up the cross at the front of the church, hoping the people will see that "not only is God interested in you; He *is* you" (*Paradise* 141, 147). To Krumholz, this scene indicates that Morrison is tweaking the religious symbol: "Morrison uses multiple interpretations to counter the ideal of purity, to reconstruct the cross as a symbol of the embrace of difference" (27). Since all the participants have divergent ideas about what the cross symbolizes, Krumholz's observation would appear to hold. The congregation's acceptance of "difference" is, however, unclear. Steward Morgan thinks that "a cross was no better than the bearer," condemning the object for the sins of the wearer, and it is clear that his twin brother is ready to stop Misner's show, ending all interpretation (*Paradise* 154). The desire to halt the demonstration is characteristic of the twins, Steward and Deacon, since they have financial and ideological control over Ruby.

Unlike the Convent, the town is physically built on literal "cross" roads, but the transitional quality of the Convent is absent. As Ruby grows, the town continues existing roads, giving the extensions new names: "So St. John Street on the east became Cross John on the west. St. Luke became Cross Luke. The sanity of this pleased most everybody" (114). Krumholz notes this ingenuity, and she reads it as the creation of a literal and figurative crossroads: "Morrison reconfigures the cross as a crossroads, a place that signifies movement, change, conjunction, meetings, and choices" (27). I see this use of the cross as grid-like and stationary. The streets named after the cross are only physically crossing, and the town is rigid and unyielding. The conventionality of the naming is illustrated by the equation of sanity with acceptance of the procedure: "The sanity of this pleased most everybody." There is no connection, meeting, or change in Ruby; for that, citizens must visit the Convent.

Indeed, the town is extremely rigid in its ideologies and the protection of the "official history" of its founding. While compiling her genealogical project, Pat Best realizes that the history of the town is based upon isolation and exclusion resulting from two "Disallowings." The first Disallowing took place during the trek of African Americans from Louisiana and Mississippi to Oklahoma in the late nineteenth century. The pilgrims who would later found Haven were turned away by lighter-skinned African Americans at a town called Fairly: "This time the clarity was clear: for ten generations they had believed the division they fought to close was free against slave and rich against poor. Usually, but not always, white against black. Now they saw a new separation: light-skinned against black" (194). The second Disallowing, the violence visited upon returning black soldiers from World War II, initiated the move from the dying Haven to a more isolated site: Ruby. Pat notes, "And just as the original wayfarers never sought another colored townsite after being cold-shouldered at the first, this generation joined no organization, fought no civil battle" (194). To keep outsiders away, the town adopts an unspoken rule of blood purity, and Pat believes that this rule caused her mother's death. According to Pat, none of the men would go for a doctor when complications from childbirth arose because "they looked down on you, Mama, I know it, and despised Daddy for marrying a wife with no last name, a wife without people, a wife of sunlight skin, a wife of racial tampering" (197).

This strict control over the citizens of Ruby is enforced silently, yet dangerously, by the ruling "eight-rock elite." Pat uses the term "eight-rock" to denote skin color of a "blue-black" and the "deep deep level in the coal mines" (193). Through legal marriages and secret "takeovers" of young girls, widows, and widowers, the bloodlines have been kept as pure as possible. Outsiders and their children are shunned, and townspeople whose spouses are not of the "eight-rock" line are disciplined through silence and isolation. The town's Christmas play even conflates the biblical Christmas story with the first Disallowing, and one by one as the bloodlines of certain families are tainted, those representatives are removed from the play (216). Richard Misner notes the preoccupation with past offenses and its connection to present stagnation: "Over and over and with the least provocation, they pulled from their stock of stories tales about the old folks, their grands and great-grands; their fathers and mothers. . . . But why were there no stories to tell of themselves? About their own lives they shut up. Had nothing to say, pass on" (161).

Similar to the insistence on controlling the meaning of the cross, blood purity, and history, a conflict over the meaning of the fading words on the town's communal Oven illustrates the rigidity of Ruby. From the original settlers of Haven through the next generation in Ruby, the families have shared the Oven, on the front of which Steward and Deacon's grandfather welded a statement that has since faded. While the older generation believes the sentence was a warning—"Beware the Furrow of His Brow"—the younger generation, with Misner's support, wants to change it to "Be the Furrow of His Brow" (86–87). The older generation believes the statement is a sacred command, while the younger generation, aware of the struggle for civil rights outside of Ruby's limits, wants it to reflect a more cooperative stance with God. Just like their control over the bloodlines and Ruby's "official" history, Deacon and Steward publicly swear to protect, with violence if necessary, the Oven's command. Reminiscent of Misner's observation that the people have no stories of their own and have only the town's history, Deacon tells the young people: "So understand me when I tell you nobody is going to come along some eighty years later claiming to know better what men who went through hell to learn knew" (86). Steward gives a more edged response: "If you, any one of you, ignore, change, take away, or add to the words in the mouth of that Oven, I will blow your head off just like you was a hood-eye snake" (87).

Consolata's ritual work with the women in the Convent stands in direct opposition to the harsh control of Ruby. The four women who have joined her in the Convent are each damaged by society. Mavis loses her twins when they suffocate in the hot car while she picks up hot dogs from the store. Her neighbors and the journalist who comes to interview her seem sympathetic, but they are titillated by the shock of the tragedy, for "the shine of excitement in their eyes was clear" (21). In addition to the loss of her twins, Mavis suffers under a domineering, abusive husband and believes that her remaining children have sided with him to kill her. When she runs away, stealing the Cadillac, her mother is unsupportive, so Mavis heads west and ends up at the Convent, where she feels a connection to Connie and decides to stay. Gigi also is wandering the country, afraid to return home to her grandfather alone, with nothing to show for her travels, and haunted by her memory of a boy shot at a march in which she participated. She recalls "the boy spitting blood into his hands" (64). Seneca is a quiet girl who, as a child, was abandoned by her mother, a woman she had thought was her sister. As she struggles through foster homes, she marks her pain onto her skin with a razor, making intricate maps of scars across her body. Once her boyfriend is jailed, she wanders aimlessly and consents to spend three weeks in "abject humiliation," catering to the needs of an older socialite, Norma Keene Fox, for five hundred dollars. At one point, she is described as a "shadow" (126). Finally, Pallas, or Divine as the women call her, is the daughter of a wealthy father and an artist mother. When she visits her mother with her older boyfriend, the two older adults begin an open affair. During Pallas's escape from her mother's home, she is chased and possibly raped by a gang of young men. Each of the women is running from a traumatic memory of violence or betrayal, or both. When they attempt to communicate with the outside world, they are ignored or told to leave, which is what occurs when the four attend Arnette's wedding reception in Ruby. They remain at the Convent because they have nowhere to go and no one to return to, and they haunt the building, each wrapped in her own painful memories.

In "'Passing On' Death: Stealing Life in Toni Morrison's *Paradise,*" Sarah Appleton Aguiar posits that most of the women may already be dead when they arrive at the Convent. For instance, Sal might have killed Mavis with the razor, and that is why Mavis had no trouble leaving the home, or Pallas might have drowned when she was hiding underwater from the rape gang (514). I do not agree that these women could be dead before arriving, since Mavis finds out that there is a warrant for her arrest, and Pallas does contact her father and briefly leaves the Convent. I read the women as physically alive upon arrival, but lacking agency and social power. They have been weakened and silenced by the trauma they have experienced and are social ghosts. When they arrive at the Convent, their lives are viewed as worthless by the inhabitants of Ruby and by most of the people they have encountered.

Although the women are silenced as a result of confrontation with and betrayal by their own families and friends, Consolata helps them work through their ghosted states, moving from "powerlessness" to "power" (Brogan 25). They move from a negative form of erased identity to a state that allows them control over the past and the direction of the present. As Consolata helps the women "unghost" themselves, through engagement and connection with each other, their own pasts, and the afterlife, boundaries begin to dissolve. By privileging liminality and having the women make templates of their bodies on the cellar floor, she blurs the line between the representational and the actual. After Consolata shares her vision of her homeland and of a singing woman named Piedade,[11] the women engage in loud dreaming as they lie within the sketched outlines of their bodies: "And it was never important to know who said the dream or whether it had meaning. In spite of or because their bodies ache, they step easily into the dreamer's tale" (*Paradise* 264). Shrieks and murmurs, accusations and love all mingle in the space of the Convent cellar. The loud dreaming allows each woman to transcend boundaries between self and other and to transcend time as each individual steps into the others' lives. For example, all the women experience exactly what it was like for Mavis when her twins died in the hot Cadillac. Each one feels as if she were actually there in Mavis's place. The women begin to mark not only their painful pasts but also personal, identifying markers on the templates in the cellar. Seneca begins to draw cuts on her image's skin instead of slicing her own, and "they spoke to each other about what had been dreamed and what had been drawn" (265). Each woman reclaims her past and faces it without feeling threatened or paralyzed.

Like Consolata's previous descent into the cellar/void, the women find strength to overcome their painful pasts through the loud dreaming episodes set in the cellar. When Soane sees the women after the sessions, she notes: "[T]he Convent women were no longer haunted" (266). Carpenter and Kolmar write, "In their ghost stories, women writers seem more likely to portray natural and supernatural experience along a continuum. Boundaries between the two are not absolute but fluid, so that the supernatural can be accepted, connected with, reclaimed, and can often possess a quality of familiarity" (12). Although the rituals that Morrison's female characters complete are supernatural in nature, the women do not view them as out of the ordinary once the healing begins. Power emanates from the interstitial spaces, and the Convent cellar is no exception. According to Allen, "In the void reside the keepers of wisdom. . . . Only the disappeared can enter the Void and . . . emerge with a small but vital pot, a design that signifies the power of meaning and of life, and a glowing ember that gives great light" (167). The Convent women enter the void of the cellar as ghosted, social outcasts and leave as healed individuals. Not only are they not haunted by painful pasts, but "life, real and intense," shifted down to the cellar (*Paradise* 264). These female characters have entered Allen's void and returned with knowledge and meaning, having learned how to integrate within a community while simultaneously facing and accepting the past.

This meaning makes them a danger to the men of Ruby, who despise the women as witches and blame them for all of the town's problems. During their meeting before going to the Convent to massacre the women, they list grievances:

> Listen, nothing ever happened around here like what's going on now. Before those heifers came to town this was a peaceable kingdom. The others before them at least had some religion. These here sluts out there by themselves never step foot in church and I bet you a dollar to a fat nickel they ain't thinking about one either. They don't need men and they don't need God. (276)

Because the women have no use for Ruby's rigid controls, the men view them as threats, even though the town's difficulties are not the women's fault but result instead from the harsh controls the men themselves have created and enforced.[12]

The men are so set on interpreting the women as evil that they blatantly misinterpret "evidence" in the Convent while they are stalking the women. They see the lipsticked message from Seneca's mother as "a letter written in blood so smeary its satanic message cannot be deciphered," and they are "alarmed" by a "series of infant booties and shoes ribboned to a cord hanging from a crib in the last bedroom they enter" (7). Far from being proof of satanic ceremonies, these objects are evidence of Pallas's child. The women's abilities to cross borders and function in spaces of healing identify them for the men as having "acquired an illegitimate strength" (Brogan 25). For the men, the women are "throwaway people," or witches, who need to be exterminated (*Paradise* 4).

Although the men do shoot and kill the five Convent women, as witnesses attest, the disappearance of the women's bodies and their subsequent reappearances as revenants to loved ones imply that death cannot stop their work. As Krumholz notes, "[T]he women have moved beyond the boundaries of representation into new possibilities of knowledge and imagination" (30). In a scene reminiscent of Beloved's questionable disappearance, Billie Delia wonders, "When will they return?" She does not believe the Convent women are truly dead, but "out there, darkly burnished, biding their time, brass-metaling their nails, filing their incisors—but out there" (*Paradise* 308). She hopes for a "miracle" and the possibility that the town will learn a lesson about rigidity and power.

Though she does not know it, Billie Delia's wish for a miracle comes true for the women's families. The women have not been destroyed. Unhampered by time or physical space, they are simply biding time until they are needed again. Each one appears to a loved one: Mavis has breakfast with her oldest daughter, who she thought had been trying to kill her; Gigi sees her father after the commutation of his death sentence; Pallas and her child visit her mother; and Seneca sees her mother in a parking lot. While Seneca and Pallas do not achieve the same peace of mind that Mavis and Gigi do, their work is continuing beyond the grave. Readers are reminded of the coda to *Beloved:* "Sometimes the photograph of a close friend or relative—looked at too long—shifts, and something more familiar than the dear face moves there. They can touch it if they like, but don't, because they know things will never be the same if they do" (*Beloved* 275). Beloved may have disappeared from 124, but she is not completely gone. She can reappear any time her cultural work is needed for anyone who may be disconnected from the past or the surrounding community. The Convent women have achieved a similar state of being in that they are free to move wherever they are needed for healing, and this open connection to another world touches a few people in the town of Ruby besides Billie Delia and the women's loved ones, including Deek Morgan, Richard Misner, and Anna Flood.

The inability of the townspeople to pin down exactly what occurred at the Convent marks a change from rigidity to a more liminal state. Misner notes, "The future panted at the gate. Roger Best will get his gas station and the connecting roads will be laid. Outsiders will come and go" (*Paradise* 306). Isolation will give way to connection and movement. Even the stories circulating about the incident at the Convent are multiplicitous. Unlike the single, town-approved message concerning the Disallowing and the communal Oven, no one has the correct tale. Lone is frustrated "by the way the story was being retold; how people were changing it to make themselves look good" (297). Misner cannot understand the stories the other two ministers tell because "neither had decided on the meaning of the ending" (297). Instead of silence, "the difficulties churned and entangled everybody" (298). There are rumblings of both disapproval and agreement as, in Philip Page's words, "all the participants' brows are furrowed in hermeneutic concentration" ("Furrowing" 638).

This openness to mediation and interpretation affects Deacon Morgan the most intensely. He begins the work of making Ruby's roads into an actual crossroads of transformation by walking the "cross" streets barefoot to Misner's home for a confessional discussion. In contrast to the single-minded resolve he and his twin brother felt before the Convent attack, Deek is now unwilling to share Steward's interpretation of the killings. He sees that he has "become what the Old Fathers cursed: the kind of man who set himself up to judge, rout and even destroy, the needy, the defenseless, the different" (*Paradise* 302). His part in the attack on the Convent women preys on his mind, showing him his dangerous single-mindedness, and his transformation begins when he encounters Consolata right before Steward kills her.

Just as Consolata serves as a spectral bridge to another realm between life and death for the four women under her care, she also gives Deacon a glimpse of this other plane of existence, and it is this glimpse into the unknown that initiates his remorse. When Consolata attempts to stop the men from firing on the three women who are running away from the building, Deacon is startled. Consolata says, "You're back" to something "above the heads of the men," probably her spirit guide. After she speaks, Deacon "needs the sunglasses, but they are nestled in his shirt pocket," and "he looks at Consolata and sees in her eyes what has been drained from them and from himself as well" (289). Like Consolata before her "conversion," Deacon needs sunglasses, but he needs them to shield his eyes from this other spiritual, liminal plane. Her ability to move among states of existence, time, and identity affects him, but only for a moment before she is shot and killed by Steward. Her death, though, does not end this effect.

Between Consolata's death and his visit to Misner, Deacon feels isolated and incomplete since he is no longer close to his identical twin, Steward, and he cannot communicate to his wife what has happened to him. At one point, he realizes that he can never speak of his feelings about Consolata's death because he would have to tell Soane

> that green springtime had been sapped away; that outside of that loss, she was grand, more beautiful than he believed a woman could be; that her untamable hair framed a face of planes so sharp he wanted to touch; that after she spoke, the smile that followed made the sun look like a fool. He might tell his wife that he thought at first that she was speaking to him—'You're back'—but knew now it wasn't so. And that instantly he longed to know what she saw, but Steward, who saw nothing or everything, stopped them dead lest they know another realm. (301)

Justine Tally reads this passage as a return of Connie as a revenant to Soane ("Reality" 40), but it is actually Deacon remembering the moments before Connie's death and his confused emotions. At first, Deacon is troubled by his surviving intimate feelings for Connie, and he wishes to hide from Soane his desire for Connie's exclamation to be a response to his return. By the end of the passage, however, he is contrasting Steward's binary thinking —he sees "nothing *or* everything"—with Connie's liminal transcendence of boundaries. He receives a glimpse of "another realm," a place between "nothing or everything" that neither Steward nor the old Deacon could understand. Now Deacon wants illumination, and he will try to understand his transformation in his talks with Misner and his new independence from his brother.

In addition to Deacon Morgan, Richard Misner and Anna Flood are affected by the fleeting view of another realm when they visit the Convent, hoping to discover some clue as to what went on and what happened to the bodies. While standing near Consolata's garden chair, they concurrently experience a vision: Misner sees a window and Anna sees a door (305).[13] Although Page interprets this scene as Misner and Anna's "leap beyond the ordinary senses, beyond the usual binary oppositions between the real and the magical and between life and death" ("Furrowing" 642), the two do not come to that conclusion on their own. The experience becomes a debate over whether it is a window or a door, not over the meaning or where it could lead: "They expanded on the subject: What did a door mean? what a window? focusing on the sign rather than the event; excited by the invitation rather than the party. They knew it was there. Knew it so well they were transfixed for a long moment before they backed away and ran to the car" (*Paradise* 305). The two run back to their reality and then proceed to banter lightheartedly over the sign rather than the meaning—a debate somewhat like the town's arguments over the faded words on the Oven. Instead of making a leap, they wish to "avoid reliving the shiver or saying out loud what they were wondering. Whether through a door needing to be opened or a beckoning window already raised, what would happen if you entered? What would be on the other side? What on earth would it be? What on earth?" (305). Whatever is on the other side, be it positive or negative, it opens up multiple interpretations. Even though the townspeople might tell versions of the story about the Convent women that make the town look better at the expense of the truth, there are truthful versions in the mix, and the townspeople have moved beyond adhering to one town-father-approved message.

Later, during his funeral sermon for Save-Marie, Misner begins to move through the opening, but he moves in confusion. He sees the window again in the little coffin: "[H]e saw the window in the garden, felt it beckon toward another place—neither life nor death—but there, just yonder, shaping thoughts he did not know he had" (307). At that moment he becomes emotional, speaking of Save-Marie's short but loved existence on earth: "He [God] is with us always, in life, after it and especially in between, lying in wait for us to know the splendor" (307). Misner is "disturbed by what he had said" most likely because, as a minister, he has been trained to see God in life's journey and afterward, but never between the two (307). After seeing the window in the garden and glimpsing where Connie, Mavis, Gigi, Seneca, and Pallas exist, he can say that God is present always, but "especially in between" the two levels.

Unlike Deacon, Misner, and Anna, who receive glimpses of what Page identifies as the "transcendent realm where Milkman leaps in *Song of Solomon,* Son runs in *Tar Baby,* Beloved disappears in *Beloved,* and Wild and Golden Grey reside in *Jazz,*" the reader actually sees this transcendent realm, or paradise, in *Paradise* ("Furrowing" 642). Geoffrey Bent views the end of the novel as supernatural overkill: "Current fashion has deemed magic *de rigueur* for visionary novels . . . [and] [t]he plethora of ghosts and spectral figures here more than fill the paranormal quota" (147). Bent misses, however, the importance of the spectral presences. Instead of being a supernatural overload or a "surreal set-piece [that] feels like a hasty afterthought" ("Worthy Women," Kakutani 8), the view of paradise at the end is the key to the novel. There is an image of a young woman with "tea brown hair" and "emerald eyes" sitting on a beach with a singing woman named Piedade.[14] This young woman appears to be Consolata reconnecting with the singing woman she described earlier to her four protégés (*Paradise* 264). The final image of the two women on the beach is not of a perfect place: "Around them on the beach, sea trash gleams. Discarded bottle caps sparkle near a broken sandal. A small dead radio plays the quiet surf" (318). Similar to the Convent women's reclamation of their haunted pasts, these are images of detritus redeemed in that a broken radio can still "play" and "trash" can "gleam." Also, the relationship pictured is one of healing and love: "There is nothing to beat this solace which is what Piedade's song is all about, although the words evoke memories neither one has ever had: of reaching age in the company of the other; of speech shared and divided bread smoking from the fire; the unambivalent bliss of going home to be at home—the ease of coming back to love begun" (318). This space seems to be simultaneously earthly, spiritual, and timeless as the two women remember events that might not ever have happened and share each other's memories in a close connection.

While the women sit, a ship sails into port: "Another ship perhaps, but different, heading to port, crew and passengers, lost and saved, atremble, for they have been disconsolate for some time. Now they will rest before shouldering the endless work they were created to do down here in paradise" (318). These closing words in the novel regarding this space echo the work that Consolata and her charges began in the Convent; only now they have been freed to continue the work unfettered by questions of reality, life, or death. This space is a true crossroads of physical and temporal space: a space of spirits.

Regarding the importance of living with spirits, Derrida notes: "[L]earning to live . . . can happen only between life and death, [and] . . . can only *maintain itself* with some ghost" (xviii). This "learning to live" is the process that Consolata used to lead the Convent women into a more connected and balanced existence, and it is the process that Piedade and others in the pictured paradise are working to continue. An openness to specters or alternate modes of existence and thought and a movement beyond binary structures is mediated through this space that Deacon, Misner, and Anna could see but not enter. This space is not only transcendent, as it functions between the actual and the magical, life and afterlife, and past and present; but its work is "especially in between," as Misner observed. Souls like Piedade, Connie, the Convent women, and also Beloved, can enter and leave at will. They move among humanity and help individuals first to memorialize and reconnect to their traumatic pasts and then to move toward reintegration into their community.

I read Beloved and Consolata as more fully developed spectral entities building from the work of Pilate and Thérèse in the previous novels by actively haunting "ghosted" characters and repairing mental damage and separation. Beloved and Consolata serve as bridges for the people they haunt, connecting individuals to cultural and personal history and generations to one another. The "endless work" that the souls "were created to do down here in paradise" is to create historical and personal connection (*Paradise* 318). The bookends of Morrison's trilogy span the spectrum of the African American experience. *Beloved* begins this epic historical undertaking by making history present for a family rent by slavery, and *Paradise* continues by illustrating the trauma after slavery and into the 1970s of a black community damaged by its self-imposed isolation and insistence on racial purity. *Paradise* is also a glimpse for readers of the liminal space that allows the Convent women, Consolata, Beloved, and other spectral figures to keep working even after death, thus rending the distinction between life and the afterlife and past and present. These spectral figures are shown in a triumphant space of spirits and transformation. In a similar manner, the tantalizing glimpses of paradise available to Deacon, Misner, and Anna imply that these characters, like Milkman, Son, and Jadine, might be ready to experience healing through the legacy of the spectral guides' work and the possibility of their return. For that to happen, they must enter the door or window and find out "what would be on the other side" (305).

CHAPTER FOUR

"The Specter as Possibility": Ghostly Narrators in *Jazz* and *Love*

In Morrison's fiction, the spectral defies compartmentalization and definition, and it can serve as a spot for the eruption of various stories and perspectives that were previously ignored. Her sixth and eighth novels, *Jazz* (1992) and *Love* (2003), are not exceptions to this supernatural rule as it operates in *Song of Solomon, Tar Baby, Beloved,* and *Paradise.* The difference is that in these two books the specter is the narrator. This use of a spectral narrator moves beyond the "unreliable" tendencies of first-person narrative voices. In Morrison's previous work, the importance of storytelling as a device for ordering the characters' impressions and foregrounding their experiences against the backdrop of historical episodes is clear. This spectral narrator is a new kind of creative voice that privileges the eruptions of various perspectives at the textual and narrative level. In *Jazz* and *Love,* the narrators fulfill the functions of previous spectral figures: their identities are fluid and indeterminate; they are guides for the characters in the novels; but, as narrative voices, they further open the texts to new possibilities and new avenues of interaction with readers.

In *Jazz,* Morrison re-creates New York during the Jazz Age. She follows her main characters, Joe and Violet Trace, as they migrate north from Virginia to escape the Jim Crow South; but even though they may physically leave Virginia, the past still haunts the couple. The action revolves primarily around Joe's affair with a young girl he murders when she leaves him for a younger man and Violet's breakdown after discovering the infidelity, which induces her to attack Joe's lover any way she can, even if she must knife a corpse. Of course, the characters are not simply affected by the affair and its consequences; layered upon these problems are Joe and Violet's haunting traumatic pasts. Operating under the surface of the plot are the horrors that Violet and Joe have each brought with them from Virginia and the family secrets they will not share even with each other. Additionally, as *Jazz* is the middle book of Morrison's historical trilogy, the traumas that Violet and Joe have experienced are directly traceable to memories and effects of slavery and Reconstruction as evidenced by the characters of Wild and Golden Gray. The reader becomes aware of these secrets through a narration that, unlike in previous Morrison novels, is from the first-person point of view; but the identity of the narrator is unknown, thus leaving the reader faced with a ghostly presence as the source of information.

In *Love,* the setting spans several decades, picking up approximately where *Jazz* left off and moving through the civil rights struggles of the 1960s and 1970s and on into the 1990s. Similar to *Jazz,* there is a plot that follows a marriage; but this time the partners are an older man and his twelve-year-old granddaughter's best friend, and the relationship that sours is the one between the young friends, Christine and Heed. The ghostly narrator, who actually is dead in the present time of the novel, murders Cosey, the wealthy older man, for the girls' protection. In this novel, the relationships are affected by class, as the wealthy Cosey simply buys his granddaughter's friend Heed from her parents, and by the patriarchy, as Cosey lords it over his household and indelibly damages the two girls through his sexual abuse of his twelve-year-old wife. *Jazz* may be part of Morrison's trilogy between *Beloved* and *Paradise,* but it shares more affinities with this later work, *Love. Jazz* and *Love* carry on the author's concern with African American history and issues of haunting, but they introduce a new motif of a spectral *narrator* who happens to be the guide for the ghosted characters.

What, then, are the implications of having ghostly narrators? Barbara T. Christian posits that part of Morrison's task as a writer is "a remapping of the historical terrain for African Americans, a terrain that had been previously charted by a master narrative from the outside, rather than from inside their experiences" (31). Speaking of *Jazz* in particular, Alan Munton writes, "Morrison has made the European novel tell a different story by imagining hitherto ignored histories which enable us to hear lost black voices" (250). As evidenced in *Beloved* and *Paradise,* Morrison's literary purpose is to bring to light the untold stories of American history and the parts that individual African Americans play in those larger contexts, and each of her books tackles a different piece of that history from slavery to the present. While completing this cultural work, though, she always focuses on the characters' personal memories of and reactions to an overarching matrix of concerns: she charts the narrative "from inside their experiences." For instance, in *Beloved,* Morrison shows Sethe's personal and violent reaction to the Fugitive Bill as an illustration of its terrible consequences, and in *Jazz,* she focuses on the experiences of ordinary folks during the time of the Harlem Renaissance, "moving away from the 'big' picture" (Peterson 206). For its part, *Jazz* initially seems to depart from Morrison's historical recovery mission. As Nancy J. Peterson notes, "*Jazz* is a historical novel that 'fails' to represent its epoch properly; set for the most part in Harlem, the novel opens in 1926 . . . it offers for full view almost none of the artistic, cultural, or political milestones that African Americans achieved in those years" (201). In *Love,* as in *Paradise,* although each novel takes place during a different span of years, the everyday lives of the characters are intricately caught up in and affected by the larger dramas of the civil rights movement. While Linda Hutcheon calls this more inclusive look at history in fiction "historiographic metafiction [where] we now get the histories (in the plural) of the losers as well as the winners" (63), when looking at Morrison's *Jazz* and *Love,* I would call her technique one of *spectralized narration,* where multiple versions of the past and the text itself are mediated through a specter. The layers interact and haunt each other, and according to Andrew Smith, this fragile layering of history in fiction causes "the present [to be] ghosted by the past" (36). As spectral narrators, the voice of *Jazz* and L in *Love* not only serve as bridges for the ghosted individuals in their respective novels, but simply by being the narrative authority, they also mediate between the text and the reader in a manner that previous Morrison novels have not. These narrators are the ultimate observers, who have the "power to see without being seen" (Derrida 8); and through their liminal mediations between "all the 'two's' one likes" (xviii), including between text and reader, Morrison privileges the space where history, memory, and lived experience are fluid components of one another, offering alternative ways of thinking and perceiving.

Much critical ink has been spilled in attempts to label the narrator of *Jazz,* who is nameless, genderless, placeless, and perhaps not even corporeal. Morrison highlighted this indeterminate identity in a 1995 interview with Angels Carabi: "I decided that the voice would be one of assumed knowledge, the voice that says, 'I know everything.' This is a kind of dominant ownership: without sex, gender, or age" (41). Critics have identified the narrator as a female voice, a community member, and the goddess from the *Nag Hammadi,* among other interpretations.[1] In the Carabi interview, Morrison also said that she wanted to approximate an actual "talking book," as if "the book were talking, writing itself, in a sense" (42).[2] What if, however, this idea of a "book-in-progress" and the reader's inability to pin down the narrator's identity are a result of the narrator's, and therefore the text's, spectrality? What does it mean for this novel if the actual narrative becomes spectralized? Once the narrator of *Jazz* is viewed as spectral, the figure's fuzzy identity, its seeming omnipresence throughout time and space, and even its bizarre layering of versions of the story, particularly in the Golden Gray sections, become important parts of its ethos. The reason why the narrative truth is so hard for the reader (and the narrator) to pin down is the same reason for the narrator's inscrutability: all of the possibilities are valuable.

This emphasis on allowing for all of the possibilities is a part of jazz music and spectrality. In the foreword to *Jazz,* Morrison discusses her creative difficulties in making "structure . . . *equal* meaning" in the novel (xix). She did not want jazz to be a "musical background." Rather, she "wanted the work to be a manifestation of the music's intellect, sensuality, anarchy; its history, its range, and its modernity" (xix). While critics have wrangled over the relation between *Jazz* and the musical genre, for my purposes it is enough to note that, for Morrison in this enterprise, the narrator could manifest these qualities of jazz music: "invention," "improvisation," and "change" (xix).[3] These mutable, ineffable, and fluid aspects recall Derrida's specter. Indeed, Morrison notes that "the jazz enables possibility" (Carabi 43), and for Derrida, the specter is possibility, always evading prescription. When discussing the need for scholars to investigate spaces of haunting, he writes, "The latter [scholar] would finally be capable, beyond the opposition between presence and non-presence, actuality and inactuality, life and non-life, of thinking the possibility of the specter, the specter as possibility"

(12). Thus the narrator, as a specter imbued with the possibilities of jazz, can transcend boundaries and limiting perspectives.[4] The point is not to convey one set story from one viewpoint but to open up the text to a multiplicity of possibilities. The narrator's spectrality is made apparent through its veiled identity, its omnipresence, and its unpredictability. It explodes the bounds of what one traditionally expects from the fictional authority.

The narrator is the ultimate silent observer. I call it a "silent" observer because, even though the first-person voice does speak incessantly to the reader, the narrator's presence, for the most part, remains unknown to the characters: "I haven't got any muscles, so I can't really be expected to defend myself. But I do know how to take precaution. Mostly it's making sure no one knows all there is to know about me. Second, I watch everything and everyone and try to figure out their plans, their reasonings, long before they do" (*Jazz* 8). When the narrator admits a love for "this City" (7), the reader is taken on a descriptive journey that soars over the cityscape, enters into apartment buildings, and watches individuals in shadow. Sharon Jessee comments on this omniscience and omnipresence as proof of the narrator's status as a goddess (143), but this is also a quality of the spectral that is not unlike Beloved's abilities to bend time and space to her will or L's powers of observation, as we will see in *Love.* This omniscience is atypical of a first-person narrator who is a character in its story, and this supernatural awareness extends beyond the setting to the main characters. Although the voice later admits to losing control of the slippery narrative it is telling, it knows a great deal about Joe, Violet, Wild, Dorcas, and Felice. While observing Joe at one point, the narrator exhibits a remarkable knowledge of his demeanor and thoughts: "I know him so well. Have seen him feed small animals nobody else paid any attention to, but I was never deceived. I remember the way he used to fix his hat. . . . The sweater under his suit jacket would be buttoned all the way up, but I know his thoughts are not—they are loose" (*Jazz* 119). The narrator becomes quite attached to its literary charges and haunts their actions and thoughts. During the confusing narrative sequence when two versions of the story of Golden Gray's confrontation with his father are told, the narrator thinks of its relationship to Gray, "I have to be a shadow who wishes him well, like the smiles of the dead left over from their lives" (161). The narrator is the "shade" of the novel, haunting the characters as a spectral voyeur.

Although the narrator can free-float through the settings and observe the characters with otherworldly impunity, it is not an infallible authority on the text because the narrative is as slippery and resistant to meaning as the specter is. There are, therefore, moments in the novel when the narrator admits to speculation and outright failure at predicting certain events. When the narrator points out that Joe does not know about his wife's past, in particular her time with her grandmother True Belle and her mother's suicide, the narrator admits that it does not completely understand Violet's state of mind either but asserts its pleasure in speculation: "[It is] worth the trouble if you're like me—curious, inventive and well-informed" (137). Morrison describes the narrator's difficulty in telling a story that is in progress: "Because the voice has to actually imagine the story it's telling, using the art of imagination, it's in trouble, because if it's really involved in the process of telling the story and letting the other voices speak, the story that it thought it knew turns out to be entirely different from what it predicted because the characters will be evolving within the story, within the book" (Carabi 41). There are two major instances in the novel where the narrator loses control of the story: in the description of the meeting between Golden Gray and Wild and in the expectation that someone else in addition to Dorcas will be killed by the end of the book.

According to Jennifer Andrews, the episode in which Golden Gray finds Wild on the way to meet and possibly exact revenge upon his African American father, Henry Lestroy, is one of the scenes "relatively untouched by critics because of their seemingly enigmatic relationship to the text's main plot" (88).[5] I believe these scenes point to the spectrality of the narrator and the narrative itself. Rather than telling the story "the way it is" with one master narrative, Morrison allows the story to escape the grasp of the narrator, and the different versions overlap and haunt each other and the reader. The reader never knows which strand is correct, but knowing this is not necessary because the narration is about process and the allowance for all possibilities. After the initial version of Golden Gray's perfunctory rescue of Wild, the narrator chides itself:

> What was I thinking of? How could I have imagined him so poorly? Not noticed the hurt that was not linked to the color of his skin, or the blood that beat beneath it. But to some other thing that longed for authenticity, for a right to be in this place, effortlessly without

> needing to acquire a false face, a laughless grin, a talking posture. I have been careless and stupid and it infuriates me to discover (again) how unreliable I am. (*Jazz* 160)

Here, the narrator freely admits its unreliability and that it requires the acceptance of several possibilities to tell properly the characters' stories. The narrator illustrates its desire to encompass all options: "Not hating him is not enough; liking, loving him is not useful" (161). Telling Gray's story goes beyond right or wrong and love or hate; to tell the tale, the narrator must account for all of its complexity and ambiguity.[6] According to Peterson, the narrator's "commitment to looking again brings more details into the picture, which pose new contradictions, and thus her former narrative can no longer offer neat evaluations" (212).

This slippery narrative tendency appears again toward the end of the novel: "I thought I'd hidden myself so well as I watched them through windows and doors, took every opportunity I had to follow them, to gossip about and fill in their lives, and all the while they were watching me. . . . So I missed it altogether. . . . It never occurred to me that they were thinking other thoughts, feeling other feelings, putting their lives together in ways I never dreamed of" (*Jazz* 220–21). Part of the narrator's surprise at the end is that another young woman, Felice, is introduced, but this does not result in violence. In trying to tell the "true" story as witnessed, the narrator loses control as it misses the characters' actual feelings and decisions. The characters, meanwhile, create a separate plot underneath, and commingling with, the narrator's story.

In another change from Morrison's previous works, there are two spectral figures in *Jazz* in addition to the narrator: Wild and Dorcas. Both women are absences that are yet palpably present in the narrative and in the characters' thoughts and memories, and both slip around the meanings that are imposed upon them. Joe sees the two as connected maternal figures, and he shoots his lover, Dorcas, to keep her from leaving him as his mother, Wild, did. Violet is confused about whether Dorcas is the rival for Joe's love—whom she should have attacked while she was alive instead of desecrating her body in a coffin—or the child that Violet never was able (or allowed herself) to have? There are critical connections between Wild, Dorcas, and Beloved, since *Jazz* is the second novel of the trilogy.[7] In particular, Peter Nicholls and Sarah Appleton Aguiar both posit that Wild is a manifestation of Beloved, showing readers where she migrated after the events of the earlier novel, and Nicholls reads Joe Trace as the child of Paul D and Beloved, physically continuing that saga in a new generation. Indeed, Morrison has hinted at the connection, noting, "Wild is a kind of Beloved. The dates are the same. . . . When you see Beloved towards the end, you don't know; she's either a ghost who has been exorcised or she's a real person pregnant by Paul D, who runs away, ending up in Virginia, which is right next to Ohio. But I don't want to make all those connections" (Carabi 43). I do not want to make those connections either; rather, I want to focus on how "Wild is a kind of Beloved," but not the same character. In my reading, she is a specter like Morrison's previous ghost and her fictional comrades, the narrator and Dorcas.[8]

A scene integral to Wild's spectrality occurs in Virginia when a young Joe Trace tracks her in the woods, desiring some form of contact so that he can know with certainty that she is his mother. Joe shows his knowledge of how slippery language can be as he asks the hiding and silent Wild to touch his hand rather than feel forced to say anything: "Just a sign, he said, just show me your hand, he said, and I'll know don't you know I have to know? She wouldn't have to say anything, although nobody had ever heard her say anything; it wouldn't have to be words; he didn't need words or even want them because he knew how they could lie, could heat your blood and disappear" (37). Later in the scene, Joe's frustration is shown primarily not to be a result of having a wilderness woman for a mother, but of not knowing one way or another whether she *is* his mother.

To be sure, Wild's existence in the woods echoes Beloved's withdrawal and the Convent women's departure, leaving possibilities of return from the margins: "[T]he son she had fourteen years ago, and ran away from, but not too far. Just far enough away to annoy everybody because she was not completely gone, and close enough to scare everybody because she creeps about and hides and touches and laughs a low sweet babygirl laugh in the cane" (37). Her presence at the margins of the community, while hidden in the cane field, places her close enough to fleetingly touch people, but never to communicate, and thus signals her spectral properties. Joe knows that other children believe she is supernatural: "The small children believed she was a witch but they were wrong. . . . She was powerless, invisible, wastefully daft. Everywhere and nowhere" (179). Certainly, we have seen from the Convent women in *Paradise* what supposedly daft and throwaway women can do, but Joe also is describing her power to haunt: she is invisible and omnipresent. She becomes a staple of ghost stories for children and adults as everyone searches for a glimpse of her: "She lived close, they said, not way off in the woods or even down in the riverbed, but somewhere in that cane field—at its edge some said or maybe moving around in it. Close" (166).

Her presence in the cane field further signals her link to the brutal past of slavery; as Anissa Janine Wardi notes in a discussion of *Love,* cane and sugar can be "an embodiment of evil as the cultivation of this cash crop evokes a particularly brutal chapter in plantation history" ("Laying" 216n8).[9] Reacting to a present danger, Joe fears that his mother remains in the fields even when whites set fire to the area, resulting in a mass migration of African Americans from that part of Virginia. He remembers the terror:

> [T]he cotton fields and the colored neighborhood around them were churned up and pressed down. One week of rumors, two days of packing, and nine hundred Negroes, encouraged by guns and hemp, left Vienna, rode out of town on wagons or walked on their feet to who knew (or cared) where. . . . The cane field where Wild hid, or watched, or laughed out loud, or stayed quiet burned for months. The sugar smell lingered in the smoke—weighting it. Would she know? he wondered. Would she understand that fire was not light or flowers moving toward her, or flying golden hair? That if you tried to touch or kiss it, it would swallow your breath away? (*Jazz* 173–74)

Wild's whereabouts and her actions are confused and inscrutable, and in Joe's memory, she becomes a part of the violent, sickeningly sweetened scene of the burning cane fields.[10] She, like Beloved before her, is tied intimately to the trauma of white violence and black dispossession. In her book *Death and the Arc of Mourning in African American Literature,* Wardi describes the haunting nature of the South as "a locus of racial terror and a consecrated landscape rich with ancestral corpses," and "an in-between place, suspended between a living community and a passed ancestral corpus" (3). For her, the South is simultaneously a location for a living African American community and a place of ancestral spirits, results of oppression and violence. This space of unresolved memory and trauma haunts the migrants even when they escape to the North.

One of the characters Joe encounters in the North is his paramour, Dorcas, and the young girl also becomes a repository for contradictory meanings much like the narrator and Wild. When Violet remembers cutting Dorcas's face at the girl's funeral, she thinks that "nothing would have come out but straw" (*Jazz* 5), but besides the preparation of the body for the funeral, this reference to straw inside of Dorcas points to her as an empty signifier laden with the interpretations of all her fellow characters: she is everyone's "straw man" for his or her own beliefs. Her guardian, Alice Manfred, sees the licentious nature of youth in her niece and attempts to guard the child against all sensuality. Violet confuses Dorcas with the child she thought she had never wanted but now fervently desires: "Was she the woman who took her man, or the daughter who fled her womb?" (109). And Joe confuses Dorcas with his mother when the girl rejects him for a younger man, shooting her when he tracks her to the house party, something he refused to do while hunting his mother in Virginia no matter how angry he became. Dorcas even participates in the diluting of her own identity when she leaves Joe precisely *because* he wants to love her for who she is: "I could be anything, do anything—and it pleased him" (191). After leaving Joe, Dorcas dates Acton, a man who tells her what to wear, where to go, and how much to eat. She notes the change: "I wanted to have a personality and with Acton I'm getting one" (191).

This tendency for characters to use Dorcas as a lens for their own fears continues in the presence of her photograph. In fact, the primary appearance of Dorcas in the present plot of the novel is in her picture—her remnant image from beyond the grave. Since Violet never knew Dorcas when she was alive, she creates a personality for the girl by investigating the traces of her life: she goes to the places where she went for entertainment, to her school, and finally to Alice's home, where she asks to borrow the photograph. The picture is, however, just as ungraspable as all the other threads of a life once lived, but Violet's attempts to understand Dorcas haunt her: "For Violet, who never knew the girl, only her picture and the personality she invented for her based on careful investigations, the girl's memory is a sickness in the house—everywhere and nowhere" (28). Like the narrator and Wild (and Beloved before them), Dorcas is ever-present and ineffable. She is portrayed in the text only through Violet's imagination or Joe's memory. For Violet, "[T]he space where the photo had been was real" (197). Joe mourns not only his murder of Dorcas, but also his inability to remember her properly: he "minded more the possibility of his memory failing to conjure up the dearness" (28). Dorcas's photograph haunts Joe and Violet in a manner reminiscent of this passage at the end of *Beloved:* "Sometimes the photograph of a close friend or relative—looked at too long—shifts, and something more familiar than the dear face itself moves there. They can touch it if they like, but don't, because they know things will never be the same if they do" (275). This photo, or trace, of Dorcas becomes just as mutable as her living personality, and in an instance of intertextuality within Morrison's canon, a trace of Beloved peeps through this photograph as well. In another layer of intertextuality, a photograph also was the seed of the novel as, according to Morrison, she found the inspiration for *Jazz* in a picture of a dead girl in *The Harlem Book of the Dead,* a collection of Van der Zee's photographs. The eighteen-year-old had been shot by a jealous lover at a party (Naylor 207). In an exercise of improper mourning, with only this image of Dorcas haunting the couple without a direct connection to her remains (both of them desecrated Dorcas's body in some manner) (Derrida 9), Joe and Violet sink into depression and are trapped in their separate obsessions with Dorcas.

For much of the novel, Violet and Joe can be described as social ghosts. They are on the margins of society, and while the narrator assures the reader in its description of "the City" that the migrants have forgotten the southern terror they have left behind—"There goes the sad stuff. The bad stuff. The things-nobody-could-help stuff. The way everybody was then and there. Forget that" (*Jazz* 7)—the reader knows from Joe and Violet's memories that they have not forgotten the past. Violet is haunted by her mother's suicide after the family's dispossession by whites and by the stories of the North that her grandmother True Belle told. Joe's unknown wild-woman mother and the violence he witnessed both in the South and in the City forever haunt him. Violet and Joe are fractured people who are always fleeing, either physically or mentally.

Violet has so much difficulty functioning in spite of her memories and trauma that she creates another persona in her mind, one that is capable of the rage and violence she will not permit herself, and this persona earns the nickname "Violent" when she attacks Dorcas's corpse for revenge. Wardi believes that "the splintering of Violet's identity . . . bespeaks migration displacement" (*Death* 118). For Wardi, Violet's "true self" is southern, while the City has transformed her into her violent alter ego. The narrator pictures her fractured personality as "cracks" into which she falls occasionally: "I call them cracks because that is what they were. Not openings or breaks, but dark fissures in the globe light of the day. She wakes up in the morning and sees . . . a string of small, well-lit scenes. In each one something specific is being done. . . . But she does not see herself doing these things. She sees them being done" (*Jazz* 22). This vision shows a lack of agency as things are finished around the house without Violet's awareness of doing the chores. Her split personality leads to her actually haunting herself. This side of her is unknown to her husband: "Joe never learned of Violet's public craziness" (22), just as she is unaware of Joe's past in Virginia before they met and of his affair, until he kills Dorcas.

Unlike Violet's "cracks," Joe Trace's very last name points to the mutability of his identity.[11] As a child, he named himself instead of taking his foster parents' surname: "I named my own self, since nobody did it for me, since nobody knew what it could or should have been" (123). When Mrs. Williams tells Joe that his parents disappeared without a trace, he believes he is the "trace" they left behind, and he takes Trace as his last name (124). Joe is the trace of Wild's presence at the margins. He is the slight evidence of her shadowy existence in space and time. Moreover, much like his lost mother, he knows how to disappear when necessary, for one of his skills at his work as a waiter and salesman is to fade into the background and let the products and service sell themselves: "I'm there but only if you want me" (122). Joe's identity is contingent upon his environment and circumstances —it is a survival mechanism for a marginalized individual. He is proud that he named himself and then, when necessary, "changed into new seven times" (123), reminiscent of Son's seven documented identities during his long exile in *Tar Baby.* Joe is adept at ghosting himself in order to function in a society dominated by oppression, as he faces white terror in Virginia, manifested in burning fields and repossessed homes, and then race riots in the North. As a result of direct experience, he concisely summarizes the dangers of migration: "Crackers in the South mad cause Negroes were leaving; crackers in the North mad cause they were coming" (128). And he notes with irony: "You could say I've been a new Negro all my life" (129). Self-erasure, reconstruction, and a longing to forget the violent past work together to trap Joe in a static present where he cannot connect to his wife or to his young lover without fragments of memories about his mother creeping into the equation.

As in previous Morrison novels, these ghosted characters can be restored only through interaction with a spectral guide that creates new and healthier connections to the past and moves them away from trauma and repression. In *Jazz,* however, there are three primary spectral figures—the narrator, Wild, and Dorcas—and they interact not only with Joe and Violet, but also with each other and the reader. By the end of the novel, the three spectral characters join and create a spectral text that mediates directly between the narrative and the reader. During Joe's journey tracking Dorcas through the city, he constantly slips in his mind, connecting Dorcas to the other woman who abandoned him: Wild. He thinks at one point, "I had the gun but it was not the gun—it was my hand I wanted to touch you with" (130–31). This is reminiscent of the scene in which he remembers trying to coax his mother's hand out of the wilderness. Later, while tracking Dorcas, he conflates the two again: "Not her. Not Dorcas. She'll be alone. Hardheaded. *Wild,* even. But alone" (182, emphasis mine). Once Dorcas and Wild are connected, toward the end of the book the narrative voice links itself to Wild. The narrator reiterates the slippage between Wild and Dorcas, asserting that Joe was really searching for "Wild's chamber of gold," and then notes:

> I'd love to close myself in the peace left by the woman who lived there and scared everybody. Unseen because she knows better than to be seen. After all, who would see her, a playful woman who lived in a rock? Who could, without fright? Of her looking eyes looking back? I wouldn't mind. Why should I? She has seen me and is not afraid of me. She hugs me. Understands me. Has given me her hand. I am touched by her. Released in secret. Now I know. (221)

The narrator and Wild know the power of secret observation, and they are both haunting presences in the text. The narrator, Wild, and Dorcas constitute a spectral trio that makes visible different layers of the past for the narrative and the characters.[12] Together, they create a tableau of the African American experience from slavery and Reconstruction through to the migration and the violence of the Jazz Age in the early twentieth century. Wild is "the embodiment of the pain and suffering of slavery" (Lesoinne 161); Dorcas portrays the perspective of the younger generation of African Americans living in the urban environment of 1920s New York, yet aware of the horror of the race riots that killed her parents; and the narrator takes these narrative threads, allows them to mingle, and then communicates them to the reader.

In a move more blatantly haunting even than the end of *Beloved,* the ghostly narrator transforms the novel into a spectral space of haunting absence and presence as illustrated by its final paragraphs:

> *That I love the way you hold me, how close you let me be to you. I like your fingers on and on, lifting, turning. I have watched your face for a long time now, and missed your eyes when you went away from me. Talking to you and hearing you answer—that's the kick. . . .* Say make me, remake me. You are free to do it and I am free to let you because look, look. Look where your hands are. Now. (*Jazz* 229)

The tables are turned: the narrator has not only been observing the characters secretly but the reader as well. Katherine Stern posits that, at this moment, Morrison "extracts the characters from the narrator's and reader's intimacy, so that reader and narrator too are alone together between the covers of the novel, 'bound and joined'" (91). This passage also illustrates the fluid, multivalent narrative that has been created, since even though the novel is ending, the narrator is inviting the reader to revise and to recompose this text. Like the end of *Beloved* and *Paradise, Jazz* ends with the possibility of return:

> Pushed away into certain streets, restricted from others . . . the shade stretches—just there—at the edge of a dream, or slips into the crevices of a chuckle. . . . It bunches on the curbstone, wrists crossed, and hides its smile under a wide-brim hat. Shade. Protective, available. Or sometimes not; sometimes it seems to lurk rather than hover kindly, and its stretch is not a yawn but an increase to be beaten back with a stick. (*Jazz* 227)

The past is never far, and acknowledging it, digesting it, and reconstituting it for the future can never end. This continuing need is why the spectral narrator draws in the reader to participate, to "make" and "remake"; the effort is communal among author, characters, and readers and includes various strands and states of existence. This powerful theme of spectral/historical/personal connection carries through into Morrison's *Love* as well.

Like Morrison's *Paradise,* her eighth novel, *Love,* garnered a mixed critical reception. While acknowledging the novel's power and place within Morrison's canon, Thulani Davis still mentions at the start of her review that it "may seem, at first glance, to fit within a group of books one could crudely call Morrison Lite, not requiring any of the heavy lifting from the reader like her masterpieces" (30). In her *New York Times* review, Michiko Kakutani calls *Love* one of Morrison's "slighter efforts," though she does praise it for being "more engaging than *Paradise,* her flatfooted and highly schematic 1998 novel" ("Family Secrets" 37). According to Kakutani, Morrison's eighth book may contain the author's "perennial themes," but she finds that the story "reads like a gothic soap opera, peopled by scheming, bitter women and selfish, predatory men: women engaged in cartoon-violent catfights; men catting around and going to cathouses" (37). To read *Love* in this manner requires one, however, to skip over the intricate layering of not only the "perennial Morrison themes" present in the novel but also the palimpsest of personal, cultural, and historical knowledge and information that forms the foundation for and ultimately threads throughout the book. As in the trilogy before it, in *Love* Morrison is still concerned with the social location of used and ignored female characters and the haunting aspects of history itself, but as in *Jazz,* she once again uses the technique of a spectral narrator—this time a deceased character.[13] Unlike any of the books before, this novel engages with the consequences of the heavy-handed patriarchal power that creates Cosey's empire and destroys Christine and Heed.

Following on the heels of the reviewers, critic Tessa Roynon points to the novel's ability to perplex discerning readers:

> Perhaps this [mixed reception] is because—appearing after the magnificent trilogy that so explicitly takes on all the grand themes of African American history—*Love* confounds readers' expectations of what a book by this author should be and should do. Only just two hundred pages long, and with a plot centered on a feud between two old women in a decayed mid-Atlantic resort town, the work initially

> impresses an authorial turning away from profound concerns, or even as a self-indulgence born of established success. (32–33)

For Roynon, this initial impression is, however, an illusion, and she and other critics have used several different frameworks in order to explore *Love.*[14] I agree that this initial view of the novel is an illusion, and while *Love* may initially appear to be a "slight" effort, the layers of haunting and history in the novel are myriad and complex. In my analysis, I focus on the importance of L as a spectral narrator, who imbues the text itself with a liminal quality, and I trace how L and Celestial function as guides for the ghosted and marginalized characters of this novel: Heed and Christine. As Davis notes, "*Love* is a rich parable about the damaging past as a demagogue ruling the present" (30). In opposition to this damaging past, L's power as the specter allows her not only to observe the characters of the novel, but also to affect them through her haunting presence and her overarching, yet unseen, control over their lives. She makes a concentrated effort while alive, and continues after her death, to counteract the negative effects of Bill Cosey that haunt Heed and Christine and their disintegrated friendship.

As evidenced by L's posthumous agency within the text, ghosts problematize the seemingly simple separation between life and death. L, like Beloved and the spectral trio in *Jazz,* is a timeless and subversive figure, and she serves as a translation point, a medium, between the warring Christine and Heed, and, most important, between the text and the reader. Inside the plot as a character and narrator, yet at the same time outside the plot since she is dead during the present action, L straddles the boundary between life and death. Because of her intimate knowledge of her fellow characters, L also illustrates how their lives are intricately caught up in larger cultural dramas. During the unfolding narrative, events of the past subtly influence and repeat during the present, and the characters' personal history is consumed by the politics and the prevailing hopes and fears of the day.

A striking example in the text of the past that continually wounds the present is Cosey's relationship to his father's legacy as an informant for whites: "*Contrary to the tale he put in the street, the father he bragged about had earned his way as a Courthouse informer. The one police could count on to know . . . all sorts of things Dixie law was interested in*" (*Love* 67–68). Because of his betrayals, "*his initials, DRC, gave rise to the name he was known by:*

Dark" (68). Cosey's career develops as a counterpoint to his father's reputation and personality: "*The father was dreaded; the son was a ray of light. The cops paid off the father; the son paid off the cops. What the father corrected, the son celebrated*" (68). Using his father's money, he builds his pleasure palace for a wealthy African American clientele. Even though the hotel is always booked when the local black population wishes to stay or have a celebration, the hotel does give this group another employment option besides the unpopular cannery, a workplace that Vida calls "a plantation" (18). Cosey is so tormented by his father's legacy that, when remembering his son's death at an early age, he tells Sandler, "[I]t was like somebody from the grave reached up and grabbed him for spite" (43). He fears his father's posthumous revenge. L even believes that Cosey marries twelve-year-old Heed to antagonize his dead father: "*Just like he avoided Christine because she had his father's gray eyes, he picked Heed to make old Dark groan*" (139). The miserly and class-conscious Dark would never have approved of a marriage linking his son to the Johnsons, a family May fears because she thinks that, for them, "*shiftlessness was not a habit, it was a trait; ignorance was destiny; dirt lingered on by choice*" (138). Shades of concern over class tinge the generational conflicts in the novel.

This anguish that colors Cosey's life and work trickles down to Heed and Christine, especially after he marries Heed, and she becomes her best friend's grandmother at the age of twelve. As the two women realize toward the end of the novel, for them Cosey "*was* everywhere. And nowhere" (189). He is the haunting hand of patriarchal power that they feel created and sustained them. He is everywhere in the novel itself as each section title lists a different role he fills, including Portrait, Friend, Stranger, Benefactor, Lover, Husband, Guardian, Father, and finally Phantom; yet while the sections reflect his presence, he never has a voice in the present action of the book because he is dead. Unlike L, who is dead but acts as a spectral guide for the characters and for the reader, he does not comment on the action as Heed and Christine work through their tortured relationship.[15] As L asserts more than once, the marriage of Cosey and Heed destroys the two girls. When Heed becomes her "grandmother," Christine feels unwanted by her family. Cosey sends her away, ostensibly for her safety since Heed does burn her bed after a contentious family dinner, but Christine senses the reason that L gives the reader: she has her great-grandfather's eyes. May becomes obsessed with keeping Christine away from Heed after the marriage. As the narrator notes, "There was a heap of blame to spread" (133). It is Christine's anger and hurt over being abandoned, over "being the only innocent one in the place" that had to go (133), that causes her to look for affection in all the wrong places and finally to return home obsessed with the Monarch house and all its childhood meanings. She tells her lawyer, "This is *my* place. I had my sixteenth-birthday party in that house. When I was away at school it was my *address.* It's where I belong. . . . If you don't know the difference between property and a home you need to be kicked in the face" (95). Christine and Heed's war, which isolates them from the world and consumes their identities, is over the approval of Cosey, the man who created their world—from the property that is the center of their fight to their perceptions of themselves as women. Even though he is dead, his control looms over their lives. Instead of creating a healing relationship with each other, they sublimate their very beings into his legacy.

Upon Christine's return home, she transfers all her anger over her abandonment onto Heed, who she believes is an obstacle to her final happiness in her childhood home. As a result of Cosey's openly cavalier sexual behavior and the distance he created by choosing Heed and rejecting his own flesh and blood, Christine cannot form affectionate and equal relationships that are not, in the final analysis, abusive, and she virulently hates and blames her childhood best friend. In contrast, from L's perspective, the hotel failed precisely because of Cosey's transgression in marrying Heed and destroying the two girls' relationship. The other reasons may have played a role, but the unscrupulous marriage caused tremendous damage to the family and ultimately to the two girls: "*It was marrying Heed that laid the brickwork for ruination. See, he chose a girl already spoken for. Not promised to anyone by her parents. That trash gave her up like they would a puppy. No. The way I see it, she belonged to Christine and Christine belonged to her*" (105). Cosey's choice of Heed for a wife is merely a choice of a plaything, and this sexual abuse does much to twist the girls' friendship into one of competition for the love of a man who does not even care for them. Morrison commented on the importance of women's friendships in an interview with Claudia Tate: "Friendship between women is special, different, and has never been depicted as the major focus of a novel before *Sula*. . . . Relationships between women were always written about as though they were subordinate to some other roles they're playing. This is not true of men" (157). For Heed and Christine, their lives and their friendship are subsumed into Cosey's desires and possessions. Their relationships with him and the control of his property become their single-minded purposes, derailing the relationship they had as children, a relationship that transcended class differences.

The friendship between Heed and Christine is the first and only healthy and open one in each of their lives, but each girl, unfortunately, is betrayed by loved ones. Christine is not the sole character in the novel rejected by her family: Heed's parents sell her to Cosey for some cash and a pocketbook. In this potent mix of class and obsession, Heed becomes a lightning rod for Christine's and May's anger, a rod that unites the mother and daughter despite their entrenched political disagreements:

> Decades of bitterness, sealed in quarrels over Malcolm X, Reverend King, Selma, Newark, Chicago, Detroit, and Watts were gone. Dead the question of what was best for the race, because Heed answered it for them. She was the throwback they both had fought. Neither won, but they agreed on the target. (*Love* 141)

Christine and May's generational disputes over African American political concerns and the feasibility of freedom movements pale in comparison to Heed's transgression of marrying into the family's wealth, although not by her choice. The conflict between poor and wealthy and Cosey's patriarchal damage will trump the larger political scene.

Heed and Christine are shells of the individuals that they could have been: they are gutted by the lack of love and care in their lives. Hilary Mantel describes the two as "ghosts, women who exist less as presences than as echoes" (2). Regardless of their hatred for one another and their long and bitter battle over Cosey's will, the two live together in the large Monarch street house, albeit in different wings. Their only contact with the outside world is Romen, a teenager who does chores around the house and yard, and Christine's occasional trips to the store or to see her lawyer. They are pretty much forgotten by the surrounding community and only exist in gossip, stories about the past, and questions of whether the two are even still alive, since they are in their seventies. They are ghosts in the large, haunted house: "It seemed . . . that each woman lived in a spotlight separated—or connected—by the darkness between them" (*Love* 25). In a discussion of the invisibility of women, Brogan posits that they "are ghostly both because they are socially unrecognized and because they have acquired an illegitimate strength" (25). At this point in the narrative, Heed and Christine are "socially unrecognized" as individuals and exist only to struggle against each other for Cosey's estate, but later the women will achieve a strength that mirrors the transformational powers of the spectral L.

The house is not, however, only an abode for the living: it also houses the dead and ghostly. Similar to its predecessors in the Morrison canon, 124 and the Convent, the house is a crossroads for the past and the present, the living and the dead, and the upper and lower classes. The house is loaded with Gothic trappings of haunting and unease: a preponderance of heavy, antique furnishings, darkness, isolation, immense space, and a looming portrait of the patriarchal builder, Cosey. The house is a nexus of hauntings: it shelters Heed and Christine; Junior believes that Cosey is haunting the building (*Love* 118–19); and the reader knows that the spectral L can check on things in the house at any time. L can sit anywhere she likes and watch Heed take care of May, for example (139). Moreover, the house represents the idea of the "present ghosted by the past" (Smith 36). Upon meeting Junior, soon to become Heed's assistant, Christine immediately thinks of Heed's desire for the property, but she puts this fear in terms of temporality, seeing Junior as "[s]ome new way to rob her future just as she [Heed] had ripped off her past" (*Love* 24). The house is the merging point for all the concerns of the novel. It is the domestic space Cosey violated, and it is the symbol of everything the two women are fighting to own. What is in dispute is each woman's hold on the Cosey name and the position of each in the world that he created. Heed wishes to hold onto her status as Cosey's wife, which means possession of his money and property, and Christine wants to reclaim her place in the family as a granddaughter, which for her includes any material legacy. They both desire a return to an idealized past in which they each held a place in the Cosey empire. For Heed and Christine, the only way they can "unghost" their true selves from the bondage of patriarchy and status through material possessions is through the transformative powers and guidance of L and Celestial, the spectral figures of this novel following in the tradition of Pilate, Beloved, Consolata, and the spectral trio in *Jazz*.

In keeping with her role as supernatural caretaker, L is a central figure and an occasional narrative voice in the novel.[16] Wen-ching Ho posits that as she is "the narrative conduit, understanding L is key to understanding the novel, because she is a vital component of its plot development, narrative structure, and perspective" (654). Thulani Davis writes, "L., whose name no one can remember, knows love as mercy. She is a perfect rendering of those shadowy African-Americans—surrogates and enablers—Morrison describes in . . . *Playing in the Dark,* as lurking, ignored, yet defining all others in so much American fiction. She is an invention of the later Toni Morrison, a compassionate mediator between warring extremes" (31). She is a point of mediation between the extremes of the Cosey family, and, as the reader discovers late in the novel, she is dead. During their reconciliation scene, Heed tells Christine that L "dropped dead at the stove" at Maceo's while "smothering pork chops" (*Love* 189). L is a ghost in the present time frame of the novel, and she is a guide for Heed and Christine, as well as for the reader through her narration. L knows the power of the liminal space between past and present and death and life. While May thinks that death means that one "[*goes*] *to heaven or hell,*" L knows, like Baby Suggs, that "*it might just be more of the same*" (135). L is reminiscent both of Beloved, though she is more thoughtful and compassionate toward her charges, and of the spectral narrator of *Jazz,* in that she is a character returned from the afterlife who secretly observes other characters. In serving as narrator of sections of the novel, she provides the reader with information from the past that helps fill in the gaps of the story.[17] Consequently, L solves the murder mystery of the novel by admitting that she poisoned Cosey with foxglove and rewrote his will in order to protect Heed and Christine (201).

L's importance is immediately clear in that she is the first and last voice in the novel. She begins in a startling manner typical of a Morrison work: "*The women's legs are spread wide open, so I hum*" (3). The novel ends with her words: "*So I join in. And hum*" (202).[18] L's humming, as literal sound and as the hum of her constant presence throughout the novel, haunts the setting, the characters, and the reader. As she points out, "*I'm background—the movie music that comes along. . . . My humming encourages people; frames their thoughts*" (4).[19] Following the possibilities of the specter and of jazz music in the discussion of *Jazz,* it would seem that these metaphoric connections are continued in the ghostly hum of L. Her hum cradles the possibilities of her text.

In addition to her ever-present hum, she often focuses on the power and the fluidity of language and words. Although L confesses toward the end of the novel that her "*name is the subject of First Corinthians, chapter 13*" (199), making her the eponymous character of *Love* much like Beloved in her book, there is confusion over her name within the story, resulting in the abbreviation of her name to a single letter. She notes:

> *Anybody who remembers what my real name is is dead or gone and nobody inquires now. Even children, who have a world of time to waste,* treat me like I'm dead *and don't ask about me anymore. Some thought it was Louise or Lucille because they used to see me . . . sign my tithe envelopes with L. Others, from hearing people mention or call me, said it was El for Eleanor or Elvira. They're all wrong. Anyway, they gave up. Like they gave up calling Maceo's Maceo's or supplying the missing letters. Café Ria is what it's known as, and like a favored customer spoiled by easy transportation, I glide there still.* (65, emphasis mine)

Even though it is unclear for the reader at this point whether L is dead or not, children *treat* her as though she is. Moreover, not only is her biological status in question, but her very name and identity are as well. L's discussion of names and their connection to actuality illustrates the slipperiness of language and emphasizes her own importance as an unknown quantity (and entity) in this novel. This concern with language becomes of ultimate importance when the reader learns that she forged the menu/will that Christine and Heed have been battling over: "*My menu worked just fine. Gave them a reason to stay connected and maybe figure out how precious the tongue is*" (201).[20] Her use of the vague term "Sweet Cosey Child" as a beneficiary in the forged will haunts Heed and Christine as they each vie for the honor of inhabiting that identity. The phrase highlights the indeterminacy present in the novel, and it privileges Morrison's concern with the fluidity of meaning, identity, and life. L presences herself in the novel through her narration, her written fake will for Cosey's estate, and the memories of the power of her words: as Heed and Christine are aware, L "*could make a point strong enough to stop a womb—or a knife*" (3).

Besides L's importance as background music underneath all that occurs in the novel and her ability to live within the slippery boundaries of language itself, L (like Beloved) is not beholden to conventional rules of temporality or physical locality. When Heed recounts to herself all her triumphs over Cosey's family and friends, she thinks, "May in the ground, Christine penniless in the kitchen, L haunting Up Beach. Where they belonged" (73). While it is obvious that May is dead, L's condition remains unclear, especially since L tells the reader that she still "glides" at Maceo's, close to Up Beach (65). Is she literally haunting Up Beach, or does she "haunt" it by constantly being in the area? Furthermore, L contradicts the placement of her "haunting" when she appears in the Monarch House, where Heed lives.

Defying the traditional connection of a ghost to a single, specific location, Morrison has L narrate various "haunts" throughout her sections. At one point, when L notes that sometimes the people we hate are the only ones who can care for us in old age, she mentions that she "*sat at the foot of May's bed or on top of her dresser sometimes and watched Heed soap her bottom, mash badly cooked food to the right consistency*" (139–40). It appears as if L can manifest herself anywhere, even in Heed's home. In addition to Up Beach and the Cosey mansion, L also haunts the famous hotel. She is the one who gives the haunting description of its abandoned interior: "*No matter the outside loneliness, if you look inside, the hotel seems to promise you ecstasy and the company of all your best friends. And music. The shift of a shutter hinge sounds like the cough of a trumpet; piano keys waver a quarter note above the wind so you might miss the hurt jamming all those halls and closed up rooms*" (7). At another moment, we know that L is actually in the hotel because, in a passage describing Cosey's disappointment with his father and despair over the loss of his son, she says, "*See that window over there?*" (104). Maceo's, Up Beach, the house, and the hotel all hold special meanings for L, but all of these places also allow her to be ever-present and practically omniscient as she watches the characters while the action unfolds. L could not help Heed and Christine if she only rewrote the will before her death: she needs to continue her transformative work after death, when she is able to move wherever needed. Indeed, it is L's ability to free-float throughout the book's settings that places her at the actual time of Heed and Christine's reconciliation. While moving through the hotel, Junior notices the smell of "baking bread, something with cinnamon," and Heed says, "Smells like L" (175).

L's spectrality and indeterminacy also affect the narrative itself, as we have seen in *Jazz*. According to Hutcheon, "Historical meaning may thus be seen today as unstable, contextual, relational, and provisional" (64), and

Morrison once again illustrates the political issues that occur in the novel through the relationships of her characters. L embodies Avery F. Gordon's definition of the ghost as a "social figure": "The ghost is not simply a dead or a missing person, but a social figure, and investigating it can lead to that dense site where history and subjectivity make social life. The ghost or the apparition is one form by which something lost, or barely visible, or seemingly not there . . . makes itself known or apparent to us, in its own way, of course" (8). In L's narrative sections, in particular, the inability to pin down exactly what happened among competing versions is highlighted as her ghostly presence circumvents a central narrative and shows where history and subjective experience collide. A prime example of this involves the various versions of the decline of Cosey's resort and the change that came over his daughter-in-law May in 1955. L discusses this in her first monologue, and she tells the reader that Cosey believed that his resort declined because "*the whites had tricked him*" by selling him undesirable land (8); May thought that "*civil rights destroyed her family and its business*" because African Americans were fighting for integration rather than coming to the hotel (8); and L believes that the fall comes because of Cosey's interference in Heed and Christine's friendship. No one has the definitive answer, but L reports all the speculations. Later, L revisits these options for the hotel's failure and focuses more tightly on May:

> *Oh, I know the 'reasons' given* [for the decline]*: cannery smell, civil rights, integration. And May's behavior did go strange in 1955 when that boy from Chicago tried to act like a man and got beat to death for his trouble. Mississippi's answer to desegregation and whatever else that wilted their sex. We all shivered about what they did to that boy. . . . But for May it was a sign. It sent her to the beach where she buried not just the deed but a flashlight and Lord knows what else. Any day now some Negro was going to rile waiting whites, give them an excuse to hang somebody and close the hotel down.* (104)

Haunted by the brutal Emmett Till murder, May's single-minded purpose becomes the protection of her property and family, no matter the cost; in fact, her fear of civil unrest possesses her so firmly that she takes to wearing a military helmet. It is this fear of radicalism and of its subsequent "punishment" that helps produce a rift between her and her daughter Christine, who joins a Black Power group. Through L's description of the resort's deterioration, Morrison introduces the larger civil rights movement as it actually affects the characters' beliefs and actions.

Morrison also allows the experiences and memories of her characters to bleed through during the sections of the novel narrated by the omniscient third-person voice, making the narrative truly multivocal and reiterating the impact of larger dramas on the characters' lives. For instance, when Christine runs away from home after completing school, she moves through a succession of bad choices and abuse, all haunted by her dysfunctional relationship with her grandfather: a failed marriage, time as a kept woman, and finally disenchantment with the Black Power group that she joins. Her disillusionment with the civil rights group is a direct result of the erasure of her agency as an individual woman. After seven abortions, she reflects, "Besides, no one stopped her or suggested she do otherwise: Revolutions needed men—not fathers" (164). Her decision to be a mother seems to rest upon the belief that children would inconvenience her boyfriend, Fruit, and it is interesting that her thoughts after aborting her babies focus on the father and the revolutionary, never on herself as a possible mother.[21] This relationship is far from equal in any aspect as she is forced to accept that "having men meant sharing them" (165). The steep decline of her enthusiasm begins when she demands justice for a young rape victim in the group. When Fruit refuses to confront the Comrade who attacked the girl, Christine realizes, "The girl's violation carried no weight against the sturdier violation of male friendship" (166). Unlike Christine, whose friendship with Heed was capriciously cut short by Cosey, this *male* friendship is sacrosanct. She continues to go about the "good work of civil disobedience and personal obedience," but she has no agency in this situation: she is silenced and her needs are not being met; she is "irrelevant" (167). Using Christine's experiences, Morrison engages the problems women experienced in the strongly male-identified Black Power movement. Although the majority of the abuse Christine experiences comes at the hands of patriarchal figures, she insists on blaming Heed for everything.

In addition to L and the spectral and multivocal narrative, the prostitute Celestial is another absenced woman who exerts power over the narrative and the characters.[22] The juxtaposition of her fleshly profession and her mystical name—"Celestial connotes divine, heavenly, of the firmament, the harmony of the spheres" (Sweeney 461)—indicates her position "betwixt" seemingly exclusive oppositions. Celestial joins L as a beginning and ending figure in the novel. L could be talking about Celestial in her first line, and the final scene of *Love* pictures Celestial singing over Cosey's grave with L humming in the background.[23] She is often pictured on the beach and is often seen at the boundary between land and water as the waves crash toward her. At one point, L sees her swimming in the waves, and when she returns to shore, "*Her hair, flat when she went in, rose up slowly and took on the shape of the clouds dragging the moon. Then she—well, made a sound. I don't know to this day whether it was a word, a tune, or a scream. All I know is that it was a sound I wanted to answer. Even though, normally, I'm stone quiet, Celestial*" (*Love* 106).[24] In this scene, Celestial is in the water and yet on the shore; she is in the clouds and yet on earth. She also wields a power that L, Heed, and Christine all desire and need.

As a prostitute Celestial can cross borders of race, class, and power. Although she may not be in a position of power such as Cosey or even L sustains, she is an independent woman, and she exercises a sexual power that affects Cosey in a manner that no one else seems capable of doing. She is a fixture on Cosey's carnivalesque fishing boat rides: "the counterfeit world invented on the boat; the real one set aside for a few hours so women could dominate, men would crawl, blacks could insult whites. Until they docked" (111). Once the boat docks, reality's hierarchies return, and Celestial is not allowed in Cosey's hotel, but "she could summon [Cosey] anytime she wanted to" (79). L says that when Cosey "*changed—well, limited—her caseload, neither could break the spell*" (106). In addition to her sexual power over him, she appears in his fantasies of domestic life in the double C's on his silverware, which may or may not reference her (104), and, if L had not stepped in, she would have owned his estate. L describes the original will: "They never saw the real thing—witnessed by me, notarized by Buddy Silk's wife—leaving everything to Celestial. Everything. Everything. Except a boat he left to Sandler Gibbons. It wasn't right" (200).[25]

Celestial also exerts a strong hold on the imaginations of Heed and Christine. The two girls see her on the beach one day and hear a man call her name. Her personal strength is clear in her wordless exchange with the two children: "The woman didn't look around to see who called her. Her profile was etched against the seascape; her head held high. She turned instead to look at them. . . . Her eyes locking theirs were cold and scary, until she winked at them, making their toes clench and curl with happiness" (188). May tells the girls to stay away from Celestial because "there is nothing a sporting woman won't do" (188). Of course, this remark creates an even brighter aura of mystery and awe around Celestial: the girls name their playhouse "Celestial Palace," and, to "acknowledge a particularly bold, smart, risky thing, they mimicked the male voice crying 'Hey, Celestial'" (188). For Heed and Christine, Celestial's liminal power is clear. It allows a woman the ability to choose to create her own space, as she is not truly controlled by her male clientele. It is significant that the two seal their reconciliation discussion with a return to their phrase, "Hey, Celestial." L brings the two friends/enemies together, and a memory of Celestial helps repair the friendship and take the focus away from Cosey.

The final reconciliation of Heed and Christine is important in that they communicate and ultimately mend their friendship, and the importance of L's spectrality becomes clear after this reconciliation, because the pair becomes open to liminality and L's legacy of spirit work. Since Heed is facing impending death at the reconciliation scene, having broken numerous bones as a result of her fall from the hotel's attic, it would appear that the two women reconnect only to be separated by death, but this is not the case. Morrison describes the scene: "Still, they avoid rehearsing accusations, a waste of breath with one of them cracked to pieces and the other sweating like a laundress. Up here where the solitude is like the room of a dead child, the ocean has no scent or roar. The future is disintegrating along with the past" (184). The women inhabit a timeless space where they can have the open conversation about Cosey's treatment of them that they could not have had as children, and their language is "sudden, raw, stripped to its underwear" (184). This section bears a resemblance in form and intent to the "threnody" from *Beloved.* There are no introductory tags alerting the reader about who is speaking; the conversation thus becomes an organic, timeless, placeless process. The resulting story/confession/reconnection is placed in the forefront, and as the opposition between the two women dissolves, their voices blend.

Furthermore, during this episode, Morrison continues her careful layering of personal and group history and memories. In a moment of partial realization, Christine says, "It's just. Well, it's like we started out being sold, got free of it, then sold ourselves to the highest bidder" (185). Heed asks her what group she means by "we": "Black people? Women? You mean me and you?" (185). It is telling that the response is "I don't know what I mean" (185), because throughout the novel all three of these levels—race, gender, and the individual experience—have been interconnected into one tapestry. According to bell hooks, black women are affected by "interlocking systems of domination, of racism and sexism" (xxxii). Patricia Hill Collins also emphasizes the multiple angles of oppression facing African American women using the terms "intersectionality" and "matrix of domination." For Collins, "[i]ntersectionality refers to particular forms of intersecting oppressions, for example, intersections of race and gender, or of sexuality and nation," and "the matrix of domination refers to how these intersecting oppressions are actually organized" (18). In Morrison's novel, each strand of the tapestry involves a different "version" of events that L narrates, summarizes, or contradicts. Christine's comment also brings Morrison's work full circle in that it references slavery and its subsequent effects on black women in particular.

After Romen has rescued them and brought them home, the text makes it clear that one woman died and the other survived the ordeal, but Morrison leaves it to the reader to interpret which one. Since Heed is in so much pain at the hotel, and the dead woman is described as having an "arm akimbo" (*Love* 195), it is reasonable to infer that she dies and Christine lives. The remarkable aspect of this return to the Monarch Street house, though, is that it does not really matter which one dies or lives because, unlike Nel and Sula after Sula's death, these two friends are still in communication. The narrator notes, "Alone, seated at the table, she speaks to the friend of her life waiting to be driven to the morgue" (198). When she asks how the dead woman is feeling, the response is: "Middling. You?" (198). As the two try to decide what to do with Junior after her treachery, it is clear that once again, in Morrison's work, death is not the end, but rather a transformative transition, or passage, of life.[26] During the discussion between the living and the dead, the pronoun "we" is used, and when the dead asks, "Do *you* want her [Junior] around," the answer is: "What for? I got you" (198). Apparently, the Cosey household can expect one more phantom member to be added to its ranks. That neither woman, according to Wardi, is surprised at this newfound ability is "a gesture that reinforces the seamless connection between love and death" ("Laying" 214). The majority of Morrison characters who have been nurtured by a spectral guide do not view death as the end but rather as a continuation of the subversive and healing power drawn from this "other side," and Heed and Christine are no different.

Critics such as Vega-González and Javier Gascueña Gahete point to the postmodern qualities of *Love,* but they do not explore the primacy of the negotiation between life and death that is emphasized through the ghostly presences of Heed and Christine and the literal ghost that helps narrate the novel. For instance, according to Vega-González, Morrison uses water as a metaphor in the novel "as a claim to freedom, fluidity, flexibility and indeterminacy." This metaphor, she notes, can "subvert the fixity of enclosed monolithic conceptions of the world and reality" (209, 211). Using the metaphor of the "ghost," my analysis also pinpoints this "fluidity," and I emphasize Morrison's penchant for looking beneath master narratives and illustrating lived history. When viewed as a cultural ghost story, *Love* exemplifies a worldview that encompasses not just life but the afterlife too—an afterlife the spectral L knows just might be *"more of the same"* (*Love* 135).

In *Jazz* and *Love,* as in previous novels, death is not the end of life, for in these two books Morrison emphasizes the spectral figure by entrusting it with the responsibility of narration. In *Jazz,* the narrator is the ultimate indeterminate character who joins with the other two ghostly presences in a kind of spectral nexus. In *Love,* the character who provides the most inside information is dead and also joins with another spectral figure to direct the thoughts, actions, and development of those characters who can be described as social ghosts. Reminiscent of the end of *Paradise,* where the reader sees that the spectral figure moves to a space on the "other side," in *Jazz* and *Love* Morrison lets the reader hear directly from these liminal figures after they have transitioned. These spectral narrators not only guide the marginalized and ghosted characters, but they also serve as a connector between the text and the reader, making the narrative itself "fluid and shifting" (Peterson 210). The successful negotiation of painful layers of personal and cultural history only can be accomplished through a connection to specters and an openness to the instability of time and space that this type of connection requires. Morrison's characters are ghosted by various issues including race, class, gender, and personal and cultural history; and the only way that the entire story of the Traces in *Jazz* or of the Cosey family in *Love* can be told is through a spectral character who can see *all* the facets of the saga, acknowledging the possibilities that are ignored in a more straightforward master narrative. "Following individual lives closely makes it possible for Morrison to (re)construct a history that remains faithful to the past but is not predetermined," writes Peterson. "Individual lives outside of such a grand narrative . . . are much more chaotic, contradictory, and unpredictable—which creates a necessary space for resistance, agency and counternarratives" (209).

The specter is the perfect narrator for this type of reconstruction because "the ghost . . . indicates that . . . there lurks another narrative, an untold story that calls into question the veracity of the authorized version of events" (Weinstock 5). There is always another layer lurking just beneath the surface, and it is through the work of characters like the first-person voice of *Jazz,* Wild, Dorcas, and L that elided individuals are empowered and all the strands of the story are made visible. This empowerment results from dismantling traditional binary oppositions. In Morrison's novels, ghosts are necessary for this spectral work of healing, connection, and transformation, and in *Jazz* and *Love* the reader is also involved in this spectral work through the ghostly narrators and their spectral narratives.

CHAPTER FIVE

"Slave. Free. I Last": Spectral Returns in *A Mercy*

In *A Mercy,* Morrison's ninth novel (published in 2008, five years after *Love*), the author goes back before the events of *Beloved* to what she calls a "pre-racial" time during the colonial period of the seventeenth century when the slippery borders between slavery and indentured servitude led to a slave population of blacks *and* whites (Houpt R1). The plot involves a small "family" that has formed at the homestead of Jacob Vaark, an Anglo-Dutch trader. While Vaark dabbles in many kinds of trade, he strictly avoids buying and selling human life. The individuals he does purchase to work his farm are all rescued from much worse situations, and his antipathy for owning other people trickles down to his slaves, who feel like a part of the family, at least until Vaark dies, leaving them all to fend for themselves. The cast of characters includes Vaark's wife, Rebekka, a mail-order bride from London; Lina, a Native American orphan of the small pox plague, who was bought by Vaark when she was a teenager; Sorrow, a hybridized orphan of a sea captain and a subsequent victim of rape; and Florens, whose traumatic abandonment by her mother to Vaark turns out to be the mercy of the title.

In this novel, Morrison revisits themes of her earlier work: the destruction of the family unit by slavery, mother and daughter relationships, obsessive love, degrees of freedom, the importance of community, class and race conflicts, and patriarchal dominance. The strongest connection can be made to *Beloved* in that a mother once again gives up a daughter to save the girl from a life of violence at the hands of the master. In *A Mercy,* the reasons for this rejection are never given to the daughter, which causes the girl to search for unconditional love in a sexual relationship and consequently to be bitterly disappointed. After a life of seeking love and acceptance from others and feeling rejection, Florens must come to terms with her own individuality. The other novels sharing strong affinities with *A Mercy* are *Paradise* and *Love.* As in these predecessors, Morrison explores in *A Mercy* the dangers patriarchy poses to women. The women on Jacob Vaark's homestead attempt to form a family reminiscent of the multiracial one in the Convent; but after Vaark dies, the legal realities of the time set in, and without a spectral guide to help them, their female community slowly disintegrates. In this novel, Morrison illustrates the haunting trauma of slavery that underlies every relationship and transaction of this time period. In a thematic return to her earlier work, she fills *A Mercy* with marginalized social ghosts reminiscent of the Breedloves in *The Bluest Eye* and everyone in *Tar Baby.* At first glance, this book would seem to be very much like *The Bluest Eye,* without a spectral guide for the ghostly characters. This time, however, unlike her predecessor Pecola, Florens seizes agency by telling her own story in writing on the walls of the abandoned house of her dead master. Moreover, there is a spectral presence in the novel through Florens's mother, but this liminal space is only available to the reader, not to the daughter. In an intriguing twist on the spectral address to the reader at the end of *Jazz,* Florens must write herself into existence.

The seeds of the downfall of Jacob Vaark's homestead lie in his entanglement in a new business venture and his greed for the possessions of the planters that he sees in Maryland and Virginia. As Vaark notes when he bests his debtor D'Ortega, the Portuguese owner of Florens and her mother, "only things, not bloodlines or character, separated them. . . . So mighten it be nice to have such a fence to enclose the headstones in his own meadow? And one day, not too far away, to build a house that size on his own property? Not as ornate as D'Ortega's. . . . And pure, noble even, because it would not be compromised as Jublio was. Access to a fleet of free labor made D'Ortega's leisurely life possible" (*A Mercy* 27). Vaark is disgusted by D'Ortega's reliance on what he see as "a captured workforce that required more force to maintain," and he is eager to prove that he can amass D'Ortega's material comforts on "his own industry . . . without trading his conscience for coin" (28).

Vaark's distaste for the slave market is clear. Morrison writes, "Flesh was not his commodity" (22), and when D'Ortega tries to force one of his Angolan slaves on Vaark for payment of the planter's debt, the visitor is very uncomfortable. Morrison makes it clear that Vaark's discomfort stems from coming face-to-face with a horror he prefers not to see. The underlying violence of the slaves' lives haunts their bodies in "wounds like misplaced veins tracing their skin" and in the attempts of the women to absent themselves from the scene with "shockproof" eyes "gazing beyond place and time as though they were not actually there" (22). These individuals are social ghosts: victims of physical and psychological torture who are attempting to hold onto their agency in spite of the erasure of being someone else's property. The physical traces of the institution that mark them haunt Vaark. Although he is fully aware of what they signal, he does not want to consciously dwell on the implications. He is disturbed by D'Ortega's silence about the scars and his obvious sexual abuse of Florens's mother. The issue of enforced silence covering a multitude of abuses is emphasized in Vaark's desire to escape: "Whatever it was, he couldn't stay there surrounded by a passel of slaves whose silence made him imagine an avalanche seen from a great distance" (22). He sees a small chip of the reality of the enforced labor that is hidden beneath the "welcoming" smells and tastes of tobacco, sugar, molasses, and cocoa (22). He realizes that the abuses have become a horrific byproduct of the trade process and its financial benefits.

While Vaark may take Florens from D'Ortega in payment for the debt because he feels compassion for orphaned children and because Florens's mother believes it is the only way to protect her daughter from D'Oretega's predation, his hands are not entirely clean. He may not want to be involved in buying and selling slaves for his livelihood, but in a crisis of conscience after seeing D'Ortega's plantation and wishing to have his own large home, he decides he can make more money by investing in sugar production on Barbados. He believes he can avoid the moral implications of slavery as long as he does not visually acknowledge its reality in his profit and trades solely at the financial level. Thinking purely in terms of money and dismissing the human suffering inherent in the plan, Vaark decides, "And the plan was as sweet as the sugar on which it was based. And there was a profound difference between the intimacy of slave bodies at Jublio and a remote labor force in Barbados. Right?" (35). After making his decision, Vaark dreams of the "grand house of many rooms" he intends to build with the profits of his venture (35), and this is the house that he will not live to see finished. The haunting institution of slavery is always already present in every relationship and business transaction of this novel, even though it is not always visible. Its violence will erupt in Vaark's life even if he never witnesses or physically participates in the slave trade and plantation system of Barbados. The enterprise has dire results for all involved.

Similar to the underlying implications of slavery and its relation to trade, the very land on which the developing American colonies are built has hidden, ghostly valences as well. The same thirst for wealth and trade underlies the shifting rulers and populations of the New World. The landscape is described as an unmoored postmodern space in that its ownership is constantly in flux, and it is a spectral palimpsest of nations and cultures. While Vaark travels to Maryland to see D'Ortega, he thinks about the chain of claims to the land over which he is riding: from Swedish to Dutch to English. He knows: "Other than certain natives, to whom it all belonged, from one year to another any stretch might be claimed by a church, controlled by a Company or become the private property of a royal's gift to a son or a favorite. Since land claims were always fluid, except for notations on bills of sale, he paid scant attention to old or new names of towns or forts" (12). Vaark uses physical geography to traverse the landscape; he pays attention to visible landmarks, the fields of various Native communities, and forests. Even in his mind, the list of claims to the land creates a haunting panorama of struggle for power in the New World, a space where political identity is always shifting, at times to the detriment of the individuals who live there, depending upon race and religion.

The repressed horrors of slavery that frighten Vaark at D'Ortega's plantation are also embedded in this fluid geography. When Vaark is speaking with D'Ortega's wife at dinner, an almost absurd exchange occurs wherein the actual nation of Portugal is confused with its colonial holdings in Angola. D'Ortega's unfeeling wife tells Vaark that the laborers pretend illness so as not to work and that this would not be tolerated in Portugal. When Vaark asks if the slaves come from Portugal, D'Ortega corrects him, "Well, the Angola part of Portugal." During the continued conversation, Portugal and Angola are confused again, and D'Ortega's wife tells Vaark that their children were not born in Angola or Portugal, but rather

Maryland, which causes Vaark to comment finally, "Ah. England" (18). The lines between what is Portugal, Angola, Maryland, and England are not concretely drawn and freely invite transgression, even as the D'Ortegas desperately try to reestablish those boundaries: at least their children were not born in Angola, even if it is a part of Portugal. Of course, the underlying harsh current of this discussion is that D'Ortega made his money by trading human life in Angola, and now he has come to the colonies in the hopes of increasing his wealth on the backs of those laborers.

Morrison continues this concern with fluid boundaries in that D'Ortega's Africans are not the only slaves in the novel. She attempts to remove the black and white binary from slavery and focus on the slippery borders between the conditions of indentured servants and black slaves, conditions that, in this time period, often were not strikingly different. This time the conflict is more hierarchical between the colonial planters and the European cast-offs and African slaves. As Morrison put it in an NPR interview, one of her aims in this novel was to "remove race from slavery" (Norris), and she cited in this interview her use of the book *White Cargo: The Forgotten History of Britain's White Slaves in America* by Don Jordan and Michael Walsh. Noting the large numbers of exiled political enemies, the poor, orphans, the kidnapped, and convicts that made up the pool of white labor in Maryland, Virginia, and Barbados in the seventeenth and eighteenth centuries, Jordan and Walsh contend, "Today, tens of millions of white Americans are descended from such chattels. It is a shame that few in America claim these largely forgotten men and women of the early frontier as their own" (19). These indentured servants rarely saw the end of their servitude. In *A Mercy,* the women Rebekka meets on the ship to the colonies are prime examples of the type of people sent to the New World for labor—prostitutes and thieves avoiding prison sentences and daughters given up by poor parents. Willard and Scully, the servants whom Vaark rents occasionally, illustrate the rarity of an end to servitude before death. Willard's time has stretched from seven years to over twenty because of minor infractions, and Scully is serving his time and the time of his mother's contract because she died while indentured. These servants haunt the margins of colonial America.

Jordan and Walsh emphasize that for the ruling elite in Britain, the people being sent into bondage in the colonies were "'surplus' people—the rootless, the unemployed, the criminal and the dissident" (12). Remarkably, considering my metaphor of the social ghost, Jordan and Walsh note that the practice of kidnapping children and adults to sell into bondage was called "spiriting" people away. The local populace called the kidnappers "spirits," and these incidents spread fear throughout urban and rural areas. These kidnappers would effectively erase all traces of their victims in Britain simply by locking them up near the docks and then shoving them on a ship to the colonies (13–14). By exploring this time period and privileging the status of free versus slave, rather than the binary of race only, Morrison continues her work at opening up language and crushing arbitrary oppositions that restrict events to a single interpretation. She also unghosts and gives voice to the experiences of countless ignored people from the primeval American moment; as Tessa Roynon posited in her review of *A Mercy,* "[Morrison] again restores the voices of the silenced . . . with a characteristic focus on the hopes, dreams and traumas of those that history forgot" (13).

By dealing with these tangled issues of bondage, *A Mercy* is, like *The Bluest Eye* and *Tar Baby* before it, full of social ghosts. Because of slavery and indentured servitude, all social life is compartmentalized into a strict hierarchy, and every boundary is policed. In this atmosphere of opposition, separation, and enforced isolation, there is no value for human connection. This is the beginning of the economic and social structures that leave the characters of *Beloved* bereft. Almost every main character in *A Mercy* has been, or is currently, marginalized. Although Vaark and his wife Rebekka own three slaves and rent the labor of Willard and Scully, they are both orphans who exist on the edges of the frontier. In England as a child, Vaark lived in orphanages and on the streets and only acquired land in New Amsterdam through the will of an uncle he had never met. Rebekka's childhood in England was haunted by nightmares of the religious quarrels that surrounded her and the horrendous punishments meted out to supposed heretics, depending on who happened to be in power. Her father gladly answered Vaark's advertisement for a wife because he would have "shipped her off to anyone who would book her passage and relieve him of feeding her" (*A Mercy* 74). Her mother only objected because Vaark was "a heathen living among savages." Religion, for Rebekka's family was "a flame fueled by a wondrous hatred" (74). Once she is married to Vaark, the two isolate themselves on his homestead. They do not meet or worship with the local Separatist community, not because of hatred, but because of doctrinal disagreements over childhood baptism and because Vaark and Rebekka think they are enough for each other. From the outside looking in, Lina realizes that this is pride and that Vaark and Rebekka see themselves as "Adam and Eve, like gods from nowhere beholden to nothing except their own creations" (58–59). Lina sees that this life cannot last because "some encircling outside thing was needed" (58). She knows that the Vaarks believe "they could have honest free-thinking lives, yet without heirs, all their work meant less than a swallow's nest" (58). As in the story of the original Adam and Eve, this Eden will not last, but more important, this failure of the Vaarks to sustain a family without outside community foreshadows the failure of the women to hold together once Jacob has died.

The female community of the Vaark homestead is a direct result of Jacob and Rebekka's lonely childhoods and their experiences of rejection. These feelings and memories spur them not only to create a home in the New World, but also to acquire other orphans as slaves, giving a home to three women who were abused in their previous situations. In an interview in 2008, Morrison explained the emphasis on the position of women in her new "pre-racial" setting: "These are women, understand: in most cases, illegal without a man. . . . It's not difference that matters—there are differences that are profound—it's hierarchy" (Houpt R1). While slavery is a major component of this novel, the emphasis is on the strict demarcations of class and power that flow from it and the resulting tenuous existence of women in the New World who are unattached to men. As Rebekka reflects during her illness, "Invisibility was intolerable to men. What complaint would a female Job dare to put forth?" (*A Mercy* 91). All of the women in the book are ghosted and damaged. Rebekka realizes after her husband's death that a widow has few legal privileges. Lina originally lived with a Presbyterian family who forcefully disconnected her from her Native American past. She was sexually and physically abused by a neighbor, discarded by the Presbyterians, and currently exists as an appendage of the Vaark family. Sorrow is haunted by her time spent on a ship of the dead after it was presumably pirated, and she is raped by the boys of the family who rescued her. Her trauma haunts her through a split personality. She has an imaginary friend named Twin, who helps her to make sense of the world and to protect herself. At one point, Twin warns her to keep her real name secret. Sorrow's situation is reminiscent of the Violet/Violent dichotomy in *Jazz* and Pecola's split self in *The Bluest Eye.* Furthermore, Florens, an African slave from the Portuguese planter, is permanently damaged by her mother's unexplained choice to keep her younger boy but to give Florens to Vaark.

Once again in Morrison's work, individuals are ghosted by their damaging encounters with various overarching social forces. Women are affected by the power and violence of men, and, as in *Beloved,* the conditions of slavery disconnect and subvert mother-love and desire. In the microcosm of the Vaark farm, motherhood plays a role for every individual. Rebekka wants to be a mother, but her children all die, which causes her to lash out against the Separatists, who tell her that her children will not make it to Heaven, and against Sorrow, who successfully gives birth. For Rebekka, this is a constant reminder of what she could not have. For her part, Sorrow finds her purpose in loving her child, and motherhood completes her. She no longer requires the companionship of Twin. In a way similar to Rebekka's desire to be a mother, Lina wants to mother Florens, and Florens desperately wishes that her mother loved her, since she does not understand her mother's purpose in giving her up to Vaark. Because the women's desires are at cross-purposes and because they are unable to fight the constraints of a society that does not legally recognize them, the women's community is doomed to break apart into their separate concerns or be preyed upon by outside forces. In this novel, there is no healing spectral guide to help the women bond in spite of their differences.

Since the novel is partially told from Florens's point of view and the most important relationship in the book is between her and her mother, I will focus primarily on her story. Florens's experience very much parallels the themes of *Beloved* in that her motivation in *A Mercy* is mother-hunger. In her mind, the primal scene of rejection—her mother pleading with Vaark to take Florens and sending her away, all while holding the hand of Florens's younger brother—colors every action of her life, and this apparition of her mother haunts her at several points in the novel.[1] Scully describes Florens as a "combination of defenselessness, eagerness to please and, most of all, a willingness to blame herself for the meanness of others" (152). Because she perceives that her mother rejected her, she lacks self-love and confidence and submerges herself in obsessive love of the free African blacksmith who builds the gate for Vaark's new home. Instead of an equal love between partners, Florens defines her sense of self through her love of the beloved. She wraps herself in a "too-thick" love and hopes to erase every rejection that she has experienced since the first one by her mother. She says, "I am here with you always. Never never without you. Here I am not the one to throw out. . . . With you my body is pleasure is safe is belonging. I can never not have you have me" (136–37). This is very close to the obsessive language that Beloved uses to describe Sethe in the threnody section. The danger of this self-effacing love is shown when Florens, in a fit of jealousy, attacks the orphan that the blacksmith has taken in and then tells the blacksmith that he owns her (141). The blacksmith realizes her lack of agency, tells her to own herself, and rejects her. This final rejection, so like the initial one when her mother sent her away and kept her younger brother, sends Florens into a rage, and she attacks the blacksmith.

Three scenes that occur during Florens's journey to find the blacksmith clearly illustrate her dangerous lack of agency as a result of the prevailing social codes in the colonies. She is searching for the blacksmith because he might be the only person who can heal Rebekka of the pox that killed Jacob. Even though Rebekka writes a pass for Florens explaining the urgency of this mission to anyone who might delay her, Florens learns a hard lesson about what it means to be a female African slave and leave her place of service. She is untethered to her master and in grave danger from strangers. Her mission is jeopardized from the start when her fellow travelers on the wagon to the next town run away while the drivers are in a tavern. These indentured servants are "certain that their years of debt are over but the master says no" (40). They are headed for work in a tannery, which, according to one of the women, will lead to certain death. Florens is unable to understand their position, but she does know that she should not remain alone in the wagon after they have escaped. At this moment, she is lost and vulnerable to anyone she may encounter, literally on the outskirts of society in the wilderness.

After seeing the plight of the indentured servants—a group composed of men, women, and young children bound by rope to one another and uncertain of their future except that it means more bondage—Florens comes across a small village in the throes of a witch hunt. This is a typical event from this time period in that the victim believes the accusations have less to do with her supposed supernatural powers than with the pasture that her family owns and which the accusers covet (109). This covert land grab also recalls the reasons for the attack on the Convent in *Paradise.* By an unlucky accident, Florens chooses the house of the victim, a girl who is believed to be a demon, to beg for food. The next morning, when the villagers come to inspect the girl, they find Florens and connect her dark skin color to their fears of the "Black Man." During the inspection of her body for marks from the devil, Florens feels robbed of her individuality. She says, "They circle me, lean down to inspect my feet. Naked under their examination I watch for what is in their eyes. No hate is there or scare or disgust but they are looking at me my body across distances without recognition. Swine look at me with more connection when they raise their heads from the trough" (113). These people fear her and treat her as an object, rather than as a human being. In a move similar to the men's misinterpretation of the lipstick message from Seneca's mother in *Paradise* as satanic, the villagers take Florens's letter, which they believe might have been authored by Lucifer. This leaves Florens without the protection of her master and the purpose of her mission. She knows she is in danger, and this experience of being a powerless object in the villagers' gaze with no human recognition has scarred her:

> I walk alone except for the eyes that join me on my journey. . . . To know if I can spring out of the darkness and bite. Inside I am shrinking. I climb the streambed under watching trees and know I am not the same. I am losing something with every step I take. I can feel the drain. Something precious is leaving me. I am a thing apart. With the letter I belong and am lawful. Without it I am a weak calf abandon by the herd, a turtle without shell, a minion with no telltale signs but a darkness I am born with, outside, yes, but inside as well and the inside dark is small, feathered and toothy. Is that what my mother knows? Why she chooses me to live without? (115)

Without the pass from her mistress, Florens lacks identity and power—she has become a non-person. She is prey for anyone who may want to rape or kidnap her. She indeed is losing "something precious"—her sense of self. She uses animal imagery for her weakness and isolation. She also connects this awareness of her race and social position to her mother and wonders whether this is why she was abandoned. The "inside dark" of which she speaks foreshadows her violence against the blacksmith, which she is leading up to in her written story, but this passage illustrates her fragmentation as she experiences multiple rejections she cannot fathom.

The third instance takes place the night before she attacks the boy at the blacksmith's house. In a dream that points to her lack of a coherent identity, she looks into water and thinks: "Right away I take fright when I see my face is not there. Where my face should be is nothing. I put a finger in and watch the water circle. I put my mouth close enough to drink or kiss but I am not even a shadow there. Where is it hiding? Why is it?" (138). Slavery, her subsequent misunderstanding of her mother, and her observations of the position of servants and slaves in this colonial world have stunted Florens's ability to know herself. Unlike Shadrack, who in *Sula* sees his reflection in a toilet and realizes his bodily existence, for Florens there is not even a "shadow" of her in the water. She is invisible; she is elided. The scene is reminiscent of Beloved's fervent desire to find Sethe's face in the water and to understand herself and her mother. This lack of her mother and of her own self structures Florens's perceptions of the blacksmith and the boy and leads to her outburst of violence. She uses this violence to make her desires known and to make a mark. She finally does make many marks, as she writes her life story on the walls of Vaark's incomplete mansion in the hope that the blacksmith will read it and understand why she was so jealous of his relationship with the boy.

Florens's defiance of Rebekka's order that no one should ever enter Vaark's house again and her construction of her memoir on the walls of that house symbolize an attempt to subvert the master-slave relationship and bring visibility to the scars of slavery—the scars that haunted the bodies of D'Ortega's slaves and Vaark's thoughts before he stopped looking and invested in Barbados. Florens supercedes Vaark as the main character not only because she received the "mercy," but also through her narration and her presence in his house. She physically outlasts him (much like Circe outlasts the Butlers in *Song of Solomon*), and she writes her story on the emblem of his great dream of profit and glory, a scheme supported by her labor. Willard and Scully think that the light in the house is Vaark's ghost haunting the building because they believe the women would never defy Rebekka's orders. But it is really Florens with her candle and writing instrument scribbling away every night. She unghosts herself by marking her life on the walls of Vaark's home, and even though the blacksmith may never see it, the reader does.[2] The reader is privy to Florens's spectral text as every other section of the book has been a portion of her writing on the wall. Text itself, as we have seen from *Jazz* and *Love,* can be spectral, and according to Julian Wolfreys, "Texts are neither dead nor alive, yet they hover at the very limits between living and dying. The text thus partakes in its own haunting, it is traced by its own phantoms, and it is this condition which reading must confront." He adds that text can be seen as "merely a conduit, a spirit medium if you like, by which the author communicates" (xii). Florens's text is her liminal conduit of communication to whoever will read it. In it, she describes the haunting primal scene of her life—the loss of her mother—and attempts to make sense of this lack and its effect on her life thus far. She achieves agency through writing and bringing order to her life experiences. Her last words in the text acknowledge that she and her mother will never know each other or understand how that moment of loss affected them but that she has learned who she is: "I am become wilderness but I am also Florens. In full. Unforgiven. Unforgiving. No ruth, my love. None. Hear me? Slave. Free. I last" (161). She has survived regardless of her circumstances, and she is demanding to be heard. Unlike her moment of despair without the master's written pass, when she saw nothing instead of her reflection, she inscribes her voice and her presence on the master's house. She breaks her silence by revising the meaning of his monument. Because of the strict binaries that control this society, this book is predominantly focused on social ghosts, but even though Florens does not understand her spectral mother, she still finds her voice. Slavery attempts to erase the mother/child bond by creating loss and absence—the ghostly parent. This time, however, the reader is able to hear from the specter because Florens's mother speaks in the final section of the novel. The omniscient narrator can reach for a connection where Florens cannot.

Florens's admission at the end of her last section that she will never understand her mother is underscored by her mother's appearance to tell her side of the story. Although an apparition of Florens's mother does appear to her several times, Florens ignores the specter and never learns why she was so easily given up. The *reader,* however, does learn this secret from the mother's spectral presence. Her mother gave her up precisely because of the violence of the master and of slavery. Through the mother's narrative of her capture, her experience during the Middle Passage, and her life as a slave in the Americas, the personal experience underlying the highly organized and lethal slave trade from Africa to the Caribbean to Maryland is unghosted and given language. Florens's mother never told her daughter about her capture and the horrific scenes she witnessed on the slave ship and on a sugar plantation. She never told her daughter that she and her brother, the little boy who Florens believes was valued more than she was, were products of rape meant to "break" the mother in for servitude (163). The mother knows, "There is no protection. To be female in this place is to be an open wound that cannot heal. Even if scars form, the festering is ever below" (163). This clearly illustrates the position of women in this society. To be a female slave is to experience a deep trauma that haunts, even if it is not visible or is in the past. This is the first step toward "rememory" and the traumatic repetition that Sethe tries to avoid and from which she tries to shield her children. Florens does not know that her mother felt that by giving her to Vaark she would protect her from rape. She cannot understand, but her writing on the wall places her experiences next to those of her mother, showing the reader the fractures and the motivations within and behind this haunted relationship.

The chaotic and disastrous dislocations of families in slavery prohibit the necessary information from being passed on to the next generation, from mother to daughter. The cycle of dispossession and silence repeats because the characters are thoroughly imbricated in their roles in relation to the larger forces at work. Unlike the characters in the post–Civil War setting of *Beloved,* the characters in this novel are still being moved like pieces in a checkers game, to borrow imagery from Baby Suggs, and there is no distance from the trauma for a spectral guide like Beloved or Consolata to help negotiate. The reader, however, through Florens's mother's spectral narrative, receives a *glimpse* of the terrible reasoning that forces a woman to give up her daughter for that daughter's best interests. She gives us a sliver of a view of the violating experiences of slavery, the labor that, throughout the book, has been silently providing for Vaark's rising profits and, at the same time, his dramatic downfall. While her mother reveals her motivations and choices through the spectral text of the novel, Florens unghosts herself through *her* text on the master's walls that narrates her life story, thereby subverting the silence that surrounds her social position. Even if Lina does burn the house, as Florens suspects she will, her story will fly through the smoke and debris over the nascent American nation. As Florens notes, "Perhaps these words need the air that is out in the world. Need to fly up then fall, fall like ash over acres of primrose and mallow. Over a turquoise lake, beyond the eternal hemlocks, through clouds cut by rainbow and flavor the soil of the earth" (161). In this novel, Morrison comes full circle as Florens, who has much in common with Pecola, seizes agency and writes her story on the physical manifestation of the very institution that has harmed her. In *The Bluest Eye,* the novel ends with sterility because the "soil is bad for certain kinds of flowers" (*The Bluest Eye* 206), but in *A Mercy,* there is hope that Florens's words, a witness to her life, may season the very soil and add her story to the mosaic of human experience and history. Her voice will not be ignored. She will last.

CONCLUSION

In her novels, Toni Morrison uses the metaphor of the ghost to assert the presence of African American history and to re-create the personal experiences of those who lived this history. This information is often ignored by hierarchical and binary ways of thinking. The spectral figure shows the power of the ghostly and the supernatural to subvert dualistic and oppressive relationships, and the figure finds ways for socially ghosted characters, who are silenced and lost in the interstices, to endure traumatic experiences resulting from slavery, dispossession, racial violence, class conflicts, and oppression. These specters form conduits of communication across generations, races, classes, genders, life and death, and past and present. In *Song of Solomon* and *Tar Baby,* the ghosted characters are torn by issues of class and race and are disconnected from their family heritage, and in *Beloved* and *Paradise,* the ghosted characters are brought into communication with previous generations and with a violent cultural and personal history that has traumatized them. In *Jazz* and *Love,* the spectral guides become the narrators, breaking down the boundaries between text and reader as they unghost the characters who have been elided by precarious interactions with history, class conflicts, and patriarchal dominance. These concerns with the ghostliness of history and individuals continue in Morrison's latest book, *A Mercy,* which, in a thematic return toward *The Bluest Eye* and *Beloved,* delineates the precarious positions of socially marginalized characters, including orphans, women, servants, and slaves, who are all trying to negotiate their relationships to power and agency in early America.

This concern with the spectral is also present in Morrison's nonfiction, particularly in her Nobel lecture and acceptance speech, which she delivered in 1993 between the publications of *Jazz* and *Paradise.* Tellingly, in her acceptance speech to the Swedish Academy, she described as part of the honor of being awarded the prize her feeling of being "pleasantly haunted" by those who had been chosen before and "delightfully haunt[ed]" by those who will be chosen in the coming years (*Nobel* 31–32). During a 2004 interview on NPR's *Morning Edition,* Renee Montagne asked Morrison how being haunted could be pleasant. "I think of ghosts and haunting as just being alert," Morrison replied. "If you are really alert, then you see the life that exists beyond the life that is on top. It's not spooky, necessarily—might be, but it doesn't have to be. It's something I relish, rather than run from" (Montagne). This idea of looking beneath and beyond the accepted surface of things is of paramount importance in Morrison's creative work, and it accounts for her frequent use of the ghost to communicate what is often lost to cultural and national amnesia. Furthermore, the themes in her novels of communication between generations, the possibilities of the shared text, and the avoidance of either/or thinking are all showcased in Morrison's Nobel lecture. Here she forecasts the paradise where her souls do their work in the spaces between, and she reiterates the generational connections among spectral guides/ancestors and their charges, who lack a coherent narrative of their origins. Since Morrison delivered this lecture during the completion of her trilogy, its emphasis on spaces of mediation indicates the unifying nature of this theme of intergenerational haunting that is present throughout her canon.

This theme of generations communally working through the past, a quality that is so important in the novels I have analyzed, is emphasized beautifully in Morrison's Nobel lecture. She tells the story of an old wise woman who is blind but who, even though she has this disability, is held in honor by her community and possesses the insight that is a key ability for so many of Morrison's spectral figures. This woman encompasses many oppositions comfortably: she is honored but "lives alone in a small house outside of town" (*Nobel* 9); she "is the law and its transgression" (10). One day, several disaffected youth come to ask this woman a question that hinges on her disability. They are "bent on disproving her clairvoyance and showing her up for the fraud they believe she is" (10). Telling her that one of them is holding a bird, they ask her whether it is alive or dead. She answers that what she does know is that it is "in your hands" (11). Morrison uses this story to illustrate the responsibility that comes with the manipulation of language because it is in the writer's hands, like the bird. For her, much of the language of the present is used for limitation and violence, not for "new knowledge" or the "mutual exchange of ideas" (17).

The young people criticize this answer, however, as the easy way out because the old woman does not even check to see if there *is* a bird in someone's hand. They want her to use her imagination and create something in place of the absent bird. They ask:

> Is there no context for our lives? No song, no literature, no poem full of vitamins, no history connected to experience that you can pass along to help us start strong? You are an adult. The old one, the wise one. Stop thinking about saving your face. Think of our lives and tell us your particularized world. Make up a story. Narrative is radical, creating us at the very moment it is being created. (27)

As shown in their litany of demands, the youth feel disconnected and ghosted. They want to know "what moves at the margin" (28). They want history as it was experienced and folklore as it was practiced. They want the generational connection that the spectral figure can provide, but she can provide this only *in tandem with* their imaginations and desires. As the old woman points out once they have finished listing their requests: "I trust you with the bird that is not in your hands because you have truly caught it. Look. How lovely it is, this thing we have done—together" (30). This exchange between the old woman and the children neatly encapsulates the interactions we have seen between the spectral figures and their ghosted charges as "a *politics* of memory, of inheritance, and of generations" (Derrida xix). The end also links to the importance of group creation of meaning and the merging of the written text into spectral mediums that we have seen at the ends of *Beloved* and *Jazz.* "The act of writing," according to Ralph Ellison, "requires a constant plunging back into the shadow of the past where time hovers ghostlike" (*Shadow* xvi). Narrative is radically and communally created, not static on a page, and it engages the past.

Finally, Morrison foreshadows in the lecture her creation of a space of spirits in *Paradise.* This forecasting gives the end of that novel a new power in her canon, a pivotal role that I asserted in my second chapter. In the story, the old woman ponders the real problem of the Tower of Babel. She does not believe the issue was that a multitude of languages stopped the builders from gaining heaven. She questions instead what kind of heaven would have been reached had the people continued: "Perhaps the achievement of a Paradise was premature, a little hasty if no one could take the time to understand other languages, other views, other narratives. Had they, the heaven they imagined might have been found at their feet. Complicated, demanding, yes, but a view of heaven as life" (*Nobel* 19). The goal is to move beyond the either/or traps in which places like Ruby and people like Milkman, Jadine and Son, Sethe and Denver, Joe and Violet, and Christine and Heed find themselves. Morrison shows characters and readers these expansive places between the rigid oppositions drawn among classes, races, genders, magic and reality, life and death, and past, present, and future. Her vehicles for this liminal journey include her spectral figures and the spectral language of her texts themselves. As she asserts, "Language can never 'pin down' slavery, genocide, war. Nor should it yearn for the arrogance to be able to do so. Its force, its felicity, is in its reach toward the ineffable" (21). Morrison's specters bring attention to the veiled spots in history and those horrifying events that defy description, those places where mainstream America does not want to shine a light. While not every character comes through the spectral moments unscathed or completely healed, each novel, from *Song of Solomon* onward, does begin in stasis and entrapment and end in possibility. In her work, Morrison gives presence to the invisible, voice to the previously silenced and unspeakable, and agency to the oppressed on the margins of society, who are refused a space in which to tell a story of their experiences.

NOTES

INTRODUCTION

1. In her discussion of *Paradise,* J. Brooks Bouson cites Morrison's original pre-trilogy wish to write a novel on the nature of "the beloved" (209).

2. The meaning of the term "magical realism" has experienced a metamorphosis from its initial birth as "magic realism" in the German post-Expressionist movement of the 1920s to encompass literature during the growth of "magical realism" in Latin America in the 1940s and 1950s. During the last half of the twentieth century, it circled the globe, particularly among postcolonial cultures (Bowers 8–9). For a history of this term see Bowers, Zamora and Faris, Chanady, and Schroeder.

3. There are echoes of the early practitioners of magical realism here in Chanady's assertion that the mode represents "a more complete picture of the world." In his 1925 article on "magic realism" as a German post-Expressionistic art movement, Franz Roh noted that his use of the term "magic" rather than "mystic" resulted from his "wish to indicate that the mystery does not descend to the represented world, but rather hides and palpitates behind it" (16). The "magic" is found within normal objects and situations. In 1949, Alejo Carpentier posited that Europe had developed surrealism and Latin America had created the magically real, what he referred to as "*lo real maravilloso americano.*" This "'marvelous American reality' does not imply a conscious assault on conventionally depicted reality but, rather, an amplification of perceived reality required by and inherent in Latin American nature and culture" (75). For Carpentier, "the fantastic inheres in the natural and human realities of time and place, where improbable juxtapositions and marvelous mixtures exist by virtue of Latin America's varied history, geography, demography, and politics" (75). Magical realism becomes a description of Latin American reality. Of course, hidden within this aesthetic belief may be a colonial view of the exotic native: even though Carpentier was Cuban, he was educated in Europe.

4. For examples of the critical attention paid to *Beloved* as a magical realist work, see Hart, Schroeder, Bowers, and Faris's *Ordinary Enchantments.* For magical realist interpretations of *Song of Solomon* and *Tar Baby,* see Stelamaris Coser and P. Gabrielle Foreman.

5. This position of women as abused, silenced, or "throwaway" characters, a phrase actually used in reference to the Convent women in Morrison's *Paradise,* is integral in Patricia Yaeger's study *Dirt and Desire,* where she identifies a deep connection between images of contamination, dirt, consumption, and burial with marginal female characters in the writings of both white and African American women of the South. This power that Brogan describes of overcoming "ghosting" through a connection to spirits and a world beyond is also discussed with a feminist bent in Gloria Anzaldúa's *Borderlands/ La Fronteras* and Paula Gunn Allen's *Off the Reservation.*

6. Other critics and theorists have dealt with the causes of and consequences from "social death" for minorities, including Orlando Patterson and most recently Christopher Peterson. Using the metaphor of death rather than that of "ghosting," Patterson notes that

slavery results in a slave's status as a "social nonperson" who has "no socially recognized existence outside of his master" (5). The slave also becomes a "genealogical isolate" because he has no claim on living blood relations, ancestors, or descendants (5). In his *Kindred Specters,* Christopher Peterson notes that scholars, like Patterson, have shown "the ways in which American culture represents racial and sexual minorities as dead—both figuratively and literally," and he sees this tendency as "accompany[ing] and reinforc[ing] the larger cultural dissimulation of mortality by making racial and sexual others stand in for the death that haunts every life" (4). For Peterson, "[T]o be without kin, or to engage in sexual and social relations that are unrecognized or unrecognizable as kinship within established norms, is to live among the ranks of the socially dead" (9). For my purposes, using the metaphor of being "ghosted" rather than "dead" implies that there is some chance of return or transformation.

7. These studies are, respectively, Jill Matus's *Toni Morrison,* Denise Heinze's *The Dilemma of Double-Consciousness: Toni Morrison's Novels,* Doreatha Mbalia's *Toni Morrison's Developing Class Consciousness,* Andrea O'Reilly's *Toni Morrison and Motherhood: A Politics of the Heart,* Philip Page's *Dangerous Freedom: Fusion and Fragmentation in Toni Morrison's Novels,* Trudier Harris's *Fiction and Folklore: The Novels of Toni Morrison,* Karla F. C. Holloway and Stephanie A. Demetrakopoulos's *New Dimensions of Spirituality: A Biracial and Bicultural Reading of the Novels of Toni Morrison,* Barbara Hill Rigney's *The Voices of Toni Morrison,* Gurleen Grewal's *Circles of Sorrow, Lines of Struggle: The Novels of Toni Morrison,* Susan Neal Mayberry's *Can't I Love What I Criticize? The Masculine and Morrison,* and John N. Duvall's *The Identifying Fictions of Toni Morrison: Modernist Authenticity and Postmodern Blackness.*

8. Three studies do skirt the edges of my aims with spectrality and deconstruction. Jeffrey Andrew Weinstock's article "Ten Minutes for Seven Letters: Reading *Beloved*'s Epitaph" analyzes the epitaph in that novel through the lens of deconstruction and the instability of language. In their book *A World of Difference,* Wendy Harding and Jacky Martin apply the critical term "interface" to Morrison's novels. For them, the "interface" is the "place where culture is produced in the friction between affronted groups" (7), and they emphasize Morrison's mission of deconstructing simplistic binaries. In his *Ghosts, Metaphor, and History in Toni Morrison's* Beloved *and Gabriel García Márquez's* One Hundred Years of Solitude, Daniel Erickson unpacks the connections between ghosts as metaphors and history and ideology. None of these studies approaches the double-sided metaphor of the ghost as presence and person, however; and none deals with the repeated spectral figures that guide characters throughout Morrison's novels.

CHAPTER 2 "Why Not Ghosts As Well?"

1. John N. Duvall sees *Tar Baby* as a follow-up to *Song of Solomon* that complicates Milkman's journey of discovery. For Duvall, in *Tar Baby* Morrison is "overtly giving up the project of ever achieving a completed self" (101). Herbert William Rice also sees this complex relationship in that for him, *Song of Solomon* is a text about "reclamation," while *Tar Baby* has no resolutions (84). Susan Willis and Karla F. C. Holloway both see Jadine and Milkman as similar questing characters and believe that Jadine fails in her quest because she lacks a guide like Pilate.

2. For takes on Morrison's use of folklore and storytelling in *Song of Solomon,* in particular the quest motif and the flying African stories, see Susan Blake, Dorothy H. Lee, Trudier Harris, Joyce Irene Middleton, and A. Leslie Harris. For discussions of African elements and diasporic connections, see Gay Wilentz, Wendy W. Walters, Keith Cartwright, and Valorie D. Thomas. Cedric Gael Bryant places the novel within African American traditions of death and the afterlife. Karla F. C. Holloway and Valerie Smith both discuss the novel in terms of community, and Michael Awkward and Stephanie Demetrakopoulos deal with gender concerns.

3. See, in particular, Joseph T. Skerrett Jr. In contrast, Jane S. Bakerman sees Pilate as a failed character. In her article "Failures of Love: Female Initiation in the Novels of Toni Morrison," Bakerman cites Pilate's inability to understand her father's messages, her isolation, and her failure to save her granddaughter as aspects of her weakness (556). I think that Pilate's strength comes from her abilities to transgress boundaries and proliferate meanings.

4. This belief that second sight results from the caul being wrapped around an infant at birth also appears in Randall Kenan's story collection *Let the Dead Bury Their Dead* (1992) and in Tina McElroy Ansa's *Baby of the Family* (1989).

5. For a discussion of female shape-shifters in postcolonial magical realist fiction, see Megan Musgrave. In "The Gospel According to Pilate," Brenda Marshall investigates Pilate's ability to manipulate stereotypes and inhabit roles, a talent that places her "outside the norm" (486).

6. Marianne Hirsch, Gary Storhoff, and Keith Byerman each explore family issues in *Song of Solomon.* Hirsch focuses on "family ideologies" (142). Storhoff identifies the Dead family as dysfunctional because of parental enmeshment, a situation that occurs when parents use their children as pawns in a competition for affection. Byerman believes that the novel is defined and driven by family problems, history, and relationships.

7. For a discussion of the Seven Days group and African American secret societies of the nineteenth century and 1960s political thought, see Ralph Story. Harry Reed also reads *Song of Solomon* against the backdrop of black politics of the 1960s, but he identifies Morrison as a Black Cultural Nationalist who hopes for "a focus on regenerating the community from within," a stance between conservative and militant black nationalism (75).

8. Karla F. C. Holloway describes Circe as "the incarnate Pilate" (69), and Harry Reed notes that "both Pilate and Circe survive partly by utilizing the past" (75).

9. Heinze sees connections between Son and Milkman; Holloway describes Son as "natural truth" (126); and Mbalia calls him the "revolutionary protagonist" (29), who exemplifies class and people consciousness. Mbalia also limns him as a successful Milkman (77). By contrast, Duvall and O'Reilly find problems with him. Duvall notes Son's violence and his rape of Jadine right before she leaves him, and he believes that she needs more than just Son to complete her identity formation (106–7, 115). O'Reilly notes that he cannot be a guide for Jadine because of his links to patriarchal masculinity, which are evinced in his violence (108). In *Fiction and Folklore,* Trudier Harris posits that he is an amoral and ambivalent presence in the trickster tradition and that Morrison switches between Son and Jadine as trickster figures in the text (121).

10. Demetrakopoulos sees Jadine in a more positive light than Holloway, who believes that Jadine wants "to strip Son of his identity" and to "suck him dry" (124–25). For

Demetrakopoulos, the American reality is such that individuals are often alienated from their pasts (131). Letitia L. Moffitt identifies the frustration of readers who are in positions quite similar to Jadine's but still condemn her choices as the "trap" that Morrison's novel has set: "The trap is in judging the characters in terms of overly simplistic, quickly formed definitions based on their apparent roles . . . readers may avoid [this trap], given that from our vantage point we are able to see multiple visions" (14). While this is a "richly duplicitous text" (Werner 63), Jadine does feel inauthentic at times, and the characters fall into the trap of seeing all their relationships as a contest of extremes. The reader may be able to deconstruct the trap, but the characters need some connection and negotiation, which is only tentatively accomplished by the end of the novel.

11. Krumholz writes, "Michael's ever-present absence is reminiscent . . . [of] Beloved's role as the historical, psychological, and symbolic presence and absence around which *Beloved* focuses" ("Blackness and Art," 268).

12. Terry Otten and Lauren Lepow discuss the island as a version of Eden and the plot as a kind of a parable of the fall.

13. On the one hand, Holloway describes the island and Thérèse as "suspended in time," powerful, and mythic, and she sees Son's return to the island as his place of safety, or his "briar patch" (127–28). Demetrakopoulos, on the other hand, sees Thérèse as a "devouring aspect of the Earth Mother" and "purely a conjurer, a curse-producing woman" (135, 137).

CHAPTER 3 "What Would Be on the Other Side?"

1. Throughout the novel, Consolata is addressed as "Connie" by most characters. When she claims her identity and her past, she insists on her full name: Consolata Sosa. I use both "Connie" and "Consolata" throughout this chapter to refer to her, depending on what scene of the book I am analyzing.

2. For a discussion of trauma and history as "difficult or painful to remember" in Morrison's novels (102), see Jill Matus.

3. While many critics interpret Beloved as an apparition haunting Sethe's home and its occupants, Elizabeth B. House makes a convincing argument that "evidence throughout the book suggests that the girl [Beloved] is not a supernatural being of any kind but simply a young woman who has herself suffered the horrors of slavery" (17). House reads Beloved as a young woman who experienced the Middle Passage and is traumatized enough to believe that Sethe is her mother. In a 1988 interview, Morrison explains that she wanted Beloved to function on many levels: "She is a spirit on one hand, literally she is what Sethe thinks she is, her child returned to her from the dead. And she must function like that in the text. She is also another kind of dead which is not spiritual but flesh, which is, a survivor from the true, factual slave ship" (Darling 247). My reading of Beloved as a spectral, boundary-crossing character allows her to inhabit these shifting identities to complete her cultural work for Sethe and Denver. She then can be whatever the characters (and readers) need her to be.

4. Similar to Brogan's use of the term "ghost" as a metaphor for female "powerlessness" (25), David Lawrence terms the inhabitants of 124 "phantoms" because they are

separated from the surrounding community, "lead[ing] sterile, isolated lives, the [baby] ghost the only member of the family who seeks the intimacy of physical contact" (50).

5. Thomas R. Edwards posits that "Beloved is *all* memory—hers seems to be a collective racial memory whose 'personal' contents mingle with recollections of the Middle Passage from Africa" (83). Carol Schmudde agrees with this evaluation of the ghost: "Morrison's narrative implies that the ghost, never named except for the memorializing word that appears on her tombstone, possesses not only the memories and experiences of Sethe's baby daughter but also the memories and experiences of several generations of her ancestors going back through the Middle Passage to Africa" (410). As a character, Beloved has no fixed subject position.

6. In her essay "Rootedness," Morrison highlights the presence of ancestors in African American literature. She notes that "[t]here is always an elder there. And these ancestors are not just parents, they are sort of timeless people whose relationships to the characters are benevolent, instructive, and protective, and they provide a certain kind of wisdom" (343). She posits, "When you kill the ancestor you kill yourself" (344). Baby Suggs (both before and after death) and Beloved are timeless ancestor spirits who give instruction to the characters of the novel, albeit in very different manners. Morrison's warning to not kill one's ancestors also points to the end of the novel, when Beloved cannot be truly exorcised.

7. For discussions of the Founding Fathers/Old Fathers/New Fathers connection and the book's interaction with "mainstream" American history, see in particular Peter Widdowson, Katrine Dalsgård, Rob Davidson, Peter R. Kearly, Andrew Read, and Marni Gauthier. The date of the Convent massacre, July 1976, is also a point of comparison between Ruby and the larger context of American history.

8. Most critics read Connie as an individual of mixed race from South America, but there are other views. Peter R. Kearly identifies Connie as a "baptized Native American woman" (12), perhaps left over from the Convent's school days, even though in the text Connie arrives in America with Mary Magna, and additionally, Connie claims no connection to the Native American girls in the Convent school: "She attended classes with the Indian girls but formed no attachments to them" (*Paradise* 225). Therese Higgins and Philip Page acknowledge Connie's affinity for the people of Ruby by identifying her as a "Black Madonna" (133) and a figuration of the "African deity Legba" ("Furrowing All the Brows" 641), respectively. Tammy Clewell believes, however, that Mary Magna rescued Connie from "a squalid life in Portugal" (137). Like that of Beloved, Consolata's identity is remarkably amorphous and difficult to establish within the text.

9. While Paula Gunn Allen is a Native American critic and *Off the Reservation* focuses on the interplay between the Native American and Western worlds, she does discuss female writers of many backgrounds in her chapter "Thus Spake Pocahontas," making the claim that their work shares a connection to the "Void" and to each other through their multivocality and boundary-crossing emphases. She also comments on African American writers, including Toni Cade Bambara, Henry Louis Gates Jr., and Morrison. Additionally, Native Americans certainly play a role in *Paradise,* particularly in the liminality of place and history connected to the Convent and to the land Ruby occupies.

10. Katrine Dalsgård describes the Convent as "indefinable" (243), and Patricia McKee notes that it is a space of "borderlessness" (210). In a fuller discussion of the

Convent's liminal positioning, Ana María Fraile-Marcos posits that it is a manifestation of Bhabha's "Third Space" and a metaphor for Purgatory (22–23). Peter Widdowson, Justine Tally, and Peter R. Kearly all read the Convent as a site of female power and security, respectively describing it as a retreat from the patriarchal (330), a "woman's space as a safety zone" ("Nature" 63), and a "strong maternal space of community" (12).

11. Since Piedade actually appears later in the text, I interpret this as evidence of Consolata's connection to the space between life and death at this point. She already is aware of the destination she shares with these women and is foreshadowing rather than simply having a vision of an ideal life or of a mother figure.

12. The attack on the Convent bears a striking resemblance to other witch hunts, particularly the episode in Salem, Massachusetts, in that the victims are on the outskirts of a highly structured society and become scapegoats for the mistakes of the accusers. Lone sardonically notes that Sargeant Person is supporting the posse because he wants to add the Convent land to his neighboring farm (277).

13. This indication of another level of existence or growth is reminiscent of the "door" Morrison said that Jadine had found at the end of *Tar Baby.*

14. Interpretations of Piedade vary. Krumholz (in "Reading and Insight") and Page (in "Furrowing All the Brows") read Piedade as an imagined lost mother figure for Consolata, and Page notes that the end of the novel is a "mystical transcendence beyond life and death, as Connie seems to blend into her idyllic visions and each of the four Convent women is spiritually reunited with her family" (646). Justine Tally reads Piedade as a metaphorical mother in the vein of "Irigaray's feminine 'Myth of Origin'" ("Nature" 70). Peter Widdowson views Piedade as a dream-figure and believes the "*real* ending" of the novel occurs earlier in the "Save-Marie" section before the women appear to their family members (333–34).

CHAPTER 4 "The Specter as Possibility"

1. Eusebio L. Rodrigues and Sharon Jessee read the narrator as a female deity, or "female immanence of the divine" (Rodrigues 261). Dirk Ludigkeit and Carolyn M. Jones both see the narrator as a jazz artist/performer. Veronique Lesoinne discusses the narrator as jazz, as sound (155), and she notes how Morrison focuses on using the sound of vernacular speech in the novel. Roberta Rubenstein calls the narrator "the voice" (4), and Nancy J. Peterson describes the narrator as fluid and unreliable, ultimately suggesting that the narrator is the book itself (216). Yvonne Atkinson identifies the narrator's power to Witness and Testify (24), and Marc C. Conner describes the narrator as a communal and choral voice (73).

2. See *The Signifying Monkey* by Henry Louis Gates Jr. for a discussion of the "talking book" trope in African American literature.

3. Critics who discuss the importance of jazz music to the novel in terms of theme or structure include Morrison herself, Caroline Brown, Jennifer Andrews, Ludigkeit, Rubenstein, Rachel Blumenthal, Rodrigues, and Peterson. Alan Munton, by contrast, takes critics to task for equating music and prose.

4. Farah Jasmine Griffin notes the haunting possibilities of the "blue note" in blues and jazz music: "Technically, blue notes are the lowered third, fifth, and seventh degrees

of a key. However, one might also speculate that at the level of content, the falling pitch of the blue note acts as the space where the absence, the terror, the fear, and the tragic moments of black life reside. In this sense, the blue note is truly the site of history and memory" (56–57).

5. Peterson offers the view that the episodes are a "stunning reworking of various Faulknerian motifs, such as long-kept secrets revealed and miscegenation" (211).

6. It is fitting that this complex and ambiguous episode should focus on Wild, the spectral figure, and Golden Gray, a complex and ambiguous figure in his own right because of his hybridity.

7. Carolyn M. Jones also connects Dorcas and Beloved as mirrors filtering memories and experiences for the other characters in their respective books. Anissa Janine Wardi posits that "conceptualizing Dorcas/Wild/Beloved as a conflated being aids in the reading of *Jazz* as a book of the dead" (*Death* 110). In addition, Morrison linked Dorcas and Beloved in an interview with Gloria Naylor when she called both of the characters "the dead girl" (qtd. in *Death* 109).

8. Caroline Brown reads Wild as "the textual embodiment of the non-hermeneutic," but she links this tendency to Audre Lorde's discussion of "the erotic" rather than spectrality (635); Lesoinne sees Wild as "the embodiment of the pain and suffering of slavery" (161); Andrea O'Reilly analyzes the mother-child relationships in *Jazz* as compared to those in *Beloved,* viewing Wild as a "lost mother," who like Beloved "exist[s] outside of and beyond the Real, the Symbiotic, the Human, in an almost timeless and supernatural place" ("In Search of My Mother's Garden" 7). Drucilla Cornell identifies the novel as an "allegory of the Wild Woman" (313), and Jennifer Andrews labels Wild "an outlaw" and a "female trickster who dwells in caves and creates her own unique domestic spaces" (93).

9. This connection between sugar and the brutality of its production appears in *Song of Solomon* when as a child Guitar becomes sick from the candy his father's white employers give him after his father is killed at the sawmill. It also appears in *Tar Baby* and *A Mercy* (2008), as sugar production, whether by mistreated native labor or slaves, provides the profits that Valerian Street and Jacob Vaark enjoy.

10. Wardi emphasizes the intertextual connections between *Jazz* and Jean Toomer's *Cane* (1923), noting that Morrison repeats descriptions of the cane fields in the southern section of the novel. Wardi reads Wild as "the southern land itself, and more specifically the personification of the African American pastoral" (*Death* 120, 121).

11. Philip Page notes that in Morrison's fiction, "characters are caught in the endless flux of becoming" and in a postmodern sense must overcome displacement to create feasible identities. Page uses "Derridean concepts" to show how displaced characters "tend to overemphasize one or the other terms of various binary oppositions" ("Traces of Derrida" 55). In another discussion of Derridean concepts, Carolyn M. Jones asserts that the "cracks" and "traces" in *Jazz* are "gap[s] in the text that must be narrated" (488), and she emphasizes that for Morrison "all rememories, as she calls them in *Beloved,* are reconstructions, complete but also incomplete" (483). In my reading, this is the entry point for the specter, with its ability to be "both—and more," as Jones describes Beloved and Dorcas. Interactions with one's haunted past bring about a form of reconstructive and transformative healing.

12. I find it interesting that part of what confuses the narrator at the end of the novel—the presence of Felice—creates another trio. A phase of the healing process for

Violet and Joe involves sharing their stories and feelings with Felice, and in the process, the three form a small family unit that continues the reconstruction of the past and the movement into the future that were prompted by the spectral group: the narrator, Dorcas, and Wild. Felice also allows Joe to properly mourn Dorcas by telling him what her final words were, giving her desecrated remains language and creating a connection between Dorcas and Joe.

13. My concept of linking *Love* back to Morrison's previous work, and her trilogy in particular, is not unique, though my thematic framework of spectrality and ghosted figures is. As Benjamin Burr notes, "[I]n each of her novels Morrison is constantly deconstructing and re-writing her own theoretical agenda. Consequently, some of [the] greatest keys for reading one of Morrison's texts are her other texts" (159). As previously discussed, I interpret the "keys" to Morrison's texts to be *Beloved* and *Paradise* working in tandem throughout her canon. Critics who make sweeping connections among *Love* and other Morrison novels include Megan Sweeney, Anissa Janine Wardi, and Hilary Mantel.

14. For readings of the novel utilizing poststructural or postmodern theory, see Burr, Gascueña Gahete, Vega-González, and Sweeney. Critics also view *Love* through thematic lenses, including gender and family (Sathyaraj and Neelakantan), the Classical tradition (Roynon), the power of love and healing hands (Wardi), the legal system and justice (Sweeney), and "watertime writing" (Vega-González).

15. While Cosey may not be "spectral" in the sense in which I am using the term, Javier Gascueña Gahete describes him as "one of Morrison's most postmodern characters ever," in that he is an absence in the present narration and a "central figure . . . doomed to an endless repetition of the interpretive acts carried out by a myriad of other 'gazers' or narrators" (265).

16. The critical response to L is varied, though most critics agree that she is central to the novel. Wen-ching Ho's essay "'I'll Tell'—The Function and Meaning of L in Toni Morrison's *Love*" focuses exclusively on L. Anissa Janine Wardi discusses L's importance as a caregiver to the other female characters in the novel as she communicates love through her hands ("Laying" 206, 212); Megan Sweeney posits that L (as well as the other women) "serves as 'something rogue' that disrupts standard disciplinary and legal equations" (455); and Susana Vega-González connects L to water, emphasizing her ability to "blur [the] line between life and death" (212–13).

17. Ho compares L to Pilate from *Song of Solomon,* linking the two characters through Morrison's concept of the ancestor-figure (660), and Wardi comments on L's similarity to the narrator of *Jazz,* noting that "both are straightforward, opinionated, and knowledgeable about their communities" ("Laying" 207).

18. L's trademark hum has received critical attention. Ho believes that it makes explicit L's presence in the novel as a type of Greek chorus since the humming provides music, and if "rhythmic dance constitutes a key feature of the chorus in establishing a lyrical mood, the rhythmic dance of the words across the page is a cornerstone of L's commentary" (666). Sweeney references the hum as a symbol of L's rebelliousness, since she teaches Heed and Christine "how to make trouble and hum a different tune that diverts discipline and punishment" (459).

19. In a discussion of *Jazz* and now L's "background" hum, it is interesting to note the presence of music in Morrison's fiction, particularly since she often emphasizes the importance of the sound of her prose: "[M]y effort is to be *like* something that has probably only been fully expressed perhaps in music" (McKay 152).

20. For an interesting discussion of the connection between handwriting and character, see Wardi. She believes that is it important to note that L's writing of the fake will by hand is one more way in which she is capable of showing love to Heed and Christine through her nurturing hands ("Laying" 212).

21. Besides this erasure of female identity, there also is a hint of a connection to Violet, who performs abortions so that her past negative relationship with *her* mother will not be reproduced, and Christine certainly does not have a healthy, reciprocal relationship with her mother, May, who is slowly losing her mind while obsessively protecting Cosey's property. Traumatic history haunts these decisions.

22. According to Megan Sweeney, Celestial can be read as a woman who "occupies every place and cannot be confined" (461). She is "outside of sanctioned domestic spaces for women" (461). She is as placeless as L.

23. It is interesting that Cosey, while labeled a "Phantom" in the final section title, does not have the transitional power that L and Celestial have after death. The two of them visit *his grave.* Both L and Celestial are liminal and negotiate borders before death, perhaps making the final state a true passage. Additionally, L and Celestial are part of a creative line of ancestors, while Cosey attempts to disown his father's sins. This scene also is reminiscent of the final scene in *Paradise,* where Piedade tenderly sings to her charge, Consolata.

24. This scene recalls the "sound" the women use to rid Sethe's house of Beloved: "They stopped praying and took a step back to the beginning. In the beginning there were no words. In the beginning was the sound, and they all knew what that sound sounded like" (*Beloved* 259). The power of the women comes from their syncretic acceptance of Christianity and African spirituality and the liminal space thus created.

25. Sweeney points out that by excluding Celestial from Cosey's will so that Heed and Christine will be provided for and stay connected, "L's narrative enacts the partiality and exclusions of the law itself" (461). If, however, L *and* Celestial are the spectral guides of this Morrison novel, then the decision to rewrite the will carries on Celestial's unique absence/presence and makes Heed and Christine indebted to her for more than their pet phrase, "Hey, Celestial."

26. Vega-González posits that Heed and Christine's reconciliation takes place as a result of the "mediation of Junior" (217). I see L as more of a mediator than Junior, since the two women are kept together because of her menu, and Heed and Christine follow L into a more accepting and aware relationship with the afterlife. While Junior is caught between the two women and functions as a counterpart to their histories, her role in the reconciliation occurs primarily because she inadvertently causes Heed's fatal accident and then abandons the women in the hotel. Moreover, Junior is left at the end of the novel locked in a room of the house waiting for Heed and Christine's judgment: her future role is unclear, and she is ancillary to the discussion about her fate.

CHAPTER 5 "Slave. Free. I Last"

1. Cathy Covell Waegner argues, "Morrison astonishingly and movingly manages to encode the entire Atlantic slave trade triangle in this picture, as well as international colonization, ethnicity, cultural/language differences, and gender issues" (91–92).

2. This uncovering of the scars of slavery through writing is reminiscent of the work of the writers of slave narratives, such as Frederick Douglass and Harriet Jacobs.

According to Jacobs, "I have not written my experiences in order to attract attention to myself. . . . Neither do I care to excite sympathy for my own sufferings. But I do earnestly desire to arouse the women of the North to a realizing sense of the condition of two millions of women at the South, still in bondage, suffering what I suffered, and most of them far worse" (Gates, *The Classic Slave Narratives* 439–40). Like Jacobs, Florens is not seeking attention. She is seeking to give voice to her life experiences by writing herself into existence on the walls of the master's house and perhaps to offer some justification for her behavior to the blacksmith. Unbeknownst to her, however, the readers of *A Mercy* also read her script, thereby broadening its audience.

WORKS CITED

Aguiar, Sarah Appleton. "'Everywhere and Nowhere': Beloved's 'Wild' Legacy in Toni Morrison's *Jazz.*" *Notes on Contemporary Literature* 25.4 (1995): 11–12.

———. "'Passing On' Death: Stealing Life in Toni Morrison's *Paradise.*" *African American Review* 38.3 (2004): 513–19.

Allen, Paula Gunn. *Off the Reservation.* Boston: Beacon, 1998.

Andrews, Jennifer. "Reading Toni Morrison's *Jazz*: Rewriting the Tall Tale and Playing with the Trickster in the White American and African-American Humor Traditions." *Canadian Review of American Studies* 29.1 (1999): 87–107.

Ansa, Tina McElroy. *Baby of the Family.* 1989. Orlando, FL: Harcourt, 1991.

Anzaldúa, Gloria. *Borderlands/La Frontera: The New Mestiza.* 1987. San Francisco: Aunt Lute, 1999.

Atkinson, Yvonne. "Language that Bears Witness: The Black English Oral Tradition in the Works of Toni Morrison." *The Aesthetics of Toni Morrison: Speaking the Unspeakable.* Ed. Marc C. Conner. Jackson: UP of Mississippi, 2000. 12–30.

Awkward, Michael. *Inspiriting Influences: Tradition, Revision, and Afro-American Women's Novels.* New York: Columbia UP, 1989.

———. "'Unruly and Let Loose': Myth, Ideology, and Gender in *Song of Solomon.*" *Modern Critical Interpretations: Toni Morrison's* Song of Solomon. Ed. Harold Bloom. Philadelphia: Chelsea House, 1999. 95–113.

Bakerman, Jane S. "Failures of Love: Female Initiation in the Novels of Toni Morrison." *American Literature* 52.4 (Jan. 1981): 541–63.

Bent, Geoffrey. "Less Than Divine: Toni Morrison's *Paradise.*" *Southern Review* 35.1 (1999): 145–49.

Blake, Susan L. "Folklore and Community in *Song of Solomon.*" *MELUS* 7.3 (Autumn 1980): 77–82.

Blumenthal, Rachel. "Improvisational Soloists in Morrison's *Jazz.*" *Explicator* 65.4 (Summer 2007): 240–41.

Bouson, J. Brooks. *Quiet as It's Kept: Shame, Trauma, and Race in the Novels of Toni Morrison.* Albany: State U of New York P, 2000.

Bowers, Maggie Ann. *Magic(al) Realism.* London: Routledge, 2004.

Broad, Robert L. "Giving Blood to the Scraps: Haints, History, and Hosea in *Beloved.*" *African American Review* 28.2 (Summer 1994): 189–96.

Brogan, Kathleen. *Cultural Haunting: Ghosts and Ethnicity in Recent American Literature.* Charlottesville: UP of Virginia, 1998.

Brown, Caroline. "Golden Gray and the Talking Book: Identity as a Site of Artful Construction in Toni Morrison's *Jazz*." *African American Review* 36.4 (2002): 629–42.

Bryant, Cedric Gael. "'Every Goodbye Ain't Gone': The Semiotics of Death, Mourning, and Closural Practice in Toni Morrison's *Song of Solomon*." *MELUS* 24.3 (Fall 1999): 97–110.

Burr, Benjamin. "Mythopoetic Syncretism in *Paradise* and the Deconstruction of Hospitality in *Love*." *Toni Morrison and the Bible: Contested Intertextualities*. Ed. Shirley A. Stave. New York: Peter Lang, 2006. 159–74.

Buse, Peter, and Andrew Stott, eds. *Ghosts: Deconstruction, Psychoanalysis, History*. New York: St. Martin's, 1999.

Byerman, Keith. "Songs of the Ancestors: Family in *Song of Solomon*." *Approaches to Teaching the Novels of Toni Morrison*. Ed. Nellie Y. McKay and Kathryn Earle. New York: MLA, 1997. 135–40.

Caldwell, Gail. "Author Toni Morrison Discusses her Latest Novel *Beloved*." 1987. *Conversations With Toni Morrison*. Ed. Danille Taylor-Guthrie. Jackson: UP of Mississippi, 1994. 239–45.

Carabi, Angels. "Interview: Toni Morrison on *Jazz*." *Belles Lettres* 10.2 (1995): 40–43.

Carpenter, Lynette, and Wendy K. Kolmar, eds. *Haunting the House of Fiction: Feminist Perspectives on Ghost Stories by American Women*. Knoxville: U of Tennessee P, 1991.

Carpentier, Alejo. "On the Marvelous Real in America." *Magical Realism: Theory, History, Community*. Ed. Lois Parkinson Zamora and Wendy B. Faris. Durham, NC: Duke UP, 1995. 75–88.

Cartwright, Keith. *Reading Africa into American Literature: Epics, Fables, and Gothic Tales*. Lexington: UP of Kentucky, 2002.

Chanady, Amaryll Beatrice. *Magical Realism and the Fantastic: Resolved Versus Unresolved Antinomy*. New York: Garland, 1985.

Charles, Pepsi. "An Interview with Toni Morrison." 1977. *Toni Morrison: Conversations*. Ed. Carolyn C. Denard. Jackson: UP of Mississippi, 2008. 17–23.

Christian, Barbara T. "Layered Rhythms: Virginia Woolf and Toni Morrison." *Toni Morrison: Critical and Theoretical Approaches*. Ed. Nancy J. Peterson. Baltimore: Johns Hopkins UP, 1997. 19–36.

Clewell, Tammy. "From Destructive to Constructive Haunting in Toni Morrison's *Paradise*." *West Coast Line* 37.36 (2002): 130–42.

Coleman, James. "Beyond the Reach of Love and Caring: Black Life in Toni Morrison's *Song of Solomon*." *Obsidian II* 1.3 (Winter 1986): 151–61.

Collins, Patricia Hill. *Black Feminist Thought: Knowledge, Consciousness, and the Politics of Empowerment*. 2nd ed. New York: Routledge, 2000.

Conner, Marc C. "From the Sublime to the Beautiful: The Aesthetic Progression of Toni Morrison." *The Aesthetics of Toni Morrison: Speaking the Unspeakable*. Ed. Marc C. Conner. Jackson: UP of Mississippi, 2000. 49–76.

Cornell, Drucilla. "The Wild Woman and All that Jazz." *Feminism Beside Itself*. Ed. Diane Elam and Robyn Wiegman. New York: Routledge, 1995. 313–21.

Coser, Stelamaris. *Bridging the Americas: The Literature of Paule Marshall, Toni Morrison, and Gayl Jones*. Philadelphia: Temple UP, 1994.

Dalsgård, Katrine. "The One All-Black Town Worth the Pain: (African) American Exceptionalism, Historical Narration, and the Critique of Nationhood in Toni Morrison's *Paradise*." *African American Review* 35.2 (2001): 233–48.

Darling, Marsha. "In the Realm of Responsibility: A Conversation With Toni Morrison." 1988. *Conversations With Toni Morrison*. Ed. Danille Taylor-Guthrie. Jackson: UP of Mississippi, 1994. 246–54.

Davidson, Rob. "Racial Stock and 8-Rocks: Communal Historiography in Toni Morrison's *Paradise*." *Twentieth Century Literature* 47.3 (2001): 355–73.

Davis, Angela Y. *Women, Race & Class*. 1981. New York: Vintage, 1983.

Davis, Thulani. "Not Beloved." *The Nation* 15 Dec. 2003: 30–32.

Demetrakopoulos, Stephanie A. "Maternal Bonds as Devourers of Women's Individuation in Toni Morrison's *Beloved*." *African American Review* 26.1. Women Writers Issue (Spring 1992): 51–59.

Derrida, Jacques. *Specters of Marx: The State of the Debt, the Work of Mourning, and the New International*. 1993. Trans. Peggy Kamuf. New York: Routledge, 1994.

DiBattista, Maria. "Contentions in the House of Chloe: Morrison's *Tar Baby*." *The Aesthetics of Toni Morrison: Speaking the Unspeakable*. Ed. Marc C. Connor. Jackson: UP of Mississippi, 2000. 92–112.

Duvall, John N. *The Identifying Fictions of Toni Morrison: Modernist Authenticity and Postmodern Blackness*. New York: Palgrave, 2000.

Edwards, Thomas R. "Ghost Story." A Review of *Beloved*. *Critical Essays on Toni Morrison's* Beloved. Ed. Barbara H. Solomon. New York: G. K. Hall, 1998. 78-83.

Ellison, Ralph. *Invisible Man*. 1952. New York: Vintage, 1995.

———. *Shadow and Act*. New York: Signet, 1966.

Erickson, Daniel. *Ghosts, Metaphor, and History in Toni Morrison's Beloved and Gabriel García Márquez's One Hundred Years of Solitude*. New York: Palgrave, 2009.

Faris, Wendy B. *Ordinary Enchantments: Magical Realism and the Remystification of Narrative*. Nashville: Vanderbilt UP, 2004.

Foreman, P. Gabrielle. "Past-On Stories: History and the Magically Real, Morrison and Allende on Call." *Magical Realism: Theory, History, Community*. Eds. Lois Parkinson Zamora and Wendy B. Faris. Durham, NC: Duke UP, 1995. 285–304.

Fraile-Marcos, Ana María. "Hybridizing the 'City upon a Hill' in Toni Morrison's *Paradise*." *MELUS* 28.4 (2003): 3–33.

Gascueña Gahete, Javier. "Narrative Delusion and Aesthetic Pleasure in Toni Morrison's *Love*." *Figures of Belatedness: Postmodernist Fiction in English*. Ed. Javier Gascueña Gahete and Paula Martín Salván. Córdoba, Spain: Universidad de Córdoba, 2006. 259–73.

Gates, Henry Louis, ed. *The Classic Slave Narratives*. New York: Signet, 2002.

———. *The Signifying Monkey: A Theory of African-American Literary Criticism.* New York: Oxford UP, 1988.

Gauthier, Marni. "The Other Side of *Paradise*: Toni Morrison's (Un)Making of Mythic History." *African American Review* 39.3 (2005): 395–414.

Gilroy, Paul. *Small Acts: Thoughts on the Politics of Black Cultures*. London: Serpent's Tail, 1993.

Goldner, Ellen J. "Other(ed) Ghosts: Gothicism and the Bonds of Reason in Melville, Chesnutt, and Morrison." *MELUS* 24.1 (Spring 1999): 59–83.

Gordon, Avery F. *Ghostly Matters: Haunting and the Sociological Imagination.* Minneapolis: U of Minnesota P, 1997.

Grewal, Gurleen. *Circles of Sorrow, Lines of Struggle: The Novels of Toni Morrison.* Baton Rouge: Louisiana State UP, 1998.

Griffin, Farah Jasmine. *"Who Set You Flowin'?" The African-American Migration Narrative.* New York: Oxford UP, 1995.

Guth, Deborah. "A Blessing and a Burden: The Relation to the Past in *Sula, Song of Solomon* and *Beloved*." *Understanding Toni Morrison's* Beloved *and* Sula. Ed. Solomon O. Iyasere and Marla W. Iyasere. Troy, NY: Whitston, 2000. 315–47.

Harding, Wendy, and Jacky Martin. *A World of Difference: An Inter-Cultural Study of Toni Morrison's Novels*. Westport, CT: Greenwood, 1994.

Harris, A. Leslie. "Myth as Structure in Toni Morrison's *Song of Solomon*." *MELUS* 7.3 (Autumn 1980): 69–76.

Harris, Trudier. "Woman, Thy Name is Demon." *Critical Essays on Toni Morrison's* Beloved. Ed. Barbara H. Solomon. New York: G. K. Hall, 1998. 127–37.

———. *Fiction and Folklore: The Novels of Toni Morrison*. Knoxville: U of Tennessee P, 1991.

———. *Saints, Sinners, Saviors: Strong Black Women in African American Literature.* New York: Palgrave, 2001.

Hart, Stephen M. "Magical Realism in the Americas: Politicised Ghosts in *One Hundred Years of Solitude*, *The House of the Spirits*, and *Beloved*." *Journal of Iberian and Latin American Studies* 9.2 (2003): 115–23.

Hayes, Elizabeth T. "'Commitment to Doubleness': U.S. Literary Magic Realism and the Postmodern." *Spectral America: Phantoms and the National Imagination*. Ed. Jeffrey Andrew Weinstock. Madison: U of Wisconsin P, 2004. 169–84.

Heinze, Denise. *The Dilemma of Double-Consciousness: Toni Morrison's Novels*. Athens: U of Georgia P, 1993.

Higgins, Therese E. *Religiosity, Cosmology, and Folklore: The African Influences in the Novels of Toni Morrison*. New York: Routledge, 2001.

Hirsch, Marianne. "Knowing Their Names: Toni Morrison's *Song of Solomon*." *Modern Critical Interpretations: Toni Morrison's* Song of Solomon. Ed. Harold Bloom. Philadelphia: Chelsea House, 1999. 141–58.

Ho, Wen-ching. "'I'll Tell'—The Function and Meaning of L in Toni Morrison's *Love*." *EurAmerica* 36.4 (Dec. 2006): 651–75.

Holloway, Karla F. C. "*Beloved*: A Spiritual." *Callaloo* 13.3 (Summer 1990): 516–25.

Holloway, Karla F. C., and Stephanie Demetrakopoulos. *New Dimensions of Spirituality: A Biracial and Bicultural Reading of the Novels of Toni Morrison*. New York: Greenwood, 1987.

hooks, bell. *Sisters of the Yam: Black Women and Self-Recovery*. Cambridge, MA: South End, 2005.

Horvitz, Deborah. "Nameless Ghosts: Possession and Dispossession in Toni Morrison's *Beloved*." *Critical Essays on Toni Morrison's* Beloved. Ed. Barbara H. Solomon. New York: G. K. Hall, 1998. 93–103.

Hostetler, Ann. "Interview with Toni Morrison: 'The Art of Teaching.'" 2002. *Toni Morrison: Conversations*. Ed. Carolyn C. Denard. Jackson: UP of Mississippi, 2008. 196–205.

Houpt, Simon. "Toni, Interrupted." *Toronto Globe and Mail* 29 Nov. 2008: R1.

House, Elizabeth B. "Toni Morrison's Ghost: The Beloved Who is Not Beloved." *Studies in American Fiction* 18.1 (Spring 1990): 17–26.

Hutcheon, Linda. *The Politics of Postmodernism*. 2nd ed. 1989. London: Routledge, 2002.

Jaffrey, Zia. "Toni Morrison." 1998. *Toni Morrison: Conversations*. Ed. Carolyn C. Denard. Jackson: UP of Mississippi, 2008. 139–54.

Jessee, Sharon. "The 'Female Revealer' in *Beloved*, *Jazz*, and *Paradise*: Syncretic Spirituality in Toni Morrison's Trilogy." *Toni Morrison and the Bible: Contested Intertextualities*. Ed. Shirley A. Stave. New York: Peter Lang, 2006. 129–58.

Jones, Carolyn M. "Traces and Cracks: Identity and Narrative in Toni Morrison's *Jazz*." *African American Review* 31.3 (Autumn 1997): 481–95.

Jordan, Don, and Michael Walsh. *White Cargo: The Forgotten History of Britain's White Slaves in America*. Edinburgh: Mainstream, 2007.

Kakutani, Michiko. "Family Secrets, Feuding Women." *New York Times* 31 Oct. 2003: 37.

———. "Worthy Women, Unredeemable Men." *New York Times* 6 Jan. 1998: 8.

Kearly, Peter R. "Toni Morrison's *Paradise* and the Politics of Community." *Journal of American and Comparative Cultures* 23.2 (2000): 9–16.

Kenan, Randall. *Let the Dead Bury Their Dead*. San Diego, CA: Harcourt, 1992.

Kingston, Maxine Hong. *The Woman Warrior: Memoirs of a Girlhood Among Ghosts*. 1976. New York: Vintage, 1989.

Krumholz, Linda. "Blackness and Art in Toni Morrison's *Tar Baby*." *Contemporary Literature* 49.2 (2008): 263–92.

———. "The Ghosts of Slavery: Historical Recovery in Toni Morrison's *Beloved*." *African American Review* 26.3 (Autumn 1992): 395–408.

———. "Reading and Insight in Toni Morrison's *Paradise*." *African American Review* 36.1 (2002): 21–34.

Lawrence, David. "Fleshly Ghosts and Ghostly Flesh: The Word and the Body in *Beloved*." *Modern Critical Interpretations: Beloved*. Ed. Harold Bloom. Philadelphia: Chelsea House, 1999. 45–56.

Lee, Dorothy H. "*Song of Solomon*: To Ride the Air." *Black American Literature Forum* 16.2 (Summer 1982): 64–70.

Lepow, Lauren. "Paradise Lost and Found: Dualism and Edenic Myth in Toni Morrison's *Tar Baby*." *Toni Morrison's Fiction: Contemporary Criticism*. Ed. David L. Middleton. New York: Garland, 1997. 165–81.

Lesoinne, Veronique. "Answer Jazz's Call: Experiencing Toni Morrison's *Jazz*." *MELUS* 22.3 (Fall 1997): 151–66.

López, Alfred J. *Posts and Pasts: A Theory of Postcolonialism*. Albany: State U of New York P, 2001.

Ludigkeit, Dirk. "Collective Improvisation and Narrative Structure in Toni Morrison's *Jazz*." *LIT* 12 (2001): 165–87.

Mantel, Hilary. "Ghost Writer." *New Statesman* 8 Dec., 2003: 50–51. Academic Search Premier. EBSCO. 18 Jan. 2008. <http://search.ebscohost.com/login.aspx?direct=true&db=aph&AN=11584010&site=ehost-live>.

Marshall, Brenda. "The Gospel According to Pilate." *American Literature* 57.3 (Oct. 1985): 486–89.

Matus, Jill. *Toni Morrison*. Manchester, UK: Manchester UP, 1998.

Mayberry, Susan Neal. *Can't I Love What I Criticize? The Masculine and Morrison*. Athens: U of Georgia P, 2007.

Mbalia, Doreatha D. *Toni Morrison's Developing Class Consciousness*. Selinsgrove, PA: Susquehanna University Press, 2004.

Mbiti, Joseph S. *African Religions and Philosophy*. 1969. 2nd ed. 1989. Oxford, UK: Heinemann, 1999.

McKay, Nellie. "An Interview With Toni Morrison." 1983. *Conversations With Toni Morrison*. Ed. Danille Taylor-Guthrie. Jackson: UP of Mississippi, 1994. 138–55.

McKee, Patricia. "Geographies of *Paradise*." *New Centennial Review* 3.1 (2003): 197–223.

Middleton, Joyce Irene. "Orality, Literacy, and Memory in Toni Morrison's *Song of Solomon*." *College English* 55.1 (Jan. 1993): 64–75.

Miner, Madonne M. "Lady No Longer Sings the Blues: Rape, Madness, and Silence in *The Bluest Eye*." *Conjuring: Black Women, Fiction, and Literary Tradition*. Eds. Marjorie Pryse and Hortense J. Spillers. Bloomington: Indiana UP, 1985. 176–91.

Mitchell, Angelyn. "'Sth, I Know that Woman': History, Gender, and the South in Toni Morrison's *Jazz*." *Studies in the Literary Imagination* 31.2 (Fall 1998): 49–60.

Mobley, Marilyn E. "Narrative Dilemma: Jadine as Cultural Orphan in Toni Morrison's *Tar Baby*." *Southern Review* 23.4 (Autumn 1987): 761–70.

Moffitt, Letitia L. "Finding the Door: Vision/Revision and Stereotype in Toni Morrison's *Tar Baby*." *Critique* 46.1 (Fall 2004): 12–26.

Montagne, Renee. "Toni Morrison's 'Good' Ghosts." NPR Interview. *Morning Edition* 20 Sept. 2004 <http://www.npr.org/templates/story/story.php?storyId=3912464&sc=emaf>.

Morrison, Toni. *The Bluest Eye*. 1970. New York: Plume, 1994.

———. *Sula*. 1973. New York: Plume, 1982.

———. *Song of Solomon*. 1977. New York: Plume, 1987.

———. *Tar Baby*. 1981. New York: Vintage, 2004.

———. "Rootedness: The Ancestor as Foundation." *Black Women Writers (1950–1980): A Critical Evaluation*. Ed. Mari Evans. Garden City, NY: Anchor, 1984. 339–45.

———. *Beloved*. 1987. New York: Plume, 1998.

———. *Jazz*. 1992. New York: Vintage, 2004.

———. *Playing in the Dark: Whiteness and the Literary Imagination*. 1992. New York: Vintage, 1993.

———. *Paradise*. 1997. New York: Plume, 1999.

———. *The Nobel Lecture in Literature, 1993*. New York: Knopf, 1999.

———. *Love*. New York: Knopf, 2003.

———. *A Mercy*. New York: Knopf, 2008.

Munton, Alan. "Misreading Morrison, Mishearing *Jazz*: A Response to Toni Morrison's Jazz Critics." *Journal of American Studies* 31.2 (1997): 235–51.

Musgrave, Megan. "Phenomenal Women: The Shape-Shifter Archetype in Postcolonial Magical Realist Fiction." *Femspec* 6.2 (2005): 65–86.

Naylor, Gloria. "A Conversation: Gloria Naylor and Toni Morrison." 1985. *Conversations with Toni Morrison*. Ed. Danille Taylor-Guthrie. Jackson: UP of Mississippi, 1994.188–217.

Nicholls, Peter. "The Belated Postmodern: History, Phantoms, and Toni Morrison." *Psychoanalytic Criticism: A Reader*. Ed. Sue Vice. Cambridge, UK: Polity Press, 1996. 50–74.

Norris, Michele. "Toni Morrison Finds 'A Mercy' in Servitude." NPR Interview. *All Things Considered* 27 Oct. 2008 <http://www.npr.org/templates/story/story.php?storyId=96118766&sc=emaf>.

O'Reilly, Andrea. "In Search of My Mother's Garden, I Found My Own: Mother-Love, Healing, and Identity in Toni Morrison's *Jazz*." *African American Review* 30.3 (Fall 1996): 367–79. *MLA International Bibliography*. EBSCO. 15 Sep. 2008. 0- search.ebscohost.com.umiss.lib.olemiss.edu/login.aspx?direct=true&db=mzh&AN=0000300192&site=ehost-live&scope=site. 15 pp.

———. *Toni Morrison and Motherhood: A Politics of the Heart*. Albany: State U of New York P, 2004.

Otten, Terry. *The Crime of Innocence in the Fiction of Toni Morrison*. Columbia and London: U of Missouri P, 1989.

Page, Philip. *Dangerous Freedom: Fusion and Fragmentation in Toni Morrison's Novels.* Jackson: UP of Mississippi, 1995.

———. "Furrowing All the Brows: Interpretation and the Transcendent in Toni Morrison's *Paradise.*" *African American Review* 35.4 (2001): 637–49.

———. "Traces of Derrida in Toni Morrison's *Jazz.*" *African American Review* 29.1 (Spring 1995): 55–66.

Patterson, Orlando. *Slavery and Social Death.* Cambridge, MA: Harvard UP, 1982.

Peterson, Christopher. *Kindred Specters: Death, Mourning, and American Affinity.* Minneapolis: U of Minnesota P, 2007.

Peterson, Nancy J. "'Say make me, remake me': Toni Morrison and the Reconstruction of African-American History." *Toni Morrison: Critical and Theoretical Approaches.* Ed. Nancy J. Peterson. Baltimore: Johns Hopkins UP, 1997. 201–21.

Rand, Naomi R. "Surviving What Haunts You: The Art of Invisibility in *Ceremony, The Ghost Writer,* and *Beloved.*" *MELUS* 20.3 (Autumn 1995): 21–32.

Read, Andrew. "'As if word-magic had anything to do with the courage it took to be a man': Black Masculinity in Toni Morrison's *Paradise.*" *African American Review* 39.4 (2005): 527–40.

Reed, Harry. "Toni Morrison, *Song of Solomon* and Black Cultural Nationalism." *Modern Critical Interpretations: Toni Morrison's* Song of Solomon. Ed. Harold Bloom. Philadelphia: Chelsea House, 1999. 73–83.

Rice, Herbert William. *Toni Morrison and the American Tradition: A Rhetorical Reading.* New York: Peter Lang, 1996.

Rigney, Barbara Hill. "A Story to Pass On: Ghosts and the Significance of History in Toni Morrison's *Beloved.*" *Haunting the House of Fiction: Feminist Perspectives on Ghost Stories by American Women.* Ed. Lynette Carpenter and Wendy K. Kolmar. Knoxville: U of Tennessee P, 1991. 229–35.

———. *The Voices of Toni Morrison.* Columbus: Ohio State UP, 1991.

Rodrigues, Eusebio L. "Experiencing *Jazz.*" *Toni Morrison: Critical and Theoretical Approaches.* Ed. Nancy J. Peterson. Baltimore: Johns Hopkins UP, 1997. 245–66.

Roh, Franz. "Magic Realism: Post-Expressionism." *Magical Realism: Theory, History, Community.* Ed. Lois Parkinson Zamora and Wendy B. Faris. Durham, NC: Duke UP, 1995. 15–31.

Roynon, Tessa. "A New 'Romen' Empire: Toni Morrison's *Love* and the Classics." *Journal of American Studies* 41 (2007): 31–47.

———. "Restoring Voice to the Silenced." *The Times* (London) 18 Oct. 2008: 13.

Ruas, Charles. "Toni Morrison." 1981. *Conversations with Toni Morrison.* Ed. Danille Taylor-Guthrie. Jackson: UP of Mississippi, 1994. 93–118.

Rubenstein, Roberta. "Singing the Blues/Reclaiming Jazz: Toni Morrison and Cultural Mourning." *Mosaic* 31.2 (June 1998): 147–64. Literature Online. 15 Sep. 2008. <http://lion.chadwyck.com>. 12 pp.

Rushdie, Salman. "An Interview with Toni Morrison." 1992. *Toni Morrison: Conversations.* Ed. Carolyn C. Denard. Jackson: UP of Mississippi, 2008. 51–61.

Ryan, Judylyn S. "Contested Visions/ Double-Vision in *Tar Baby.*" *Toni Morrison: Critical and Theoretical Approaches.* Ed. Nancy J. Peterson. Baltimore: Johns Hopkins UP, 1997.

Sathyaraj, V., and G. Neelakantan. "'Dragon Daddies and False-Hearted Men': Patriarchy in Toni Morrison's *Love.*" *Notes on Contemporary Literature* 35.5 (Nov. 2005): 2–4.

———. "Family and Parenting in Toni Morrison's *Love. Notes on Contemporary Literature.* 36.4 (Sept. 2006): 9–10.

Schmudde, Carol. "The Haunting of 124." *African American Review* 26.3 (Autumn 1992): 409–16.

Schroeder, Shannin. *Rediscovering Magical Realism in the Americas.* Westport: Praeger, 2004.

Scruggs, Charles. "The Nature of Desire in Toni Morrison's *Song of Solomon.*" *Arizona Quarterly* 38.4 (Winter 1983): 311–35.

Skerrett, Joseph T., Jr. "Recitation to the Griot: Storytelling and Learning in Toni Morrison's *Song of Solomon.*" *Conjuring: Black Women, Fiction, and Literary Tradition.* Ed. Marjorie Pryse and Hortense J. Spillers. Bloomington: Indiana UP, 1985. 192–202.

Slemon, Stephen. "Magic Realism as Postcolonial Discourse." *Magical Realism: Theory, History, Community.* Ed. Lois Parkinson Zamora and Wendy B. Faris. Durham, NC: Duke UP, 1995. 407–26.

Smith, Andrew. *Gothic Literature.* Edinburgh: Edinburgh UP, 2007.

Smith, Valerie. "*Song of Solomon*: Continuities of Community." *Modern Critical Interpretations: Toni Morrison's* Song of Solomon. Ed. Harold Bloom. Philadelphia: Chelsea House, 1999. 29–39.

Snell, Marilyn Berlin. "The Shaman and the Infidel." 1991. *Conversations with Isabel Allende.* Ed. John Rodden. Austin: U of Texas P, 1999. 237–46.

Stepto, Robert B. "'Intimate Things in Place': A Conversation with Toni Morrison." 1976. *Toni Morrison: Critical Perspectives Past and Present.* Ed. Henry Louis Gates Jr. and K. A. Appiah. New York: Amistad, 1993. 378–95.

Stern, Katherine. "Toni Morrison's Beauty Formula." *The Aesthetics of Toni Morrison: Speaking the Unspeakable.* Ed. Marc C. Conner. Jackson: UP of Mississippi, 2000. 77–91.

Storhoff, Gary. "'Anaconda Love': Parental Enmeshment in Toni Morrison's *Song of Solomon.*" *Style* 31.2 (Summer 1997): 290–309.

Story, Ralph. "An Excursion into the Black World: The 'Seven Days' in Toni Morrison's *Song of Solomon.*" *Modern Critical Interpretations: Toni Morrison's* Song of Solomon. Ed. Harold Bloom. Philadelphia: Chelsea House, 1999. 85–93.

Sweeney, Megan. "'Something Rogue': Commensurability, Commodification, Crime, and Justice in Toni Morrison's Later Fiction." *Modern Fiction Studies* 52.2 (Summer 2006): 440–69.

Tally, Justine. "Reality and Discourse in Toni Morrison's Trilogy: Testing the Limits." *Literature and Ethnicity in the Cultural Borderlands*. Amsterdam: Rodopi B.V., 2002. 35–49.

———. "The Nature of Erotica in Toni Morrison's *Paradise* and the Em-body-ment of Feminist Thought." *Eros USA: Essays on the Culture and Literature of Desire*. Ed. Cheryl Alexander Malcolm and Jopi Nyman. Gdansk, Poland: Wydawnictwo Uniwersytetu Gdanskiego, 2005. 60–74.

Tate, Claudia. "Toni Morrison." 1983. *Conversations with Toni Morrison*. Ed. Danille Taylor-Guthrie. Jackson: UP of Mississippi, 1994. 156–70.

Thomas, Valorie D. "'1+1=3' and Other Dilemmas: Reading Vertigo in *Invisible Man, My Life in the Bush of Ghosts*, and *Song of Solomon*." *African American Review* 37.1 (2003): 81–94.

Todorov, Tzvetan. *The Fantastic: A Structural Approach to a Literary Genre*. Trans. Richard Howard. Cleveland: P of Case Western Reserve U, 1973.

Vega-González, Susana. "Toni Morrison's Water World: Watertime Writing in *Love*." *The Grove: Working Papers on English Studies* 11 (2004): 209–20.

Vickroy, Laurie. "The Force Outside/The Force Inside: Mother-Love and Regenerative Spaces in *Sula* and *Beloved*." *Understanding Toni Morrison's* Beloved *and* Sula*: Selected Essays and Criticisms*. Eds. Solomon O. Iyasere and Marla W. Iyasere. Troy, NY: Whitson, 2000. 297–314.

Waegner, Cathy Covell. "Ruthless Epic Footsteps: Shoes, Migrants, and the Settlement of the Americas in Toni Morrison's *A Mercy*." *Post-National Enquiries: Essays on Ethnic and Racial Border Crossings*. Ed. Jopi Nyman. Newcastle upon Tyne, UK: Cambridge Scholars, 2009. 91–112.

Walters, Wendy W. "'One of Dese Mornings, Bright and Fair, /Take My Wings and Cleave De Air': The Legend of the Flying Africans and Diasporic Consciousness." *MELUS* 22.3 (Fall 1997): 3–29. MLA International Bibliography Database. 4 Feb. 2009.

Wardi, Anissa Janine. *Death and the Arc of Mourning in African American Literature*. Gainesville: UP of Florida, 2003.

———. "A Laying on of Hands: Toni Morrison and the Materiality of *Love*." *MELUS* 30.3 (Fall 2005): 201–18.

Watkins, Mel. "Talk with Toni Morrison." 1977. *Conversations With Toni Morrison*. Ed. Danille Taylor-Guthrie. Jackson: UP of Mississippi, 1994. 43–47.

Weinstock, Jeffrey Andrew, ed. *Spectral America: Phantoms and the National Imagination*. Madison: U of Wisconsin P, 2004.

———. "Ten Minutes for Seven Letters: Reading *Beloved*'s Epitaph." *Arizona Quarterly* 61.3 (Autumn 2005): 129–52.

Werner, Craig Hansen. *Playing the Changes: From Afro-Modernism to the Jazz Impulse*. Urbana: U of Illinois P, 1994.

Widdowson, Peter. "The American Dream Refashioned: History, Politics, and Gender in Toni Morrison's *Paradise*." *Journal of American Studies* 35.2 (2001): 313–35.

Wilentz, Gay. "Civilizations Underneath: African Heritage as Cultural Discourse in Toni Morrison's *Song of Solomon*." *African American Review* 26.1 (Spring 1992): 61–76.

Willis, Susan. *Specifying: Black Women Writing the American Experience*. Madison: U of Wisconsin P, 1987.

Wolfreys, Julian. *Victorian Hauntings: Spectrality, Gothic, the Uncanny and Literature*. New York: Palgrave, 2002.

The World: The Journal of the Unitarian Universalist Association. "A Bench by the Road: *Beloved* by Toni Morrison." 1988. *Toni Morrison: Conversations*. Ed. Carolyn C. Denard. Jackson: UP of Mississippi, 2008. 44–50.

Yaeger, Patricia. *Dirt and Desire: Reconstructing Southern Women's Writing, 1930–1990*. Chicago: U of Chicago P, 2000.

Zamora, Lois Parkinson, and Wendy B. Faris, eds. *Magical Realism: Theory, History, Community*. Durham, NC: Duke UP, 1995.

Zamora, Lois Parkinson. "Magical Romance/Magical Realism: Ghosts in U.S. and Latin American Fiction." *Magical Realism: Theory, History, Community*. Ed. Lois Parkinson Zamora and Wendy B. Faris. Durham, NC: Duke UP, 1995. 497–550.

———. *The Usable Past: The Imagination of History in Recent Fiction of the Americas*. Cambridge, UK: Cambridge UP, 1997.

INDEX

African influences, 7–8
Allen, Paula Gunn, 149n5, 153n9; on the "Void" and women, 87
Anzaldúa, Gloria, 149n5
Ancestors, 2, 7, 15; Baby Suggs as, 77, 153n6; *Beloved* as, 153n6; in *Beloved*, 153n6; in *Love*, 156n17, 157n23; in Nobel lecture, 146; relation to social death, 149–50n6; in "Rootedness" (Morrison), 18, 30, 153n6
Ansa, Tina McElroy, 8, 151n4
Awkward, Michael, 19, 50, 151n2

Beloved. See Morrison
Beloved-type, 1, 19, 38, 69, 156
The Bluest Eye. *See* Morrison
Bouson, J. Brooks, 88, 149n1
Bowers, Maggie Ann: on *Beloved* as magical realism, 149n4; on history of magical realism, 149n2; on Morrison and magical realism, 6
Brogan, Kathleen, 20, 76, 80, 86; *Beloved* as memorial, 75; concept of ghost, 12, 73, 152–53n4; women and absence/invisibility, 12, 20, 92, 94, 149n5; women's haunted literature, 1, 82
Buse, Peter and Andrew Stott, 10–12

Carpenter, Lynette and Wendy K. Kolmar: on women writers' ghost stories, 68, 93
Cartwright, Keith, 151n2
Chanady, Amaryll B., 4–5, 7, 149n2, 149n3
Collins, Patricia Hill, 12–13, 128
Creative Hauntology, 81
Crossroads: 124 in *Beloved* as, 69; in *Love*, 120; in *Paradise*, 83, 87 (Paula Gunn Allen), 89 (Krumholz), 95, 99; in *Song of Solomon*, 39

Davis, Thulani, 115, 116, 121
Demetrakopoulos, Stephanie A., 70, 150n7, 151n2, 151–52n10, 152n13
Derrida, Jacques, 9–12, 14, 65, 66, 75–76, 80–81, 83, 84, 99, 103, 104, 111, 147
Duvall, John N., 19, 28, 150n7, 151n9

Ellison, Ralph: *Invisible Man*, 13, 19; *Shadow and Act*, 147
Erickson, Daniel, 150n8

Fantastic: connection to magical realism, 4, 149n3; as literary mode, 4–5
Faris, Wendy B., 3; on *Beloved* as magical realism, 149n4; on history of magical realism, 149n2
Faulkner, William, 69, 155n5

Gates, Henry Louis, Jr., 153n9, 154n2, 158n2
Gilroy, Paul, 6
Gordon, Avery F., 9, 13–14, 20–21, 27, 124
Gothic, 13, 28, 115, 120
Grewal, Gurleen, 150n7
Griffin, Farah Jasmine, 154–55n4
Griot, 38, 52

Harding, Wendy and Jacky Martin, 150n7
Harris, Trudier, 70, 73, 150n7, 151n2
Haunted house trope, 1; in American literature, 69; in *Beloved*, 68–73; in *Love*, 119; in *A Mercy*, 141, 143; in *Song of Solomon*, 47
Heinze, Denise, 49, 58, 60, 150n7, 151n9
Higgins, Therese E., 7, 153n8
Historiographic Metafiction, 17, 103
Holloway, Karla F. C., 61, 80, 150n7, 150n1, 151n2, n8, n9, n10, 152n13

hooks, bell, 128
Hutcheon, Linda, 17, 103, 123

Invisibility (also see Ellison and Brogan), 1, 148; African American women and, 13; in *The Bluest Eye*, 20, 23; and magical realism, 5; in *A Mercy*, 137; women and, 12, 87, 120

Jazz. See Morrison
Jordan, Don and Michael Walsh, 135–36

Kenan, Randall, 8, 151n4
Krumholz, Linda, 73, 84, 88–89, 94, 152n11, 154n14

Living-dead, 8
López, Alfred J., 5–6
Love. See Morrison

Magical Realism 3–6; history of, 149n2–3; in Morrison's work, 6, 149n4; influence on Morrison, 6; Morrison on, 6
Matus, Jill, 150n7, 152n2
Mayberry, Susan Neal, 150n7
Mbalia, Doreatha, 45–46, 150n7, 151n9
Mbiti, Joseph, 7–8
A Mercy. See Morrison
Migration, 44, 109, 111–12, 113
Morrison, Toni, *Beloved*, 1, 2, 6, 16–17, 20, 26, 33, 35, 39, 65–83, 94, 98–101, 102–3, 111, 114, 145, 147; *Beloved* connected to *A Mercy*, 131, 136, 138–39, 143; *The Bluest Eye*, 16, 19–27, 53, 132, 136, 138, 144, 145; *Jazz*, 11, 16–18, 21, 33, 78, 81, 98, 101–16, 120–21, 123, 129–30, 132, 137, 141, 145, 147; *Love*, 1, 11, 17–18, 21, 29, 32, 101–3, 105, 109, 115–32, 145; *A Mercy*, 1, 15, 17–18, 131–45; the Nobel lecture, 145–48; *Paradise*, 16–17, 20, 29, 31, 33, 35, 39, 52, 63, 65–67, 69, 78, 81–103, 109, 114–15, 129, 132, 140, 145–48; *Playing in the Dark*, 2, 121; "Rootedness," 18, 30, 41, 153n6; *Song of Solomon*, 1, 6, 9, 15–16, 19, 21, 26, 35, 37–53, 64–65, 98, 101, 141, 145, 148; *Sula*, 16, 19, 27–35, 64, 79, 118, 128, 141; *Tar Baby*, 1, 6, 16, 21, 37–38, 39, 53–65, 69, 98, 101, 112, 132, 136, 145
Music, 39, 44, 121–22, 123, 156n18; the "blue note" in jazz and blues, 154–55n4; jazz, 104, 154n3; Morrison on, 6, 156n19

NPR, 135, 146
Nobel Prize, 2, 146

O'Reilly, Andrea, 150n7, 155n8
Otten, Terry, 152n12

Page, Philip, 20, 95, 150n7, 153n8, 155n11
Paradise. See Morrison
Patterson, Orlando (social death), 149–50n6
Peterson, Christopher (social death), 149–50n6
Peterson, Nancy J., 129–30; on *Jazz*, 103, 107, 154n1, 154n3; on *Jazz* and Faulkner, 155n5
Playing in the Dark: Whiteness and the Literary Imagination. See Morrison
Poststructural, 2, 7, 9; connection to magical realism, 6; in *Love* criticism, 156n14

Rice, Herbert William, 150n1
Rigney, Barbara Hill, 12, 75, 150n7
"Rootedness: The Ancestor as Foundation." *See* Morrison

Schroeder, Shannin, 4, 5; on *Beloved* as magical realism 149n4; on history of magical realism, 149n2
Shape-shifting, 42, 151n5
Slavery, 2, 3, 8, 102–3, 148; in *Beloved*, 66, 68, 70–71, 73, 75, 77–78, 80–82, 152n3; connection to social death, 149–50n6; in *Jazz*, 109, 113–14, 155n8; in *Love*, 128; in *A Mercy*, 17, 131–37, 141–45, 157–58n2; in *Paradise*, 99; in *Song of Solomon*, 16, 39; in *Tar Baby*, 60

Smith, Andrew, 103, 120
Social death, 149–50n6
Social ghosts, 7, 9, 12–16, 19, 149–50n6; in *The Bluest Eye*, 20–21, 27; in *Jazz*, 111; in *Love*, 120, 124, 129; in *A Mercy*, 132, 133, 136, 138, 142, 143; in *Paradise*, 82, 85, 92–93; in *Sula*, 32; in *Tar Baby*, 53
Spectrality, 1, 2, 12, 14, 16, 17, 35, 37, 64, 150n8, 155n8, 156n13; in *Beloved*, 66–67, 68, 76, 81; Derridean concept of, 10–11; in *Jazz*, 104–5, 106, 108; in *Love*, 123, 127; in *Sula*, 30; in *Tar Baby*, 53–54, 59
"Spectrality Effect," 9–10, 16; in *Beloved*, 66, 68, 76
Spectralized Narration, 103, 104
Sula. See Morrison
Supernatural, 1, 7, 11, 37, 65, 101, 145; in African American fiction, 3, 8; in *Beloved*, 70, 77, 152n3; in *The Bluest Eye*, 24; in *Invisible Man* (Ellison), 13; in *Jazz*, 105, 108; in *Love*, 121, 155n8; and magical realism, 4–6; in *A Mercy*, 139; in *Paradise*, 84–85, 98; in *Song of Solomon*, 40–41; in *Tar Baby*, 60, 64; in women's literature, 68, 93
Song of Solomon. See Morrison
The South, 149n5, 155n10, 157–58n2 in *Beloved*, 69; in *The Bluest Eye*, 21, 22–23; in *Jazz*, 101, 109, 111–12; in *Song of Solomon*, 39, 42, 46, 49–50; in *Tar Baby*, 53, 58, 59

Tally, Justine, 81, 96, 153–54n10, 154n14
Tar Baby. See Morrison
Till, Emmett, 45–46, 124
Todorov, Tzvetan, 4–5

Wardi, Anissa Janine, 109, 111–12, 128, 155n7, 156n13, 156n14, 156n16, 156n17, 157n20
Weinstock, Jeffrey Andrew, 1, 130, 150n8
Willis, Susan, 59, 150n1
Wolfreys, Julian, 142

Yaeger, Patricia, 149n5

Zamora, Lois Parkinson, 2; on connections between poststructuralism and magical realism, 6; on ghosts, 3–4; on history of magical realism, 149n2